JACK ⟨ W9-CAT-578

"THE DEAN OF TRUE CRIME AUTHORS"
Washington Post

CHARMER

"A MESMERIZING ACCOUNT OF EVIL . . .
ESSENTIAL FOR TRUE CRIME READERS
AND RECOMMENDED FOR A
GENERAL AUDIENCE."
Library Journal

"OLSEN JUST GETS BETTER AND BETTER"
Harry N. Maclean, EDGAR Award-winning author of
In Broad Daylight

"INCREDIBLY RIVETING . . .
HIS BEST BOOK YET . . .
A FASCINATING, MANY-LAYERED
TRUE-LIFE THRILLER"
Joseph Bosco, author of *Blood Will Tell*

"COMPELLING READING . . .
JACK OLSEN IS A FIRST-CLASS WRITER
CAPABLE OF MAKING HIS
TRUE CRIME BOOKS READ LIKE
GOOD THRILLERS."
Minneapolis Star-Tribune

"BRILLIANT . . .
CHILLING AND REMARKABLE"
Carlton Stowers, author of *Innocence Lost*

Charmer

THE TRUE STORY OF
A LADIES' MAN AND HIS VICTIMS

JACK OLSEN

AVON BOOKS ◆ NEW YORK

AVON BOOKS
A division of
The Hearst Corporation
1350 Avenue of the Americas
New York, New York 10019

Copyright © 1994 by Jack Olsen
Published by arrangement with the author
Library of Congress Catalog Card Number: 94-4420
ISBN: 0-380-71601-1

Published in hardcover by William Morrow and Company, Inc.; for information address Permissions Department, William Morrow and Company, Inc., 1350 Avenue of the Americas, New York, New York 10019.

The William Morrow edition contains the following Library of Congress Cataloging in Publication Data:

Olsen, Jack.
    Charmer: a ladies' man and his victims / by Jack Olsen.
        p.   cm.
1. Serial murders—Washington (State)—Mercer Island—Case studies. 2. Murderers—Washington (State)—Mercer Island—Biography. 3. Russell, George, Jr.   I. Title.
HV6534.M43045   1994
364.1'523'09777—dc20   94-4420
                                                           CIP

First Avon Books Printing: November 1995

AVON TRADEMARK REG. U.S. PAT. OFF. AND IN OTHER COUNTRIES, MARCA REGISTRADA, HECHO EN U.S.A.

Printed in the U.S.A.

RA   10   9   8   7   6   5   4   3   2   1

To Su
always Su

The greatest terror a child can have is that he is not loved, and rejection is the hell he fears. . . . And with rejection comes anger, and with anger some kind of crime in revenge for the rejection, and with the crime guilt—and there is the story of mankind.

JOHN STEINBECK,
EAST OF EDEN

"Jimmy," I said consolingly [to author James Baldwin], "you're only twenty-one, you're very gifted and have lots of friends." "Friends!" he exploded. "But no lover! And no money! What good is talent without recognition?" "I'm in the same boat," I said. "Oh, no, baby, we're in different boats!" he cried. "You're white!"

HAROLD NORSE,
MEMOIRS OF A BASTARD ANGEL

Wouldn't they be surprised when one day I woke out of my black ugly dream, and my real hair, which was long and blond, would take the place of the kinky mass that Momma wouldn't let me straighten? . . . Because I was really white . . .

MAYA ANGELOU,
I KNOW WHY THE CAGED BIRD SINGS

PART ONE

MYSTERIOUS GEORGE

THE POLICEMAN WONDERED what the big dog was doing on North Mercer Way. There were already too many mutts on the island, upsetting trash cans, befouling gardens, murdering sleep. Some were downright dangerous. But . . . a loose St. Bernard? On a main thoroughfare?

As the cop approached in his patrol car, he noticed a small head bobbing behind the dog. The boy looked nine or ten. He was leaning backward, hauling on a leash. The child grimaced and the dog drooled. In the semi-darkness, it looked like a racetrack scene: a hot-walker leading a rank horse. Then the policeman saw that the child was black.

Out of some 15,000 local citizens, only a handful boasted African ancestry. Retired basketball superstar Bill Russell was one, but this boy was definitely not Russell's son Bill Jr., nicknamed Buddha. The cop knew most of the island's ethnic citizens by sight; they were law-abiding professionals, like their white neighbors.

He made a mental note to check out the newcomer. When trouble came to the police department of Mercer Island, Washington, a green suburbia five minutes from Seattle, it seldom came in the form of blacks. It came in the form of boys.

Seventh grader Boris Brockett had already met the child with the St. Bernard and liked him right away.

3

He was short, like me. Had a big, round, bubbly face, big eyes, a loud infectious laugh. He's your best friend in a second. He emphasized that his name was George Russell *Junior.* I asked if he was related to Bill Russell and he said he didn't think so. I got the idea he didn't want to get personal.

My mother took one look and said, "Watch out for that boy. He's trouble." But after she got to know George she was totally charmed. He was polite, respectful. Even as a little kid, he had this uncanny ability to make you like him—an easy style, warm, very southern. His favorite food was "GREE-its." He called me "BOE-riss." When I asked him what part of the South he was from, he shrugged. He finally said he was from Maryland. I thought GREE-its must be fish eggs.

For Boris Brockett, it was the beginning of something he would learn to call "The Mystery of George."

THE BOYS OF Mercer Island specialized in making "forts," some in trees, some hidden in the woods or in long-abandoned loggers' shacks and shelters. George took Boris to his own. It was modest by his later standards, well hidden in the woods above the old Islander Tavern and concealed with blackberry bushes, vine maples and a prickly aggravation called devil's club. George said that Boris would be his first and only visitor. This fort, he stressed, was "off limits to the world."

It developed that he had others. Most of them were little more than slits, places where he could see and not be seen, where he could hide himself and his possessions from the rest of the world. Even as a twelve-year-old, he seemed to enjoy outwitting others, sometimes making the game more interesting by offering hints and clues.

To their parents' dismay, George and his new friend Boris began playing indoor basketball with rolled-up sweatsocks and curtain rods. "We pretended to dribble the sock and then shot at the curtain rod. You got one point if it hung up, two if it went through."

It wasn't long before young Brockett noticed that the wear-and-tear on the rods wasn't being evenly divided between the two households. "We played at my house, but George seemed reluctant to invite me home. For Mercer Island, his place was a little on the small side, not much lawn, no waterfront, lots of bushes and trees— Doug fir, blue spruce, cedar, maple, some apple and pear trees left over from when it was an orchard. Another lot blocked them from Lake Washington, but they could walk to the water. There wasn't much furniture; they'd just moved in. Downstairs they had a carpeted rec room with a pool table. George and his little sister Erika had their own rooms."

On his second visit Brockett encountered the Russell boy's mother, Joyce Mobley. In later years he had difficulty finding the right word to describe her. He tried out "dignified" and "austere" before settling on the unlikely "ominous."

"She was small," Brockett explained, "like George— slender, short black hair, a nice face, looked like Coretta Scott King. She had a thin voice, not threatening or overbearing, sounded a little British. George said she taught school—English, drama, black history, stuff like that.

"Tell ya one thing, she didn't make you feel overly welcome. Her look kept ya quiet. You didn't hear *her* talk about GREE-its. George was kinda subdued around her and so was I. She . . . scared me. But don't forget—we were trying to slam-dunk our socks in her living room."

When Boris asked George why he was a "Russell" and she was a "Mobley," he explained in a few words that his natural father lived back East; the man George now called "Dad" was his mother's second husband, Wonzel Mobley. Boris attempted another personal question and George turned away. He never invited his friend home again.

At first, teachers at North Mercer Island Junior High were delighted with the new student. His IQ was high and he radiated quickness and energy. It didn't take long for most of his southern accent to disappear, and soon he was parroting the intonations common to most citizens of the island, including the handful of blacks. Early in the seventh grade he informed the school newspaper that he intended to become a flier. The selection of such an orthodox ambition suggested that he was trying to fit in rather than stand out; many Boeing and Northwest Airlines personnel lived on the island. George impressed classmates with a skillfully wrought model of an aircraft carrier and said he would be stationed on one someday: "I can't wait to make my first carrier landing." Nobody scoffed. He had a ferret's reflexes and a fighter pilot's small, wiry build.

His early grades proved disappointingly low. He had the vocabulary of an English teacher's son but seemed to have difficulty transferring his thoughts to paper. His teachers were patient; the Mercer Island system had unusually high standards, and struggling newcomers were an old story.

As the months went by, he showed no improvement, and some of his teachers decided that he just wasn't a scholar. Perhaps, they theorized, schoolwork came too easily and he was bored—a common problem among gifted children. It was a convenient theory, and George was happy to embrace it later, trying to justify his ruined life.

An eighth-grade science teacher described him as "bright but immature, small for his age, antsy, hyper, all over the place. You couldn't get mad at him. He wasn't the least bit malicious. He kept us all laughing, but he just wasn't interested in schoolwork. He wanted to play. As long as I knew him, he was a playful little boy."

George confided to his friend Boris, "I only pay attention in classes I like. I don't need those goofy little art classes. I always feel like, Let's speed this up.''

After school he read sport and adventure books, comic books featuring soldiers and mercenaries, and novels like *Huckleberry Finn* and *Beau Geste*, which he seemed to find easier to start than finish. He always seemed a book or two ahead of his classmates and an assignment or two behind. He was often truant, explaining that he had to babysit his sister.

> *Police work, with its trappings of violence and authority, exerts an irresistible attraction for some sociopaths.*
>
> —MICHAEL NEWTON,
> *SERIAL SLAUGHTER*

The two-lane road called Mercer Way meandered past the Russell house and girdled the island in low hills and arcs. Teenagers with raging testosterone considered it unmanly to slow down on the unbanked curves, and Metro bus drivers used the section in front of the Russells to make up time. For years the understaffed police department had fought a losing battle to slow the pace.

A few of the radar cops began to notice a small tan face peering through the blackberry bushes at night. Sometimes the boy was with the St. Bernard, sometimes alone. On one soggy fall evening he was walking in what later became known as "the George Russell strut"—fast, purposeful, hands in pocket—when an officer rolled down his window and struck up a conversation. He said later that it was like talking to another adult. The next night the bemused cop gave the boy a lift in a rainstorm.

After that, George seemed attracted to men in uniform. A policeman named Glendon Booth, bête noire of every mischievous youth on the island, recalled, "The first time I saw Georgie, he was in trouble for some petty thing, maybe truancy, and the Youth Bureau'd given him some work around the station. He was thirteen or fourteen, a little bitty kid, well dressed, frail, innocent, very likable. He could charm your socks off. He was the last kid on Mercer Island you'd expect to turn into our biggest nightmare.''

Soon "Georgie" had become a fixture at the rundown Mercer Island police station, squeezed into the first floor of an old apartment building. "He'd come around a couple times a week," said a juvenile officer, J. C. Goodman, "and we'd let him straighten things up, wipe the blackboards, sharpen pencils, empty the trash. We thought, Hey, if we're giving him some responsibility, maybe we're helping him a little bit."

Before long, the boy had his own semi-official cubbyhole and was telling classmates that he wanted to be a policeman instead of a pilot. "It was the first time we ever took in a kid like that," said Booth, "but there was something different about him." The officers bought him pop and snacks. He seemed to revere every cop except the black ones.

Among his early assignments, he was shown how to file papers and roll a passable set of fingerprints. Later he learned how to purge reports to keep the media from obtaining confidential information like informers' names and addresses. Now and then the half-pint kid answered the phone in his pipsqueak voice—"Mercer Island *Poe*lice!'' Sometimes he pedaled downtown for cigarettes and snacks, confiding to friends that he was on official business.

After a few months his tête-à-têtes with the cops turned more personal. "We'd talk one-on-one," a patrolman named Manny Rucker recalled. "He listened to your troubles like you were the most important person in the world. You'd have to keep reminding yourself you were talking to a kid."

It took awhile for the amused officers to realize that they were getting little information in return. By now they knew that their star volunteer lived with a dentist named Wonzel Mobley and his dignified wife, Joyce, and that he often babysat the Mobleys' infant daughter, Erika. But where did Georgie Russell fit into the family?

When the friendly policemen asked questions, the boy dodged. They sensed his discomfort and didn't press. It seemed a little odd that a child barely in his teens would be turning a bunch of cops into a substitute family.

Some of the men suspected that Georgie's cheerful exterior might be a cover. "We wondered why he didn't illuminate things," said J. C. Goodman years later. "If we got too nosy, he made it plain he didn't want to talk about his homelife. So we just stopped asking. Hardest thing in the world for a bunch of nosy cops, but we liked Georgie enough to give him space. What was bothering him? He never would say."

One day Sergeant Glendon Booth approached Dr. Wonzel Mobley on a nonpolice matter. The dentist was a light-skinned African-American in his thirties, medium in height and weight, relaxed and graceful in his motions. He dressed stylishly, wore a conservative Afro and glasses, and had a small scar between his eyes. His looks put Booth in mind of the actor Bill Cosby.

The cop couldn't resist throwing in a question about Georgie's origins, and Dr. Mobley's response stuck in his mind for years. "I lived in a boardinghouse when I was going to dental school in Washington, D.C.," the dentist explained, "and this little orphan kid was living there. I picked him up and put him under my arm."

Booth waited for the rest of the story, but there didn't seem to be more. The cop figured Mobley was just tight-lipped. Some men were like that; it didn't mean anything one way or the other. Whenever any of the Mercer Island officers talked to the dentist in the ensuing years, he seemed to go out of his way to emphasize that Georgie Russell was *not* his son.

An early brush with the law was attributed to an excess of youthful spirit. With two other seventh graders, George sneaked into a waterfront home. The archcriminals made toast and left.

Soon afterward George's friend Boris Brockett and two other junior high school students stole several electric guitars from a store called Musicwest and transferred them to their fort.

The excited Boris was disappointed that his blood brother wasn't impressed by the exploit. "That was a *bad* move, BOE-riss," George admonished him. "What were you thinking, man?" Some of Mercer Island's black students affected a humble act, but George always spoke out.

"Dunno," Boris said, surprised by the reaction. "Maybe we can sell the stuff to a rock band."

"Great," George said sarcastically. "Who's gonna buy hot guitars?"

Boris admitted that he hadn't thought the matter through. The excitement had been in the act itself. The stolen instruments had become a burden and somehow would have to be returned.

That evening there was a knock on the Brocketts' front door. In front of the boy's mother and father, two juvenile officers flashed a warrant for his arrest. "They came on like Joe Friday," Boris recalled with chagrin. " 'We got the goods on ya! Ya better come clean!' "

The case ended in a stern lecture. "The probation officer sure got our attention," recalled the grown-up Brockett. "Shaped me up nice and early. I got a new respect for the Mercer Island cops. They nailed our ass good. They weren't such a comedy anymore."

THE POLICEMEN WERE impressed by their mascot's help in the Musicwest case. It wasn't often that they cleaned up a hot burglary in less than twenty-four hours. Not only had Georgie fingered the culprits, but he'd led police to the loot.

A few days later he shared valuable information about some stolen bikes. It seemed the half-pint kid was something more than likable conversationalist and handyman. He had the instincts of a cop.

George began spending more time around the police station and even went on an occasional patrol, scrunching down in the seat and observing quietly, sometimes taking notes. He studied police procedures, pored over "wanted" posters and field reports, and listened to endless war stories.

The lawmen had finely honed instincts about human behavior, and to most of them, he still seemed to be concealing a load of trouble beneath his smile and robust laugh. J. C. Goodman, a stocky, jovial cop known for his rapport with young criminals, recalled, "You couldn't help feeling sorry for him. Myself and Sergeant Smith, we tried to help him out 'cause even though he didn't want to talk about it, we could see his personal life didn't seem to be going real well. So we gave him even more to do, kept him busy around the station."

By the time George Russell entered the ninth grade, his friendship with his old pal BOE-riss had faded. "I changed and George didn't," Brockett recalled. "I was getting interested in girls. George was, too, but he was secretive about it. It was something else he kept to himself: how he felt about girls. His style attracted younger kids. I preferred older company."

In later years Brockett realized that he'd never really known his blood brother. It was more of The Mystery of George.

SOME OF THE Mercer Island policemen observed a symbiosis developing between George and younger kids. A patrol cop had a theory: "He was always skinny, didn't reach five foot till high school, and I think he felt sort of intimidated by people his own age. He could be a big shot with the littler kids. He craved that attention, people looking up to him. It was something he didn't seem to be getting anywhere else."

Now and then there was a hint of trouble at home. Mercerites tended to know their neighbors' business, but the Mobleys kept to themselves, even at the risk of being criticized by a small but dedicated black caucus for remaining a little too detached about local race relations.

To his friends in the police department, George continued to insist that his homelife was uneventful and happy. He loved his parents and half-sister Erika, and he claimed to enjoy babysitting while his mother taught college and his stepfather drilled teeth. He recounted games of Monopoly and Scrabble and backgammon played at the family hearth. He talked about romping with Max, riding dogback, harnessing the St. Bernard to a wagon and hauling groceries from the Safeway. He told warm, funny stories about his dog's relationship with a neighbor's beagle.

"That little Francesca bosses him around!" said the wide-eyed child. "She barks, he listens. He won't let other dogs near. She eats out of his pan!" He seemed amazed, and the cops were tickled by his boyish innocence.

BY HIS MID-TEENS George's popularity was still high, but he seemed to have few intimates. "He had dozens of friends," one of them recalled, "and every friendship was shallow." Only a select few ever visited his house.

"He wouldn't hesitate to use his parents for status," his childhood friend Tom Haggar recalled. "He'd say, 'My dad's a dental surgeon. My mom's a college professor. We live on the water.' He'd use them to make an impression, but he wouldn't follow through by inviting you home."

As official dentist of the University of Washington football team, Dr. Mobley had good seats at Husky Stadium, and one Saturday George invited a classmate. Twenty years later the friend remembered every detail.

His stepdad was a nice guy, funny, talked about jazz and cars and sport. He owned an Austin Healey, a Ferrari, a Lamborghini, but you'd usually see him in a little Volkswagen convertible. He said he could never get the performance cars to perform. After the football games the three of us went into the Husky locker room and talked to the players. Then he drove us to his apartment in Leschi, on the Seattle side of Lake Washington, across the lake from Mercer Island. It was a neatly furnished pad that hung over the water. He said you could fish off the balcony. He gave us a snack and a pop, and then we drove back across the bridge to Mercer Island.

After we'd gone to a couple of games, I began to wonder about the family situation. Seemed like George was always outside, running around. I never went into his house. You didn't know if his mom was still there or not. I didn't know if his dad lived at home or in the pad at Leschi. It almost seemed like conscious deception, and George was a part of it.

There are very definite aspects to our culture pattern which give psychopaths encouragement. In America we put great

*value on the acquisition of material gain, prestige, power,
personal ascendance, and the competitive massing of
goods.*

—WILLIAM KRASNER,
"THE PSYCHOPATH IN OUR SOCIETY,"
NEUROTICA II (1948)

Despite its high per capita income, Mercer Island was a
social Sahara for most young people. The standard lament—"There's nothing to do"—was as much a part of
island cacophony as the croaking of frogs, the twitter of
towhees and juncos, the rumble of trucks crossing the island
on Interstate 90.

Proud parents pointed out that no house was more than
five minutes from a tennis court, playing field, gym or pool,
no more than ten minutes from a country club or public
beach. Organized sport was encouraged, some said *over*-
encouraged.

The kids complained that there were too few places to
socialize at night. There were two or three fast-food joints,
a convenience store, a video arcade, an aging bowling alley
and a downtown shopping area whose establishments, like
Chick's Shoe Repair and Hal's Texaco, darkened early.
There was no movie theater, no skating rink, no mall or
dance hall. Many of the teenagers' activities necessarily
took place in the woods, floored with trillium, huckleberry,
wild strawberries, licorice fern and moss, and dotted with
tall cedar stumps bearing slashes where pioneer loggers had
inserted their springboards. Some boys maintained their
forts and tree houses into the college years; a few resembled
small apartments, with butane heaters, futons and bars.
George's classmate Michael A. O'Hara remembered.

Most Mercer kids were bored shitless. At night, our parents
warned, "Don't go off the island." We felt trapped. There was a
whole different world across the bridges, west to Seattle, east to
Bellevue, but we had to stay on an insulated island six miles long.
Sex was for others; our girls were "No sex, please. We're

from Mercer Island.'' My prom date slept in her gown, when a simple "no" would have made her point.

We ended up making Mercer Island mischief. Dope was big; so was vandalism. For kicks we'd drop a cherry bomb in the park toilet. Or egg houses. Or deface lawns. We used to pull up the junior high principal's primroses and dump 'em at school. We siphoned gas so we could drag. Anything that wasn't bolted down was a target. We had keggers in the woods—crazy drunken kids whooping and hollering till the cops broke it up. We ran them ragged. We referred to the cops as "dufes" or "weasels." Juvenile crime was always the biggest problem on Mercer Island. Every cop functioned as a juvenile officer. Of course the most common crime was running away from home.

IN MAY, 1973, A month after George's fifteenth birthday, he and two classmates disappeared from school. The next afternoon the runaways were arrested in Cle Elum, a little town fifty miles east in the Cascades, and a Mercer Island juvenile unit was dispatched to pick them up. One of the officers recalled: "They'd told the local deputy they were on a ski trip from North Mercer Junior High. Said they didn't know how to ski, so they wandered into Cle Elum to look around. It was a good story. The deputy asked for their phone numbers, and George and one kid gave their right numbers because they knew nobody was home. George had prepped the third kid with the number of a phone booth, but he panicked and gave his home number. So they were caught. But it was all planned out like the Brinks robbery, and most of the thinking was done by George."

Juvenile officers asked George why he'd wanted to run away in the first place. Was he unhappy? Mistreated? George replied in his effusive style that he had *wonderful* parents who gave him everything a boy could ask.

Then why run away?

"We heard you guys were trying to frame us for a burglary," George replied with a straight face.

The cops were puzzled. Later they realized that the comment was an early indication of a pattern. When George got into trouble, he blamed someone else or claimed it was misunderstanding. He stubbornly refused to accept blame or responsibility, a standard symptom of the behavioral defect once labeled "psychopathy," renamed "sociopathy" after the movie *Psycho* had muddied the definition in the public mind, and eventually known as "antisocial personality disorder." By any label, these so-called antisocials had failed to develop a conscience, a capacity for empathy, an emotional attachment to mankind. The syndrome, accompanied by extreme narcissism, often prefigured a life of crime.

A few months after the runaway incident the police department's mascot masterminded another adventure, well recalled by an admiring friend.

Me and George and another guy liked guns, so we got all scrubbed up and took a bus to the gun exchange in Seattle. Then he led us to a pornie movie house called the Green Parrot. We went down the back alley and up the fire escape into an empty building and climbed through the rafters to a big cooling fan. We skinnied through a ceiling hatch and dropped into the men's bathroom. Our clothes were smudged; we were a mess.

The movie was about a hillbilly family. The man's getting a blow job in a rocking chair. The woman says, "Why you go limp, big daddy?" She looks up, says, "Big daddy's daid!" It was so corny, we were laughing out loud.

They showed a famous old short. A knock on the door, guy says, "Pizza delivery!" A woman answers and he unzips his fly and says, "Here's your pepperoni!" Oh, we loved it. We're laughing so hard we get caught and have to run out the exit doors.

George went back a couple days later with a black kid from Mercer Island. They pulled the ceiling hatch and looked into the men's room and there's a guy standing in one of the stalls. They wait and wait for him to leave and finally another man walks in and the two of 'em do anal sex. George's friend had a 'fro comb in his hair and it fell into the men's room and *everybody* ran.

I always wondered how George learned about the Green Parrot. How'd a fifteen-year-old kid even *know* about something like that? I asked and he just kinda winked.

It was Mysterious George again. His classmates were getting used to the act.

GEORGE WALTERFIELD RUSSELL Jr. entered high school in September, 1973, one of the smallest boys in his class. Mercer Island High was top-rated and a little snooty, not without justification. To the embarrassment of coaches and teachers, an unofficial jeer sometimes went up from a few patrician islanders when opposing teams scored:

> *That's all right.*
> *That's okay.*
> *You're gonna work for us someday.*

A high percentage of graduates went on to successful careers, but many failed totally; there didn't seem to be much middle ground. No one knew exactly why.

The Mercer Island *Reporter,* an energetic hometown booster, sometimes alluded to the problem in stories about troubled students. It seemed that the island had always been hard on adolescents. Many of the first settlers were Jews and Scandinavians who crossed the lake from Seattle before World War II and established their own social order in the bucolic setting. Later immigrants were of a different sort: newly affluent, hard-driving, self-made members of the upper middle class—Boeing executives, lawyers, airline pilots, sales reps, medics, stockbrokers, insurance men,

merchants—*winners*, with an unhealthy contempt for losers. A Condé Nast study in 1961 described the island as
"upper-level suburbia" and noted that seventy-two percent
of the husbands and fathers were "professionals, owners,
managers or officials." A third of the wives and mothers
were college graduates.

Seattle columnist Jean Godden described Mercer Island
as a place "where poverty means driving last year's Mercedes." By 1989 the median value of homes had risen to
$400,000, with waterfront averages higher. The lifestyle ex-
erted heavy pressure on the young, as Michael O'Hara
learned early.

There was so much gossip about lawns, clothes, hair, vacations, how much money you had, your dad's job. You were
always nervous that your neighbor was gonna get a new car;
if he did, you'd have one within three months. Everything was
a competition: bigger boats and boathouses, homes with four-
car garages, country club and beach club memberships, great
seats at Husky and Seahawk games, trips to Palo Alto to visit
the kid at Stanford Law. We called it "keeping up with the
Larsons." It wasn't enough to have a beautiful home with a
white picket fence and tulip beds and pruned roses and
bleached rockeries and a lawn that sloped to the lake. You had
to push, keep climbing, shove that fucking rock. If you weren't
upgrading, you were downgrading.

We kids were, you know . . . different. Eight-year-olds wore
Brittania shirts, designer jeans, fifty-dollar Adidas sneakers.
You'd see teenagers carrying leather golf bags. We spent our
summers lolling in our parents' boats or their Eldorados, swimming in heated pools, shooting pool in billiard rooms with
mahogany paneling. We played cards on octagon-shaped tables
covered in felt, with woven-leather pockets for the chips. We
had drag races on Island Crest Way: Mercedes 450s, Lancias,
Audis, classic cars, Porsche 911s. You didn't see many Chev-
ies or pickups.

Our mothers did their nails and their hair and their gardens,
rearranged our living rooms, reupholstered our furniture and
then re-reupholstered. When the house was crammed with possessions, they held lawn sales. You'd see Eames chairs, Steu-

ben glass, Tiffany lamps, sit-down lawn mowers, customized golf carts sitting out in the rain. The object was to open up space for more possessions, not to make money.

Islanders flew to Hawaii the way most people go to the beach. We joked: "How do Mercer Islanders say hi? '*Aloha!*' " We had dueling vacations. If a neighbor said, "We're going to Fiji," a proper response would be "We're going to Angkor Wat." One of my high school friends was dragged to the Canary Islands. *Hated* it.

Some of us were permanently stressed; nowadays I guess they'd call it "dissociated." Every day we wondered, How can I achieve this kind of a life on my own? How can I ever measure up to Dad? Counseling was a growth industry. We lived to graduate and get away. For a kid, Mercer was the worst place on earth to build self-esteem and confidence, unless you had a therapeutic family. You'd never get any feeling of self-respect from the community at large. We borrowed esteem from our parents and friends, but we always knew it was an illusion. When we left "The island," as we usually called it, or "the Bubble," or "Poverty Rock," when we were no longer shielded by our parents' bank accounts, what would we become? Garbage collectors? *Homeless?* Some did.

B Y THE TIME George Russell entered high school, his fellow students had noticed his size and agility and dubbed him "The Fly." Unlike some black children, he didn't waste much time practicing basketball shots, but he seemed to have a playmaker's moves. Some called him "Leapin' George," after Leapin' Lee Winfield of the Seattle Super-Sonics. But he was also called "Chicken George" or "The Mouth" because he chattered so much and claimed too many fouls. He was still a gameplayer—chess, backgammon, checkers, poker—but he was so skilled by now that he complained to friends that he had to play beneath his skill to get a game. He traded sports cards, stamps, coins, often getting the worst of the deal. He seemed to be deliberately losing in an effort to ingratiate himself. He was the kid who retrieved the home run, wiped the muddy football, raked the track. He was lavish with his praise of his fellow students' outfits, hairdos, and cars.

His close friend Tom Haggar basked in the light of George.

He was so bright, so entertaining. He had an incredible memory. He wanted to be a writer and kept an ongoing list of our dead schoolmates. He'd sit in his room and write out their stories—good stuff, publishable. He had stacks of yachting magazines, how to find the right sailboat, how to make your own, how to rig for storms, hurricanes. Stuff on motorcycles, guns. We read spy magazines, went to spy movies.

It's odd, considering the way things turned out, but in our adolescence we weren't big on girlie magazines. We read 'em, but they weren't a special interest. Mainly we were dreamers; anything was possible. We'd smoke a joint and ramble on. We'd get on our bikes and ride to Luther Burbank Park, "The Burb," and talk about sailing around the world. George had maps of every ocean on his walls. He figured out the winds, how to cross the Indian Ocean, how to handle the currents at Tierra del Fuego.

We read *Popular Science* and decided we were gonna build a submarine. We went down to my dock and got two plastic garbage cans with locking tops, made a seal, locked 'em and put a hole in the top, screwed a hose into it. Then I said to George, "We gotta be crazy." We both started laughing. George said, "This'll never work." He was right.

We decided to open a restaurant in a little house on the water. Two teenagers! That idea died in about an hour. We knew we were dreaming, laughed about it, kidded each other.

He wanted to be a detective, but we didn't buy the crime magazines. He was into CIA stuff where you nicked somebody with an umbrella tip and they died three weeks later. Spies, intrigue. He had secretive ways; he'd stand outside my room at night and flash his little light till I saw him.

He'd say things like, "People in lighted houses can't see out their windows. That's important to remember."

I'd say, "Why's that important?" and he'd just shrug and smile. Nothing seemed to bother him; he got along with everybody. No, I take that back. George didn't like to be excluded.

From *anything*. If he got left off a team or didn't get invited to a party, he'd sulk. I always wondered, What the hell did George get left out of when he was a little boy in Maryland? Was that what made him this way? I never found out.

EVERY AFTERNOON THE neighborhood boys assembled in Larry Victor's big yard to play games: baseball, Wiffle ball, basketball, touch football. "We played Army," a friend recalled. "George always won. Before you could take two steps, you were dead. He had eyes like a falcon's."

In one-on-one basketball, George would pretend he was Bill Bradley or Bob Cousy and his opponent Julius Erving or Spencer Haywood. In football, George would be Sonny Jurgensen against Joe Namath. Friends noticed that George never picked a black athlete. He seemed uninterested in the racial studies that his mother now taught at the University of Washington or anything connected with the African-American culture. In complexion, he was the darkest of the four members of his immediate family, but the slightest reference to his race or color brought a scowl or a heavy blink of his big brown-black eyes.

"As a kid, George never wanted to be referred to as black," Glendon Booth recalled twenty years later. "You could get him hackled up real quick."

He was visibly annoyed when a high school coach mentioned that Bill Russell Jr. was developing into a better basketball player. "Buddha's headed for the NBA and you're not."

George complained to his friends. "Why'd he compare me to Buddha? Why not compare me to a white kid?"

Mercer Island High School teams were known as the Islanders, and a logo about six feet tall scowled over the school gym: a savage South Sea warrior with Polynesian features and a bone through his nose. The symbol seemed to go with the pickaninny statuary and hitching posts still to be found on the island. The logo lasted for ten years till more delicate sensibilities prevailed.

George Russell Jr. wasn't one of the complainants. Said a classmate: "George didn't make waves. The remark he heard more than any other was, 'George, you're the whitest guy I've ever known.' I think he liked that. But it was never easy to tell what George was thinking."

His romantic life seemed typical for a high school student. He went from crush to crush, suffered devastating turndowns, drew up checklists of girls he coveted but was afraid to approach, big names on campus like Alice Levy and her friend Mary Strome, Wendy Calvert, Linda Campbell, Kathy Adams—schoolyard beauties, unattainables.

"God, they were darling girls," George's friend Tom Haggar recalled, "but they wouldn't let us close. They were class officers, shopped at Nordstrom, had bigger houses, bigger boats, boyfriends in college. There were exceptions, but Mercer Island High generally produced prudes. A girl and her pants were seldom parted. It was tough on all of us, not just George. The only guys who consistently made out were the jocks."

After a while the color that George disdained gave him entrée to the high school elite; he was the perfect token, a walking proof of his friends' tolerance. But therein lay other problems, as Haggar recognized early.

> They treated him like their favorite eunuch. He projected the image of the pet black, and that was fine with the socialites. But they left him out of things that mattered. They pretended to accept him as a friend because they knew they'd never have to take him seriously. I always felt this helped to cause the rage that came out later, 'cause he was tight with lots of girls, and they tempted him like they tempted the rest of us, but they never let it go anywhere. George was permanently excluded and knew it. Those lily-white soshes were *never* gonna put out for the local black guy.

George just kept suffering. Never complained—that would've been uncool. But we all felt that pain, not just George. Racing hormones!

He rarely confided about girls; it was another subject he wasn't open about. He told me he wanted love, not sex. He was always looking for the ideal woman to put up on the pedestal. But the ideal woman wasn't looking for him.

IN HIGH SCHOOL George was a dervish, with a robust laugh and gleaming smile, but he seemed increasingly shallow to brighter classmates. When his typical teenage dreams proved unattainable, he turned to tricks and schemes, like the field trip to the Green Parrot. Students marveled at his street smarts, the slick way he circumvented rules and regulations. To younger boys who seldom journeyed across the Interstate 90 bridge into Seattle without their parents, his knowledge of the big city was impressive. Everyone wondered where he'd learned so many hustles and scams.

Led Zeppelin played Seattle at twelve dollars per ticket. George told his friend Michael O'Hara how to beat the cost.

He told me to meet him outside the Kingdome fence an hour before the concert. When I got there he was wearing a parking attendant's jacket, brown-and-orange polyester. So uncool, so unlike George. It put me in hysterics.

He flips a bundle over the fence and there's an attendant's jacket inside. I slipped it over my clothes and walked right into the Kingdome parking lot. George and I are directing traffic as we edge toward the employees' entrance!

I slipped out of the outfit in the men's room so George could bundle it up for another friend. He got nine of us in. We were in total admiration. How did a teenage kid from Mercer Island outwit Kingdome security? He was always doing things like that. It seemed like scams had become his life.

As his GPA sank steadily lower, George sought out younger students and was less involved with his peers. Despite his high energy level, he came across as essentially bored. He had a newspaper route but tired of it. He signed up for extra PE and handed out towels in the school locker, then quit. He never stuck to anything, and he always sought the easy way. He stole pills from his stepfather's dental supplies and shared them around. He showed up with marijuana and explained that it came from a stash he'd found at home.

Classmates suspected him of stealing from school lockers. He was caught lifting a rare penny, valued at about thirty dollars, from a friend's coin collection, but talked his way out of it. When he came afoul of the law, it was often in the company of younger children engaged in bubblegum crime: trespassing in the park, curfew violation, shoplifting, drinking, popping Valiums.

Michael O'Hara was sympathetic.

> A lot of us were just drifting, not just George. Half the high school smoked pot. Maybe twenty percent took harder drugs—acid, mushrooms, hash. Maybe ninety percent drank. We spent a lot of time in our forts, smoking, drinking. On Friday nights the cops would come stormtrooping through the woods and George would disappear. Interpol couldn't've found him. After the cops left, he'd climb out of his foxhole, grinning. He loved to outwit people and especially cops.

GEORGE STILL TALKED about becoming a detective, but his old friends on the police department began to worry about his behavior. When he was about sixteen, he received some unsolicited advice from Patrolman J. C. Goodman: "Look, Georgie, a police career is still doable, but you have to get yourself straightened around. You can't be on the periphery of all this minor criminal bullshit. Hang around with kids your own age. Grow up! Show us the effort, we'll help ya.''

Goodman and his colleagues kept after their sometime helper. "We tried to be somebody in George's life that, 'Okay, George, we like you for who you are, but we've got rules and you don't break 'em. You break the rules, there's punishment.' We tried to give him another image of a cop other than somebody who is going to smack you upside the head if you mess up. 'Cause as kids're growing up, that's the thought of cops.''

George continued doing odd jobs at the police station, but increasingly he seemed drawn to the night and the streets. With younger companions he was chased from several parks after curfew. Glen Booth and a few other cops suspected problems at home; else why would such a young boy be running loose at all hours?

"The Mobleys were a little distant for Mercer Island," Booth recalled. "This is a closed community where you know everybody's mom and dad, first name, last name, sister's name, dog's name. But we heard very little about George's people.''

The Mobley parents seemed oriented to Seattle, across the lake, where Wonzel practiced his dentistry and Joyce was active in Black Arts West, a theater group. George later claimed that his mother taught drama to Ron Glass, one of the detectives on the TV hit *Barney Miller*, and that she worked with the talented actor Danny Glover. George spent a lot of time babysitting his half-sister Erika, and he still seemed to love the bright little girl and enjoy her company.

A contemporary detected an undercurrent of trouble after a rare visit to the Mobley house. The parents didn't appear to be speaking. Little Erika was the obvious favorite, and George was barely endured. It wasn't surprising. Erika's energy and brainpower went into schoolwork, George's into mischief. Unspoken tensions filled the air.

It soon developed that Joyce Mobley, holder of a master's degree and much in demand for her incisive lectures on black studies, planned to accept a teaching position at the University of Maryland, three thousand miles away.

"They both wanted out," an intimate confided. "Wonzel was seeing a white businesswoman, and Joyce hated the idea of being in the same town with the two of them, maybe running into them socially. She needed to get as far from the situation as possible. She and Wonzel finally agreed that Erika would move to the East with Joyce but spend summers and vacations on Mercer Island. When it came to George, it was, 'You take him,' 'No, *you* take him.' *'No, you take him! . . .'*

"Wonzel ended up with a sixteen-year-old kid who was already stealing him blind. You gotta give the man credit; he tried to do the right thing. Think about it. They weren't even blood."

JUST BEFORE CHRISTMAS, 1974, Joyce and Erika Mobley moved to College Park, Maryland. Close friends noticed a dampening of George's customary bumptiousness, a slippage of spirit that he typically tried to gloss over with words. He explained to a few close friends that his mother had wanted him to go with her, but he just couldn't bring himself to leave Mercer Island. "Within thirty-five minutes I can ski, sail, fish, go boating, practically any activity I want. Who'd trade this for Maryland?"

Some found the explanation unconvincing. George had always been bored with the outdoors; he was a creature of 7-Elevens, discos, hiding places, cozy living rooms with VCRs and video games. No one was surprised when he seemed to lose all interest in school.

TOM HAGGAR REMEMBERED the excitement when Dr. Wonzel Mobley's new mate moved in.

Kris was nice to us, prim, proper, respectable—and gorgeous. When she arrived, all us adolescent boys went, Ooh-la-la! I'm sure she tried to play down her looks, but she was twelve years younger than Wonzel and still a knockout. She really had our motors running. George's mother had always worn hats and glasses and looked like a professor. Not unattractive, but . . . Kris was different.

Right from the start she tried hard to work with George, change his ways. And she helped Wonzel to fit into the neighborhood. The older and wealthier people had always considered him "the black guy," but Kris arranged cookouts and get-togethers. Old islanders said, "My God, Dr. Mobley's black, but he's not that different!" It was an astounding discovery for some of those dinosaurs. Pretty soon the Mobleys were the only racially mixed couple in Emmanuel Episcopal Church.

My mom wound up crazy about Kris and very fond of Wonzel. After that, they were always a part of our lives.

A<small>T ABOUT THE</small> time the new Mrs. Mobley settled in, piquant stories from confidential police files began circulating in the corridors of the high school. Several parents called to complain that their children's reputations were being tarnished by leaks of juvenile information that was supposed to be secret by law. After a quiet investigation, J. C. Goodman and his colleagues came to the reluctant conclusion that their friend Georgie was running his mouth. Apparently he was using police information to inflate his insider image with schoolmates.

"We had no proof," Goodman recalled, "but it was obvious. We hated to cut him loose. We never told him why. We just said, 'Georgie, you can't come around here anymore.' You could see it bothered him. Bothered us, too. You couldn't *not* like the guy, no matter how bad things got."

* * *

George acted unfazed, but friends realized he'd suffered a blow. All he'd talked about was going to college to study criminal justice and law enforcement before attending a police academy and climbing the ladder to the exalted position of homicide detective, where he could exercise his talents for solving puzzles. Now that he was banned from the station house, he seemed bewildered and lost.

As always, exclusion affected his behavior. In his junior year he cut classes, drank, stole, popped pills and smoked pot. He became a regular in juvenile court, often talking his way to freedom. He had an excuse for every malfeasance, and if he was caught with other boys, he didn't hesitate to point a finger. George was spiraling downward.

I feel personally that there was such a really smart, valuable person in there if it could've been touched at one time—but it wasn't. He could've been the brain surgeon that saved lives instead of being prosecuted for killing them.

—MICHAEL WASHINGTON, D.D.S.

Shortly after word reached police headquarters that Dr. Wonzel Mobley had finally lost all patience with his stepson, George was dispatched to the off-island home of Dr. Michael Washington, Wonzel's old classmate at Howard University dental school. According to the bold new blueprint, George would spend his senior year at Inglemoor High School, majoring in English and drama, his mother's favorite subjects. The prevailing philosophy would be "tough love," and Dr. Washington would be the guru.

The dentist seemed an inspired choice. Like George's mother and stepfather and most of the African-Americans in their circle of friends, he was a self-made man who'd become a success against odds that would have defeated most whites. With George, he was gentle but firm. He saw the boy's problem as too much spare time and too little discipline, and he intended to keep him busy. Years later George still recalled Dr. Washington's first words of advice: "I don't care if a man's black, yellow or green. There's nothing that a human being can't accomplish through hard work and diligence."

At first, Mercer Islanders missed George, if not his peccadilloes. The general feeling was that he was a likable boy— at a distance. As usual, his family reserved comment. Only a few friends knew what was going on, and they were asked to butt out and give George a chance at rehabilitation.

Patrolman J. C. Goodman was surprised to run into his former mascot at a hardware store in an outlying Seattle area called Totem Lake. "We'd all wondered where he went, why he wasn't causing any more problems on the island. I met the dentist he was staying with—a tall, good-looking, muscular guy. Very nice, very responsible. Just what George needed."

Five or six months later George reappeared on Mercer Island, walking his St. Bernard, Max. It was the same old scenario: the brown-and-white dog pulling and jerking, "The Fly" holding on for life. A patrol cop asked how things were going. With his customary panache, George told about great times at Inglemoor High, how challenging it had been to make a new start off the island, how Mike Washington's principle of "tough love" had pointed him in a new direction.

But he told his friend Tom Haggar a different story.

George could hardly discuss it without shaking. Dr. Washington had warned him that a black person had to work harder and longer and faster. That formula was gonna save George's ass. Dr. Washington didn't understand that George's only ambition was to get by *without* working. They were bound to clash.

The first morning Dr. Washington came into George's room at four forty-five and said, "Up and at 'em, man! The kennel needs to be cleaned. The dogs need to be washed and fed.''

Horror!

George said every day started at dawn, except hunting days, when they'd get up at two. They'd drive a couple hours, and Dr. Washington would throw a big pack on George's back, hand him a thirteen-pound shotgun and lead him into a slough at full trot. They'd hunch down on a patch of ice and Dr. Washington would say, "Now we're gonna shoot some ducks.''

They'd wait for hours. Ten-degree weather, snow, slush, wind. Dr. Washington would jump up and fire a few shots. God forbid he hit anything, because George said he had to clean it. George told him, "Hey, we can buy these things at the market for five bucks apiece. Already cleaned!''

They'd get home late, smelling like duckshit, and George would have to wash the dogs, clean the kennel and gear, oil the shotguns, eat dinner and break out the books. This was against everything he'd ever stood for.

Dr. Washington kept thinking that George would adjust, finish high school, maybe serve a hitch in the service, followed by college at government expense and a high-paying profession, like him and his old friend Wonzel. They thought George would slide right into the program. He was an enigma to all of them: Wonzel, Joyce, Dr. Washington, all those black overachievers who pulled themselves up by their own intelligence and hard work. George couldn't relate to them any more than he could relate to a wombat. Too bad. It might have saved his life, and a few others.

THE EXILE'S RETURN to Mercer Island coincided with the exodus of his classmates to college. Once again he found himself abandoned. He quickly regrouped his band of juveniles, and when he wasn't leading them into mischief, he began hustling them out of their cars and money. Servile with adults, he seemed to enjoy victimizing the young. The cops watched helplessly at the exercise in control.

"He developed a buncha wanna-be George Russells," said a juvenile officer. "They met in video stores, Denny's, the 7-Eleven. There'd be a hundred kids milling around that store. King George would go inside and buy beer for them, stash it in the woods.

"He also supplied weed and discipline. He never liked to fight, but he kept those kids cowed. It was almost impossible to prosecute him 'cause the kids were too scared to snitch. If they got outa line, he'd flash his knife.

"He'd take one of the rich kids aside and say, 'Lend me your car, I'll be right back, I gotta pick up a friend.' The kids were too afraid to complain when he kept it a day or two. That became a habit; he was 'borrowing' cars the same way ten years later."

One day Sergeant Glendon Booth spotted him putting a stranglehold on a boy who reached to his chin. "This punk wasn't cooperating," George explained, as though that covered the matter. The child's parents declined to press charges.

Then he beat up a nine-year-old boy for putting a slug in a video machine. "It offended his sense of control," Booth explained. "It was okay for *him* to slug those machines, but nobody else."

He broadened and refined his portfolio of scams. "Leapin' George" would pick out a parked car and bet that he could clear it in a single bound. He would jump over the hood and collect the money, explaining that he hadn't promised to clear the roof.

One day Booth and a partner took up positions on a hillside to check the 7-Eleven action through binoculars. They saw George emerge with several six-packs and disappear into the woods. They also saw drugs change hands. When the cops patted him down during the arrest, he had a kitchen knife up each sleeve and several Baggies of weed.

A tolerant judge put the clean-cut young man on probation, but before long George was arrested again and charged with criminal trespass, possession of marijuana, second-degree burglary, possession of stolen property and a popular offense called "nuisance noise." He'd just turned eighteen and was tried in District court. He was sentenced to three days in King County Jail, reoffended and served four days, reoffended and served thirty-two more. His arrest record grew, mostly minor offenses ("those little Tic-Tacs of trouble," as he discounted them later).

In his first few years after high school he often slid off the hook. Mercer Island's judges were tolerant, especially after hearing his sob stories in court. Even when he was caught in the act, he would argue that it was a misunderstanding. Now and then he made the more grandiose claim that he'd been railroaded. At trial he always maneuvered for the last word. Once he told a judge, "I'm innocent, Your Honor, but according to what these cops are telling you, you'll find me guilty, so what the heck—I plead guilty." The bemused judge let him off with another warning.

WITH EACH SUCCEEDING high-school graduation ceremony, George became more estranged from contemporaries and more dependent on his wits. In between legitimate jobs that seldom lasted more than a month or two, he began a steady routine of petty theft and other misdemeanors. His easiest marks, besides his wanna-bes, were old friends and neighbors. Tom Haggar and his family became prime victims.

George *lived* at night. He would hide in bushes and learn your habits. He was patient; he'd watch a house for a week if that's what it took. He could slip through any opening. He got into one house through the dog port!

He knew that our doors were always unlocked and the keys were always in our Jag. So when I was away at college, he started borrowing it after midnight. When he finally got caught, he told the cops he had permission.

This was just *too* much, and our family decided we had to do something. We put together a complete dossier—arrests, convictions, plus everything he'd gotten away with since junior high—and presented it to the judge. When you saw it on paper, it was an eye-opener. George ended up serving thirty-five days. It was his longest stretch, and everybody hoped it would straighten him out.

When he was released, did he stay away from our house? Not George! He made it a regular target. We had a sliding glass door; that was his entry point. My mom had a stash of silver dollars that she gave out as rewards. George took six or seven at a time; I guess he figured she wouldn't notice. Think about it: The guy's slipping into our house at night, risking a felony burglary charge for pocket money! There had to be some other motivation, but we didn't learn what it was till it was too late.

Other stuff began disappearing. I came home from college on a break and ran into him at Luther Burbank Park. From thirty yards away I recognized my old orange coat. He was wearing my sweater and pants.

He asked if I wanted to get high. He looked terrible, wasted, like every other bum on the street. It brought a lump to my throat. George was the brightest, the most interesting kid I'd ever met. He still had that smile, that big laugh. But you could see he was lost.

I said, "George, that's my down coat."

He said, "Oh, is it?" He sounded kind of vague. "Here, let me give it back," avoiding the question of where he got it.

I said, "Chrisakes, no! I don't want it back." It was beat-up, dirty

I felt guilty because of this huge gulf between us. I said, "If you'd asked me for the coat, George, I'd've given it to you. The point is, how did you get it?"

He evaded an answer. I wasn't gonna push.

THE MERCER ISLAND Police Department began picking up persistent complaints of a night-prowling nomad with dark skin. It appeared that George was stepping up his depredations.

Sergeant Glendon Booth called on Dr. Mobley and learned that George had taken liquor, money and clothes before being banished from the house. An older rumor persisted: that George's advances toward the dentist's young wife had made the home situation intolerable.

He found shelter with a friend till the friend discovered that his worldly goods were disappearing piece by piece. Then it was back to the street. Booth and his colleagues received a flurry of reports.

> He was sleeping in abandoned houses, under neighbors' houses, in high grass, in his old forts. He removed the vent from the swimming pool heating duct and crawled in there. Did the same with the grate at a bank. It was like Goldilocks and her bears; folks would come home and find the bed messed up, the heater turned on, food on the table. If there was snow on the ground you could track him in and out of every yard on the north end. The Ferris family had a boat cabana, and they'd come down in the morning and find him wrapped around the base of the toilet. A friend let him sleep in his crawl space.
>
> There was an old garage back in the woods near his home, and he finally moved in there. No heat, no light, no toilet. We'd shine our police flashlights through the blackberry bushes and he'd peek out and yell, "No problem, Officer. Thanks for checkin'. I'm fine." Then he'd say, "How's the wife? How's everything at the station? Gee, I'll have to drop in and see you guys...."
>
> Some of those nights it was below freezing. We didn't have the heart to turn him out.

The vagabond also slept in parked cars, vestibules, hallways, under the canvas covers of parked boats. His old friend Patrolman Manny Rucker took a bad fall while trying to roust him from the second floor of a construction site in downtown Mercer Island.

"How ya doin', Officer Rucker?" George said in a plaintive voice as the damaged cop limped past him at the booking station. "Gee, I hope you're okay."

"I'm fine," Rucker answered. "Just bruises."

"Thank God it's not worse," George said in a grateful tone.

Rucker asked, "What do you give a damn?"

"Man, anytime you get caught for something and a cop gets hurt, they charge your ass for assault!"

"George," said the indulgent policeman, "you don't have to worry. It's my own fault for climbing up in the rafters."

George kept repeating, "Thank you, Officer. Oh, thank you. . . ."

He was acquitted of criminal trespass.

SERGEANT GLEN BOOTH became one of the first to realize the extent of the nighttime incursions and what they might portend.

George would try every car door he passed, looking for change, cigarettes, cassette tapes—small stuff. Then he'd sell it or trade it. He'd go to parties and leave with a ring or a watch.

Mostly he operated in the north end of the island, where he was raised. The south end was uphill, and George was lazy. When we stopped him, he was usually on foot, unless we caught him on a stolen bike, and then he'd say a kid loaned it to him.

"What kid, George?"

"I dunno. I just met him."

I bet he stole a hundred bikes on Mercer Island, mostly from boys that thought he was their friend.

At heart he was still a kid looking for excitement. Folks would go on vacation and he'd open up the garage, roll out their BMW and ride around. "Taking and riding," we call it. A constant problem.

Then he moved up to gutsier stuff. He'd lift somebody's wallet, and if he was caught, he'd smile and say, "I was just teaching him a lesson." Everything was a game. He'd meet some rich family and cultivate them till he learned where they hid their keys. Then they got burgled.

Long after they knew he was stealing them blind, some of his neighbors couldn't bring themselves to turn him in. How could you hold a grudge against good old George?

You asked how he was doing, he'd give you ten minutes on how things were fine with him and his dad and Kris and his new baby brother. How was his mom? "Oh, great, teaching back East, giving lectures. She just sent me a nice birthday present. I talked to her on the phone last night," et cetera et cetera.

Most of it was bullshit. He was living on the street. He didn't have a pot to piss in or a window to throw it out of. Dr. Mobley had me check his closets and under his beds because George was sneaking back in at night and they didn't want to confront him. I got the impression that George was still bothering Kris, too. I agreed that this could turn dangerous.

Most of the time George just avoided us cops. Talk about balls! He got hold of a scanner and punched in all our channels: Mercer Island, Bellevue, State Police, King County, the feds. When a police officer went on a toilet break, George knew. When duty rosters were posted, George knew. Every time we stopped him, he had the same things: scanner, miniature chess and backgammon sets, a *Playboy* or *Penthouse* and pictures of girls.

We seldom nailed him for burglary, usually had to settle for criminal trespass, which just means we caught him where he didn't belong. He'd trip an alarm and we'd drive up and he'd be doing the George Russell heel-and-toe down the street with the scanner at his ear. "Hi, Officer. How's it going?"

He did a long string of burglaries on First Hill. Chippy stuff. He was a major criminal of minor crimes. People would call us and say, "I had forty dollars in my wallet when I went to bed. I heard a noise in the middle of the night, and now I got twenty." Or they'd say, "My front door's open. I'm sure I left it closed." Or "I heard somebody downstairs, but nobody answered."

We knew it was George. Who the hell else would ignore thousand-dollar rings and steal a Mickey Mouse watch? He'd hit the same house three or four times. I began to suspect there was a sexual aspect to it. In nighttime intrusions, there often is.

If we could've caught him with the goods, things might've been different. But he had ratholes. We'd find his stash in the woods and couldn't tie it to him. It was like connecting a squirrel with his acorns. Loot didn't stick to him long. He'd trade it or hide it or give it away. George had as big a need to give as he had to take, but first he had to have something to give—earrings, rings, bracelets, all from his burglaries.

For a while I wondered why he didn't shift his operation to Seattle or Portland or even farther, somewhere he wasn't known and the whole town wasn't on his ass. I told him a dozen times, "Georgie, why don't you act up somewhere else? Why shit where you eat?"

He'd always laugh and act like he didn't know what I was talking about.

Well, it wasn't that hard to figure why he stuck around. George's MO required intimate knowledge of the area: hiding places, trails that went from nowhere to nowhere, support troops, flunkies, inside information, a steady supply of victims and forgiveness. He needed heated boathouses and gazebos and vacation houses, and hot cars to "take and ride." A setup like this takes years to develop. He couldn't survive in a strange place. To most Mercer Islanders, he was still a pet black, a token. I don't think he ever heard the word "nigger" in his life, but that's what he'd've encountered in a lot of other places. And he knew it. And so he stayed and stayed. And stayed.

In LATER YEARS one of George's friends described the central concerns of most Mercer Islanders in their early twenties: "marijuana, malls, Bolivian marching powder, sex, movies, Big Macs, snowstorms, car radios at full bass, hoops, Frisbees, throwing a football, swimming in Lake Washington, arguing, gossiping, soaps, jeans, backgammon, chess, high-tops, being cool, the electric slide, the lambada, getting hammered, stoned and ripped."

George Russell's superficiality went largely unnoticed because it was the norm. Like many of his peers, he'd always been capable of spending a whole morning picking out a shirt at Bellevue Square, then discarding it when he saw the same style on someone else. Even when he was wearing stolen clothes, he looked down on those whose jeans bore the wrong label. He was a Mercer Islander.

Against the odds, he still seemed to cling to his view of himself as a future detective, heroically solving the Northwest's backlist of unsolved homicides—the fantasy of his early teens. He liked to jump into emergency situations, take names, direct traffic. He was in his glory when any cop acknowledged him. He spotted a man masturbating in a car on the lakefront, flagged down a police car and assisted with the arrest. He wore a Seattle PD cap and carried a school patrol badge.

One night he flashed the badge at a barmaid. "I work with the police department," he confided. "Special agent. I heard there's a lot of coke dealing around here and I'm gonna infiltrate it." His drinking companions became nervous and left.

Too late, he tried to recover his standing with the Mercer Island officers. Some of the older hands enjoyed his company in spite of themselves, but kept a wary eye. In his twenties he began spending more time in jail—short stretches, two days, a day, a week. Judges and counselors were reluctant to write him off; he'd always known how to dazzle authority figures. He inundated jail guards with palaver, agreed with their generally conservative opinions, and listened to their personal problems like a talk show host. When anyone told a joke or made a wisecrack, he laughed raucously and clapped his hands. When he repeated a quote, he wiggled the index and middle fingers of each hand.

"The first time I went to visit him in King County Jail," said Tom Haggar, once his best friend, "he'd been there less than a week and was already a trusty—handing out milk, running errands, working in the dispensary. Jail was the closest George ever got to the pension system he really needed: three meals a day, cable TV, full medical and dental. He figured that King County Jail beat Dr. Washington's tough love. If only they'd let him sleep a little later . . ."

There were a few flare-ups with other prisoners, most of whom were street-savvy blacks, jailed for crimes up to and including murder. It didn't take them long to recognize that when George acted like a "brother," he was doing an impression. The painful word "oreo" was thrown at him again, as well as more derogatory terms: "house nigger," "Tom," and the ultimate jailhouse insult, "snitch."

A puzzled look flickered across his face in the presence of the ghetto patois known as blacktalk—"Yo, blood, what be shakin', bro?" It was a perfectly comprehensible tongue to those who'd spoken it all their lives, but George treated it like Sanskrit. His own speech reflected the genteel English of his surrogate parents and his natural mother. He said "transpired," "*was* graduated" instead of "graduated," "incarcerate," "interacts," "consensus" instead of "consensus of opinion," "issue-wise," "time-wise." He admitted to friends that he had a "forte" for getting in trouble, pronouncing it in the musical way: "for-tay." He eschewed vulgarities like "hopefully" and Reagan-era affectations like "point in time" and "guv-mint." He over-enunciated, widening his lips and lengthening his vowels, giving some the impression that he was talking down, or that he suspected they were deaf. Except for a few consistent errors—"excape," "expecially," "disheeveled," "between you and I," "tolerable" for "tolerant"—he sounded like a well- rounded, well-schooled Mercer Islander. And *white*. People who spoke to him only on the telephone were surprised when they learned his color.

In jail he concealed his disdain for African-Americans, but he confided to a white inmate that he'd seldom had black friends and never dated black females. He wasn't above an occasional racist reference—"You're just taking advantage of the poor nigger"—but only when there was something to be gained by such amiable obsequy. Despite his aversion to those with dark pigmentation, he learned the ghetto art of "doin' the dozens," exchanging highly stylized rhetorical insults, most of them beginning with personal references to one's mother or sister. But pejoratives had never rolled trippingly from his tongue, and he seemed to prefer to sit in his cell and work out chess problems, write letters, and read.

IN BETWEEN JAIL sentences, he expended large amounts of energy avoiding work. Because he was a known thief and high school dropout, his employment prospects were limited. He didn't appear to be interested in a regular job, even as a cover for criminal activities. In his twenties he spent a few days on a construction crew, worked a shift at a fish processing plant, clerked for a week or two in a hardware store, labored briefly for a hot tub company, and clerked in a video game shop in the sumptuous Bellevue Square shopping center nicknamed Belsquare. He didn't like to carry ID and bragged that he had no Social Security number.

His fortunes improved when a friend hired him as assistant manager of a teen disco on Mercer Island, Tonite's the Nite. He checked IDs, collected tickets, worked the velvet chain, and stole receipts. He gained a reputation for playing favorites, passing friends to the front of the line and cracking down on troublemakers. He seemed to enjoy his taste of power and control.

A security guard recalled: "He would lose it real easy whenever a kid would question his authority, especially if the kid was female. They'd say, 'Well, who are *you*?' and George would yell, 'Hey, bitch, I'm the guy that's gonna throw your ass outa here.' "

His sharp temper didn't seem to square with his hearty laugh and jolly air. Flushed with drink, he sometimes sounded like a felon in search of a felony. When a barroom acquaintance complained to George that her boyfriend had hit her, he responded, "Where's the guy live? Let's go! We'll blow up his car. I'll show you how."

He continued to wear a good face for the police, but now and then the temper showed through. "We had a complaint that he was causing trouble at a private party," recalled Patrolman Tom Kettells, one of a new breed of Mercer Island officers. "We found him hiding under a bed.

" 'Okay, George,' we said, 'come on out.' He knew we couldn't arrest him.

"He says, 'I'm just helpin' these guys clean house.'

" 'They want you *out*, George.'

" 'I'm staying.'

" *'You're outa here!'*"

"George completely lost it. He slobbered, he spit, went crazy. Called us white trash, honkies, bigots. *Screaming!* He'd always kept his temper concealed. Whenever I handled him after that, I didn't think of him as cute little George or the station mascot. I thought of him as a mean son of a bitch."

A bartender began calling him "the schizo" because his personality changed so profoundly after drinks. Cool lovable George annoyed women and barely avoided fights with their boyfriends. He seemed to revel in baiting females, then slipping away to stir up trouble elsewhere. A friend said, "George tried to surround himself with girls, but he never really liked 'em. You only had to watch him five minutes to see it. Nobody knew why."

In two flourishing years at Tonite's the Nite he escalated from stealing nickels and dimes to a steady take of a hundred-odd dollars a night, usually by palming tickets and reselling them, or by pocketing receipts at the concession stands. Between his salary and thefts, he enjoyed a new affluence. He showed up in a cherry-red BMW 320i with mag wheels, flared fenders and other hot rod accoutrements—"Resada red," as he described the car to his friends, "the only one in the state." When he was asked where he got the money, he explained that the new car was in his stepfather's name and he was paying it off on his disco salary—"No sweat, no problem."

He drove the hot car in the tradition of Mercer Island's doomed young losers. The high school had more than its share of juvenile suicides, maimings, injury accidents and so-called shit-faced fatals. George's classmate Michael O'Hara remembered their dead friends and acquaintances.

Tom Olson was dragged to death behind a Volkswagen driven by Mad-dog Maddox. Kevin Harris was killed in the same accident. Sweet little Brenda Poole died in a motorcycle accident. So did Tyler Cox, one of our stars, two days after graduation. Pete Dawson, a great kid, was joyriding his motorcycle at a kegger when he crashed head-on with another bike and was blinded. He got his law degree and now he's an attorney in Seattle. A Mercer Island success story!

It seemed like every week it'd be, "Oh, did you hear about what's his name? He killed himself." "He went over the embankment on East Mercer Way." "He got mangled in a car crash. . . ."

A few years after George and I left Mercer Island High, Jason Perrine put Lynrd Skynyrd's *Freebird* tape on the car stereo, gunned the engine and piled into the junior high school wall. His girlfriend Dawn lived; Jason didn't. When I read about it in the Bellevue *Journal American*, I thought, Another day on Poverty Rock.

My friends found a million ways to die. Alan Sidell stuck a pipe in his car and killed himself in his parents' driveway. Our Little League right fielder snapped on weight belts and walked off his boat. Another teenaged kid hanged himself in his foyer so his body would be the first thing his parents saw when they got home; later his mother drowned under strange circumstances. John Stickney blew himself up with blasting powder. John Borst, our bandleader and basketball trainer, parked in the school smoking area where the heads used to hang out and killed himself with carbon monoxide.

There were others. The cops were cooperative, and a lot of

suicides were marked down as "leukemia," "kidney failure," things like that. Mercer Island was a hell of a place to die.

To his regular companions, George Russell seemed in a hurry to follow tradition and mangle himself in his new BMW. He took Tom Haggar and another friend for a spin on West Mercer Way, and within a few minutes they were pounding his back and begging him to pull over. "He was doing sixty in a thirty-five zone," Haggar recalled, "weaving back and forth across the center line. It was worse than bad driving; it was like . . . psychotic. He claimed he knew all about performance cars 'cause he'd driven his dad's Ferrari, but you could see he didn't have a clue."

Three weeks later George rolled the car on West Mercer Way. As always, he had an explanation: "The cops checked the skid marks and found out that those special T-7 nylon tires have no traction till they're warmed up."

It was also the tires' fault when he totaled a friend's Datsun on a drive up from California. At 5 A.M. he spun off Interstate 5 near Redding and broke through the median rail, fracturing his femur. He blamed the accident on a blowout, but police suspected he'd fallen asleep at the wheel.

Later he lost control of his 1981 gold Honda Civic, wiped out a fence and crashed into a tree. When police arrived, he was on his feet, babbling. A report noted, "Russell denied driving the car stating it had been stolen. He stated he just happened to be driving by and found his car crashed there so he got in it and tried to drive it out. Russell stated to me, when I arrested him, 'You're lucky. If I had a gun you would be dead.' "

He had equally surreal explanations for lacking a valid driver's license and using plates stolen from a friend. He was sentenced to a day in jail. After that he became the personification of the old Don Adams joke: "In L.A., somebody's hit by a car every ten hours. If I was that guy, I'd get outa town."

* * *

One dark night George was cycling at top speed when he failed to notice a Mercedes turning sharply in his path. He went up and over the big car, breaking the windshield and snapping the hood ornament with his knee.

His old friend Patrolman Manny Rucker arrived at the scene. "Georgie says, 'I got my eyes closed. Is that you, Officer Rucker?'

" 'Yeah, Georgie, it's me.'

" 'Well, I can't see. I think I got glass.'

" 'Just lay there.'

" 'Well, how bad am I hurt?'

" 'Not too bad. You got a cut across the top of your eye and your knee's tore up. Just sit there and relax.'

"I thought, Georgie, Georgie, when're you gonna stop hurting yourself like this?"

As usual, he was due in court on various misdemeanor charges, and the day after the biking accident a note arrived on the stationery of "Wonzel M. Mobley, D.D.S., P.S."

Your Honorable Judge,

This letter is to inform you that George Russell is in serious condition at Harborview Hospital as a result of being hit by a car. . . . George is looking at 6–8 weeks of recovery time per his team of Doctors. He had immediate surgery on his right knee, fractures on the fifth vertebrae of the spinal column (neck area), and very deep lacerations on his face which will require plastic surgery. . . . Thank you for your kind consideration on George's behalf.

Respectfully submitted,
Dr. and Mrs. W. M. Mobley

A handwritten signature read, "Wonzel and Kris Mobley." The dentist and his wife were standing by their troublesome ward.

* * *

A few months later George limped into court with Kris Mobley at his side. She explained to the judge that he'd been well behaved until his mother moved to Maryland. Under the circumstances, didn't he deserve another chance?

George disagreed with the approach but didn't disavow her words. He told a friend later that "a lot of negative remarks about my mom started that day in court. I thought what my stepmom said was ridiculous."

The judge let him off with a suspended sentence.

> *[The psychopath] hits upon conduct and creates situations so bizarre, so untimely, and so preposterous that their motivation appears inscrutable. Many of his exploits seem directly calculated to place him in a disgraceful or ignominious position.*
>
> —HERVEY CLECKLEY, M.D.,
> *THE MASK OF SANITY*

Inevitably, George Russell was fired from Tonite's the Nite for tapping the till. No more velvet chain, no more passing in his friends, no more manhandling kids. He took the news of his ouster without a show of emotion, beyond rage. The disco had provided prestige and income that few high school dropouts could match, and it was the center of his universe. Now he was permanently banned.

George planned his revenge. He knew that manager David Israel banked the weekend receipts early every Sunday. But what if the night depository was jammed? Wouldn't Israel just drive to his apartment and lock the money overnight in his car? The rest would be easy. George had made an art form of entering parked cars.

Just before dawn, a month after the firing, Israel drove his Chevy Vega up to Rainier Bank to drop off $15,000 in gate receipts. He tried to insert his key in the depository and found it stuffed with toothpick stumps. But instead of locking the money in his car, he secured it inside his apartment.

At 5 A.M. one of Israel's neighbors looked out his window and saw a slender black man trying to break into a Vega in the parking lot below. Mercer Island Patrolman Tom Kettells and his partner got the call. Kettells was an ex-Marine, six-four, 240 pounds, an aggressive young sharpshooter who despised criminals. "I just arrest everybody I can get my hands on," he explained. "To me, that's what police work is—get the creeps outa there."

Kettells was in his eighth month on the force, and one of his least favorite creeps was about to put a permanent stain on his career.

I'd handled George before: trespass, selling to minors, nothing heavy. Some of the older cops said what a great kid he used to be, but to us newer guys he was just another asshole. He was more visible now; kids at the 7-Eleven told me he'd been kicked out of his house for hitting on his stepfather's wife. I didn't know if it was true, but Kris Mobley was terrified of George. You could see it in her eyes.

When we reached the parking lot, George was on his bike, scooting out the back.

I yelled, "George!"

He stops and comes back. He's yakkin' about how he can explain everything, but I'm not listening. He had a bunch of toothpicks in his pocket. His big G.I. Joe combat knife had paint flecks that matched the car he'd been prowling. I put him in my patrol car and ran the plate. It came back to "David Israel." George says, "I *told* ya! Dave's my friend! He lets me sleep in his car. Call him! He'll tell ya."

Officer Callahan and I took him to our station in the Shorewood Apartments. Israel came down and told me about the toothpicks he'd found in the night depository. George is yelling, "Let me talk! I can clear this thing up." He was like Ted Bundy and every other psychopath: He thought he could convince you of anything. But if you kept him talking, his lies would get mixed up, and you had him good.

I started putting the toothpicks in an evidence bag. George

is watching me carefully. He says, "What're you doing with those?"

I said, "Well, George, they're evidence. You've been fooling with a bank machine. That's a felony." I'm blowing smoke, making it up as I go along. "What I'm gonna do, George, I'm gonna have the lab compare these to the ones that came from the bank. If they match up, it's a federal crime. You'll probably do ten, fifteen years."

We're writing up the paperwork and George is trying to talk us into kicking him loose. I said, "No way, George. This is big-time felony, man."

I put him in a holding room and the next thing I hear is glass breaking. George was halfway out the window. He'd reached under the toggles and removed the heavy wire mesh and broke the plate glass with a phone book.

I just missed grabbing his foot. The hole he went through was barely big enough for a rabbit. We followed the blood to the apartment house next door, then up the stairs, then back down. We lost him in the weeds. Dogs were no help. George was *gone*.

The chief chewed me out good. I had it coming. A rookie cop shouldn't lose a prisoner. *No* officer should lose a prisoner. It was the worst sin. I took it personal.

We didn't think George would leave the island. I talked to Dr. Mobley and Kris; they said they hadn't seen him. My impression was that they sincerely wanted to cooperate.

We began hearing from informants: George was hiding in a boat; he was under somebody's house; he was living in a cave; he was here, there. We knew he couldn't run far 'cause he had pins in his hips from one of his car wrecks. Twice we chased him on foot and he got away. We had a helicopter over him but he disappeared in the woods. A canine unit tracked and lost him three times.

We posted a five-hundred-dollar reward, and a bunch of tips came in. The whole island was looking for him. I was working graveyard, eleven to seven-thirty; I'd go home in the morning and take a two-hour nap and go after him on my own time. He showed up at Denny's and the Safeway, went sunbathing at Clark Beach and Seward Park, but by the time we got the calls he was gone. The Mercer Island *Reporter* ran a story and we started hearing from housewives. They thought every shadow was George. People asked what kind of stupid god-damn cops couldn't catch a black fugitive on a white island.

He kept taunting us, daring us. It was Dungeons and Dragons to him. Our informants told us how he was going around bragging that we'd never catch him. He'd be sighted along a road and slip into the woods. He knew every bush. He did things like flipping you the bird and running off. He knew police procedure—we couldn't shoot him.

Dr. Mobley called and said some of his clothes were missing. Between the Mobley house and the lakefront house, there's a rockery and about fifteen feet of shrubs, and I hid down there every night, waiting for George. The Mobleys never knew I was there.

He was loose for two weeks when we got a tip that he was hiding out with a friend on the north end of the island. I started watching the address. I'd park my car a block away and walk up. I'd go back there about a dozen times a night, creep around the back of the house, through the carport, look in the lower windows.

I finally spot him walking behind the bushes along West Mercer. I'm in full uniform, wearing an extra twenty pounds of equipment, but I figure I can outrun him with those pins in his hips.

He doesn't see me standing between two parked cars. A marked police car drives by and I watch him peeking through the underbrush at it. My mind's made up. This time the son of a bitch isn't getting away. I had a heavy nightstick and I figured I'd chop his legs at the knees.

I crashed through the bushes and by the time he sees me it's too late for him to run and he's like frozen in place. He smacks himself on the head so hard that his eyes cross and falls on his knees. I'm still ten feet away.

He starts saying, "I give up, I give up! *Don't hit me!*" J. C. Goodman drove up to help. George is bawling and screaming like a girl. He thought I was gonna kill him. We cuffed him and took him to the station. He told me, "It wasn't you I was escaping from, Tom, honest. It was Officer Callahan." He got Callahan aside and told him the reverse. Then he claimed that he knew where I was all the time and he cou-ld've gotten away if he wanted to. That was just George's personality. He had to be right every time. He had to be the man you couldn't fool.

There was an ugly scar on his arm where he'd gone through the window. He claimed a nurse friend of his had taken him to the hospital in Seattle and they gave him twenty-five stitches. The stitches popped open the second day and he went back in for more treatment. The hospital never reported it to police.

We added "escape" to all his other charges and George ended up with his first felony conviction. I was pretty proud of that. He served ten months in county jail.

When he got out, I stayed on his ass. He was sly. He baited us, did things to throw us off. One day I caught him walking down the street with a woman's purse. I thought, This time I've got him good.

I open the purse, and there's not a thing in it. No ID, nothing.

He says, "I bought it at the Goodwill. I'm gonna give it to my girlfriend." Maybe he stole it; maybe it was a setup, trying to throw me off. He was capable of devious shit like that.

He stole a Sony Walkman from the Calvos' house. By the time I caught up with him, he had a Walkman, but it wasn't the one he'd stolen. Later I found out he'd raced over to Luther Burbank Park and traded with a kid. That was George, always a step ahead. . . .

He ran the streets *all* night *every* night. One morning around sunup he tells a thirteen-year-old paperboy, "Hey, I'll help ya." After they finished, George bought the kid a pop. Kid thought it was great, took George home to meet his family. *Don't ever take George home!* They gave him a sandwich.

The next morning the kid's halfway through his paper route. He passes his house and sees George walking out the door with a purse in his hand. George says, "I found your mom's purse in your front yard and I was just bringing it back."

The boy woke up his mother. The purse had been on her nightstand. So we had George for burglary two—a very rare event. He served another short sentence.

Then a video camera nailed him for theft. They'd just installed three of 'em at the Chevron station where George hung out. A bunch of scratch lottery tickets turned up missing, and good old George was the star of the surveillance film. Every time the gas station attendant went outside, you'd see George's hand slide over and grab more tickets. He'd fold 'em into a newspaper and transfer 'em to his pack. He did that three times and split.

When Patrolman Ken Wegner caught up with him, George flung about two hundred losing tickets down the hill, but he held on to a bunch of two-dollar and five-dollar winners. Even when he knew he was about to be arrested, he couldn't bear to throw the good ones away.

He tells Wegner, "You're supposed to *pay* for these? I thought they were the free kind."

After he was convicted of theft, he whined that we were out to get him. I took him aside and said, "You better believe it, man!" Whenever I'd escort him to court, even if it was just for a traffic warrant, I'd put him on a chain with other prisoners, or I'd hobble him. It was justifiable since he'd escaped on me. Tell ya one thing, he was the last prisoner I ever lost.

B Y HIS MID-TWENTIES George was adrift and didn't seem to care, but he stubbornly remained on Mercer Island. He'd carefully compartmentalized his minimal social life; one group of acquaintances knew nothing about the others, and only the police knew the details of his crimes.

"George didn't confide," an old friend explained. "He only *seemed* to. There were people he would steal from, and some he wouldn't go near. There were girls he wouldn't try to put his arm around, and others he tried to screw full-bore. He was a street psychologist. He knew who he could push and who not."

Relations with his family seemed to vacillate between cold and downright hostile. He would worm his way back into the house, only to be banished for another theft, an inappropriate remark, another embarrassment. Thanks to Kris, the Mobleys were now involved in island society. A son had been born, a gifted, athletic child, a perfect synthesis of his handsome biracial parents, and the chocolate-skinned George seemed more estranged than ever.

Even his St. Bernard came to a bad end. In later years some of the neighbors claimed to see a reflection of George in the animal. They felt that George, with his antisocial ways, shouldn't have been allowed to train such a large dog. The result, some claimed, was an oversize pit bull.

"Max wasn't your typical docile St. Bernard," said a neighbor. "He was territorial, grouchy, too big for the Mobley lot. Some of us felt it was pushy of them to impose on our space that way."

Max's love affair with the beagle Francesca continued unabated, but he was intolerant of other animals. He tangled with a neighbor's German shepherd and bit halfway through its neck before George conked him with a frying pan. Then Max knocked a seven-year-old boy off his bike and bit his face, leaving permanent scars. After an insurance settlement, the St. Bernard disappeared. George explained to friends that he'd developed bone cancer and was put to sleep at the Fred Hutchinson Cancer Clinic in Seattle. No one had ever heard of a dog being treated at the famous clinic, but George sounded convincing.

Policemen like Tom Kettells and Glendon Booth were watching George so closely that he was confined to crimes like selling beer to minors. For a time he reestablished a few of his police contacts. After he was arrested for smoking a joint, his old friend J. C. Goodman told him, "Now, George, I'm not gonna force you to do anything, but you can work this off. You know the drill. You can give me somebody bigger, and we can recommend to the prosecutor that they drop the charges."

George leaped at the chance. Soon he graduated to stings, helping to set up sellers and buyers. He did a credit card sting for Goodman, but he usually worked narcotics.

"He became a professional information peddler," another sergeant recalled. "He'd phone tips to Crimewatch.

He did it for return favors, for money, for fun. He seemed to enjoy rolling over on his buddies.''

One friend learned the hard way. "George told me he wanted to buy three grams of pot. Turned out the cops were watching the whole transaction from a Dodge Aspen in the Safeway parking lot. They didn't just arrest me; they impounded my Volkswagen. I wondered why they didn't arrest George, but I found out later he'd engineered the whole deal.''

George even tried to work for Tom Kettells, but the burnt young cop was leery. "I popped him with a stolen color TV," Kettells recalled. "He told me it was his, but the owner's name was etched into the set with a soldering iron. George says, 'Tom, I wanna work this off.' I said, 'No way, George. You're goin' to jail.'

"After that I decided to use him the way he tried to use me. If I didn't have the goods on him, or it was some little thing, I'd let him help me make an amphetamine case or even coke. If I had him good, I'd let him serve the time. Then I found out he was telling his wanna-be rat pack that he couldn't get arrested 'cause he knew me and the other cops. He'd show 'em his scanner. I cut him off.''

When word spread that George had turned full-time snitch, he lost the last of his childhood friends. "We saw him working with cops on drug busts," one recalled. "He got beaten up a few times, but he wouldn't stop. Nobody wanted anything to do with him. He wasn't invited to parties. We stopped playing basketball with him. He couldn't get a date.''

True to form, George retreated into the company of younger children. Ever since high school, he'd used them for companionship, for money, for power and control. Now he began using them for sex.

Laura Green was fourteen but looked younger. She had warm brown eyes, delicate features, a silly giggle and an unexpectedly sultry voice. She spoke slowly and hesitantly, reflecting childish doubts. She was thoughtful, outgoing, nonjudgmental, guileless, the very opposite of many Mercer Island teens. She'd developed the habit of frugality and usually saved most of her allowance. She worked hard—babysitting, delivery work, copying—and had already put aside five hundred dollars toward college. She was inexperienced in sex and unschooled in its byplay and games. She was perfect for George.

I still don't know how it happened. I didn't have a neurotic need for an older man and I wasn't a victim of an unhappy childhood or bad parenting. I had a good childhood and my parents were great. They never made me feel that sex was dirty or obscene and they weren't uptight about it. They were bright, professional people, upper middle class. Sex didn't seem dirty to me, just something to look forward to. When I was little, I dreamed I'd be a teacher, or I'd grow up and marry a gorgeous guy and live on a houseboat in Florida. Or I'd own a store or a restaurant. Normal dreams.

A few months after my fourteenth birthday, in between the ninth and tenth grades. I was planning to go to Christian camp for a week, and I was hanging out with my best friend V—— and some other girls. They were smoking a little pot, but I'd tried it twice and didn't like it. I'd also tried some heavy petting, not much, and I smoked cigarettes. My sins! I guess I was pretty average for my age.

One hot summer afternoon V—— and I were smoking behind a Dumpster when this black guy walked past, then stopped. He came over and talked to her, but he didn't even look at me. He was good-looking, slender, not tall, talked fast, laughed a lot. He looked about twenty. His nails were real long; I thought that was probably for cocaine. I figured, That's *his* business.

I could care less that he was black. I'm not prejudiced; it

doesn't matter to me if you have purple hair and five thumbs on each hand, as long as we can communicate. Actually I found his skin tone kind of exciting. He was pretty much the only black person I'd seen on Mercer Island.

At the one-week camp I became a born-again Christian. I talked about religion constantly, bored my friends to death. I still smoked, but I didn't drink or fool around.

One night some other girls and I went to V——'s house for a party. Her parents were the kind of people who grew pot in their bedroom and didn't hassle her, so we'd go to the 7-Eleven and buy candy and Ding Dongs and bring 'em home for a party. It was me, V——, who was thirteen; her sister, B——, who was sixteen, and another thirteen-year-old girl. I was surprised when George showed up with beer. He still didn't pay much attention to me.

As the night went on you could see that we were giving him something he needed. Made him feel good, laughed at his jokes, hung on his words. We thought he was *cool*. He seemed totally comfortable in the company of four girls, talking about ourselves and our friends. He gave the impression that he totally cared. He'd ask questions to draw you out. I thought he was just about the most interesting man I'd ever met. I never stopped to think, Why's this guy hanging around kids? Why isn't he working, or at college?

We saw a lot of George. We went with him to Luther Burbank Park and Denny's, sat up talking till all hours. Kids are used to being ignored by grown-ups, and here comes a guy who'll spend two hours discussing why thirteen-year-old Kevin snubbed twelve-year-old Sara in the lunch line the other day, and whether it means Sara should confront him about it or play it cool, or maybe take Tyler for a fall-back boyfriend. He'd get so intense, you'd think he was discussing world problems or the H-bomb. It couldn't have been an act. He was *concerned*. Nobody could fake the interest he showed in our lives.

He always had books in his pack, deep stuff, not junk. He used big words and he knew *everything*. When I'd be at V——'s for a sleepover, he'd show up around midnight and tap on the window. We learned to expect him. We wouldn't sleep. Just before daylight he would open the window and disappear. Mysterious! Exciting!

He always had money. One morning he took us to Winchell's Donuts in Bellevue and paid with a hundred-dollar bill. I'm going, Oh, my God, he's a drug dealer! It scared me, 'cause I was beginning to have a crush on him.

He could see we were freaked about the money, so he said, "You guys need to learn not to jump to conclusions. Didn't I tell you I made a lot of money managing Tonite's the Nite? Well, I saved it." He flashed a big roll. "Here!"

That eased my mind. The next time he came over to V——'s, I was laying on her bed smoking, and he said he'd never go out with a girl who smoked. I put out my cigarette. I knew he noticed, but he didn't comment. The next time I saw him, I said, "Hey, George, I quit smoking." He seemed pleased.

He seemed to know every teenage kid on the island—who they went out with, what they did with each other, whether they were fooling around. I didn't realize it at the time, but he had this terrific capacity for gossip. *People* magazine was his Bible. He could talk all night about Donald Trump and TV stars and stuff like that. I never asked myself if this wasn't odd. A grown man so involved in talking about his friend Lynn Brown, for example, and how she was sleeping around, and how she once met him at her door naked but he turned her down because she was just a silly nympho. Nowadays I would say, "Who cares, George?" But to a teenage kid it was fascinating.

Around four one morning he started talking about devils and demons. He told about two Satanists in San Francisco who were trying to draw a pentagram on the floor and couldn't get it right. George said, "If you're safe inside a pentagram, you can conjure up demons, talk to 'em, get 'em to do things for ya, money, anything you want." Then his voice turned deep, hushed, and he said, "But if you step outside the pentagram, hon—they'll *kill* ya!"

We girls hugged each other harder. He said the cops found one of the guys dead the next morning, laying outside the pentagram, squashed flat, blood everywhere. There was no way anything could have fallen on him. It was the demons.

I started to cry. George patted me on the shoulder and started talking about how you could use Ouija boards to conjure up demons. He said demons can be good, but they're *always* dangerous. He said the devil could take a pencil and spin it on its axis and kill everybody in the room who's not a Christian. He made me so scared I threw away my mom's Ouija board.

A couple of nights later George was giving us his usual playful hugs, and we were laughing and kidding. We would lay on the bed and he'd put his arms around us and not let go. *Incredible* hugs. It was exciting, but I didn't connect it with sex. Everybody on Mercer Island hugged. Everybody said, "Love ya!" It was just friendly.

We asked him if he did drugs and he said the devil had frightened him off. He said he was high on coke one night and broke a mirror and when he bent down to pick it up he saw the devil's red leg behind him. He said he dumped all his drugs after that, and he put everything else in his room under a white blanket.

He said he could speak in tongues, but he only did it when the Holy Spirit entered into him. To somebody who'd just been to Christian camp and gone forward to accept Christ, it was very impressive.

One night V—— started teasing him about sex. She asked, "What turns you on?" He said, "Nature." And we were like, "No, George, we mean *really*."

And he said, "I hear ya, and that's my answer. Nature turns me on." It seemed like he didn't want to open up.

So I said, "George, what gives you an orgasm?"

He looked like he didn't understand, so I said, "George, what makes you come?"

He changed the subject. You could see it was something he didn't want to talk about. To me, it just made him seem more lovable. He was like a shy adolescent.

We stayed up all night, and in the morning we took the bus to Seattle, to Pike Place Market, a tourist place where a lot of kids hung out. On the way I told V—— I was getting a crush on George. That made her start playing up to him, hugging, flirting. I thought, Oh, no, he's *never* gonna like me if she's always in his arms. It made me feel so bad.

At the market V—— wouldn't stop flirting. George saw me crying. That told him how I felt about him.

I went to one of the stalls and bought him a pin that said, "Luv ya, George." He said, "*You* wear it." So I put it on.

A couple nights later V—— fell asleep on her bed and

George started talking about God and how great it was that I was a Christian and didn't drink or use drugs and how I'd quit smoking for him. We hugged and kissed and talked about God; then his hands started moving and he showed me where to put my hand. I didn't think it was inconsistent with my religion. George was very religious; how could it be wrong? I was attracted to him even more. I was a virgin, but most of my friends were making out. I knew Mercer Island girls who'd slept with ten or twelve guys. I wasn't shocked. It was just the way things were.

George and I talked for two hours, and then he led me into V——'s laundry room and asked if he could go down on me. I didn't know the expression. When he explained what he meant, I thought, Wow! This guy really wants to be *with* me.

We made regular love for the first time at a party, and it hurt real bad. The next night he came over to my house after my parents were asleep and knocked on my window. We talked a lot and then did it again, and the next night, and the next. We worked out a set of signals. If I hung a blouse in the window, it meant "Too dangerous, stay away." If the coast was clear, George would tap his long fingernails on the window and shine his penlight.

After we'd been together for about a week, he said, "Can I go down on you again?"

I thought, What's the matter with the normal way? It wasn't as though he couldn't get hard. He was *always* hard.

It seemed like he was just trying to see me have an orgasm, to get my reaction. He said he wanted to get me horny so he could lick my juices. He said he liked my taste and wished he could drink me with a straw. I didn't know if he was weird or just trying to make me feel good.

Then he made me go down on him. I mean, I didn't have any choice. He acted kind of loving about it till I resisted; then he turned a little mean. After that he made me do it every time. It didn't seem like he really cared how I felt. He'd go down on me till it hurt, like it was for his pleasure, not mine. I'd yell, "Stop!" and pull away, and he'd drag me back. He was rough but not really abusive. I loved him, but if he'd been cruel, I'd have stopped then and there.

My parents' bedroom was upstairs at the other end of the house. My older sister knew what was going on, but I swore her to secrecy. George and I were pretty quiet. He'd be with me five or six hours and leave when the sun came up.

We never used protection; George said we didn't need it. Sometimes he pulled out.

Once we fell asleep and almost got caught. We heard Dad in the shower, and George said, "*Shee-it!* Gotta go!" It was daylight. He sneaked home by the back way.

He seemed to enjoy taking risks. On the way to my house, he'd jump fences, cut through yards, get chased by dogs and cops. He was stopped a few times but talked his way out of it. "I'm just taking a shortcut. I'm sorry if I bothered you. I'm George Russell, live on North Mercer Way. Maybe you know my dad? He's a dentist. . . ." A radical line of bullshit. It always worked. People *wanted* to believe George.

In public he treated me like his girlfriend. We swam at Luther, went to a movie and a couple of concerts in Seattle. Took the bus, or went with friends. But mostly it was midnight sex at my house. I wouldn't know he was coming over till he got there. Sometimes he'd be in my room when I got home from a babysitting gig or one of my jobs, and I'd be, "*George!* How'd you get in?"

He never explained, and we passed over it. It was odd 'cause he could've shined the light or tapped on my window to get in. He seemed to prefer to sneak in. Maybe he just wanted to stay in practice.

Sometimes he wouldn't show up for a week or so. He'd explain he was out doing his job as a narcotics cop. He showed me how they'd communicate by touching a nose or an ear, and it would be a signal that he had to drop everything and meet his crew somewhere. That was all he would say about his job.

He was secretive about his family, too. It was like he'd come from a test tube. I never knew where he went when he wasn't with me or hanging out with us kids. He wouldn't even tell his middle name. It turned into this big thing:

"C'mon, George, what's your middle name?"

"I'm not gonna tell ya."

"What's it start with?"

"*W*. That's all I'm gonna tell ya."

I finally dragged it out of him: "Walterfield." I asked where his folks came from and he acted like he wasn't sure: "We lived in Florida and I looked like Buckwheat; that's all I know." He said he would've been an April Fool's baby, but his mom held out till midnight so he could be born on April 2 and not be teased the rest of his life. But he never told me what year.

He claimed he knew nothing about George Walterfield Russell Senior. He said the only father he'd ever known was Wonzel Mobley. Dr. Mobley's wife Kris was only twelve years older than George.

George never referred to the Mobleys as "step" this or "step" that; it was always "my sister," "my dad," "my little brother." The only exception was Kris; he called her his "stepmom," even though they weren't really related. It was like he wanted to belong to a regular family. Don't we all?

It didn't matter how many times I tried to learn more about his family, he just kept turning me off. Or he told stories about them that sounded made up, like he wanted me to believe they did all these great things together. One day he said, "My little brother was playing baseball and I said, 'Hey, five dollars if you hit a home run!' The next pitch, *whack!* A home run! He's amazing." Does that sound made up or what?

His favorite person in the whole world was his half-sister Erika. Evidently they'd been tight before she went East with their mother. Now she was at Yale and he just missed her to pieces. When she visited Mercer, he treated her like God's gift to earth, took her everywhere, introduced her as "Erika, my baby sister." There was something unreal about that, too, like he was trying to convince himself of a closeness that didn't exist.

He seemed to regard personal questions as an attack. He'd glare at me without answering. I thought, If we're gonna get married, I have a right to know.

He let slip about a time the family was on a driving trip and he deliberately tried to dump baby Erika at a gas station. I thought, *Erika?* The visiting royalty?

He told how he'd carried the baby inside the station and left her in her bassinet. Just before they drove off, the attendant ran out and said, "Hey, is this baby yours?"

That story bothered me. My own family was tight and loving and I couldn't understand how anybody could hate their sister enough to try to dump her at a gas station. George just giggled and acted like it was no big deal.

His real mother, Joyce, was a touchy subject. For a long time he wouldn't talk about her except to say she was a hotshot professor and genius. Little by little I found out that she'd taught English at Tufts and lectured on black culture. George said she'd also taught at Maryland and the U. of Washington, and her lectures were in big demand. Now she was married to a famous guy named Corrigan. He'd been chancellor of the University of Massachusetts before becoming president of San Francisco State. George said his mother was on the faculty.

He talked as though him and his mom and his new stepfather were real tight—he referred to Dr. Corrigan as "Bob"—but little things made me wonder. I asked him for a picture of himself and he said he'd get one from his mom. When it didn't show up he mumbled something to the effect that she didn't have any.

I said, "Your mom doesn't have her own son's *picture*?" He ignored me, and when I mentioned it again he got mad. After that I noticed that anything about his mother set him off. It only made him more fascinating.

When we were at a rock concert in Seattle, some of my friends gave me a lot of crap. They said, "George robs people." "He's a cat burglar." "He's a pimp," he's this, he's that. They said, "Ya know, George is twenty-eight. His class graduated ten years ago."

I'm like, *What?* I got really nervous 'cause I didn't know anything about this side of George.

I confronted him, and he laughed and said, "Twenty-eight?" He made it seem like a joke. "I'm thousands of years old. I'm an angel of God." Then he said he was a *lot* younger than twenty-eight.

I noticed he still didn't come out and tell how old he was. I really didn't care. Later I found out he was *exactly* twenty-eight, twice my age. He said, "If you want to piss me off, send me a birthday card or a Christmas card." I asked him why and he like sloughed me off. Then he said, "I don't see any age difference between us. Laura, I love you."

He gave me a ring and told me it belonged to his grandmom. I thought, He must really like me to give me an heirloom like that.

Just before school reopened in September, my parents caught me in a lie about where I was spending the night. I was with George, but I told 'em I was having a sleepover with a girlfriend. The next day my mom enrolled me in a private school.

George and I kept seeing each other, but we had to be careful.

Then he called and said he was in King County Jail on trumped-up charges: stealing a TV and some lottery tickets, and selling beer to minors. He explained that somebody else stole the TV and he was just caught with it. He'd taken the lottery tickets by mistake and returned every one. And he said he always bought beer for kids; he hung out with them, didn't he? What were friends for? He didn't mention that it was a business with him, buying a six-pack for three bucks and selling it for five. That was just about his main source of income. Plus stealing and selling dope. But I didn't know about that till later.

His bail was three hundred dollars and he only had a hundred. I put up the rest. I was like, No big deal, it's just a mistake. I was, I love George and he loves me. He paid me back in a week.

Two months after school started, he wrote from jail and said he'd have to serve thirty days on the fake charges. A cop named Kettells was using him as an example. It was the first letter I ever got from him—full of optimism and weird punctuation. He'd once told me that he cut a lot of classes in high school; he must've cut the week they taught apostrophes. He wrote, "A lot of the guy's . . ." "Congrat's on your grades. . . ." "It make's me appreciate you more. . . ." His spelling was better, but not perfect: "Has your puppy popped the bed yet?" . . . "Thanks alot . . ." "We could elope alright . . ."

It was a surprise, because his spoken English was as good as my parents', and they were college educated. I began to get the idea that there were several different Georges.

He used a lot of cute expressions in his letters from jail. He wrote, "I know it's a bitch for you, but stay strong! O'Tay? . . ." Now I can see he was writing down to the fourteen-year-old. He actually wrote, "Remember, absence makes the heart grow fonder!" and "A journey of a mile begins with a single step." Is that tired old crap or what?

He always stressed how well he was getting along. He was

helping other prisoners with their legal papers and making them laugh with his jokes and wisecracks, "plus I've thrashed everyone in chess for extra respect." That was George—in control, even in jail. At the time I didn't see it as odd.

He'd given me some poems that Erika had written when she was at Milton Academy near Boston, prepping for Yale, and asked me to hold on to them till he got out. They were very sophisticated and sensitive, a world better than George's. In one letter he referred to Erika as "my sister whom I love more than anyone on earth." He told me how she kept herself in terrific shape and ran six miles every day. I found out that the rest of the Mobley family called him "Russ," but Erika called him "Russy." She's the one he tried to dump at the gas station.

He always claimed that he loved his mother, told me how she sent him presents and phoned from San Francisco to see how he was doing. Once I made the mistake of asking, "Why did your mom take Erika and leave you?" and he went into a long explanation about how his mom *didn't* leave him, she *wanted* him to come along, but she left the decision to him; she loved him too much to force him to leave his friends, and he just decided to stay on Mercer Island.

All I really cared about was that he loved me and said so in writing. He wrote, "I think about you so much, that I once called a guard by your name!!" That made me feel great.

I thought he would be in jail for thirty days, but then he wrote that it might be longer. "Mercer Island Court might try to give me more time . . . but whatever they do it will be the last time they do anything to me. . . . I'm through letting M.I. mess with my life. And that includes most of the people too."

I didn't understand what he meant by Mercer Island "messing" with his life. How can an island mess with your life? He always got along with people, and now he was acting like his hometown was to blame for him being in jail.

He taught me a code based on a Harold Robbins novel, in case he would have to write secret stuff that nobody except him and I could understand. I wondered what secrets he had to tell me. He scared me when he wrote, "If I can't get work-release then you can RamboLaura me out of here. (j/k). . . ." "J/k" was shorthand for "just kidding." He also put in a lot of happy faces and "(smile)," meaning that he was smiling as he wrote that passage. I wasn't sure what he meant by RamboLaura-ing him out of jail, but it made me kinda nervous.

He worked out a way to communicate by phone. I had a phone in my bedroom, but it rang all over the house. So exactly at one A.M. I'd dial Look's Pharmacy and let it keep ringing till George broke in on call waiting. That way there'd be no ring in my house.

It worked for a while, but then he began having problems with the jail phone, so we went back to writing letters for a while.

He called me "my love" and told me I was the only "positive" thing in his life. He said we'd get married in four years when I was eighteen and wouldn't need my parents' permission.

That old stuff about his sister and the gas station still bothered me, so I asked him about it in a letter. He wrote back, "I have to admit that story about me trying to get rid of my sister is a true classic because its true. And if it wasn't for that gas station guy my sisters picture would be on the back of a milk carton." He seemed to think it was cute. I still thought it was scary.

He told me to be tough—"That way you can keep me in line in the future. If I get out of line you can threaten to do surgery with a dull, rusty butter knife on certain parts of my body."

I wrote that I would pray for him every day, and he asked me to pray for some of the other prisoners instead of him. "Some guys are going to go to Prison for 5, 10, even 20 *years* or more. . . . So my little bit of time is nothing." He wrote, "Remember, we have *forever*."

He said he was polishing his poems and short stories and learning how to draw. I loved it when he called me "Gorgeous Girl," "hon" and "babe." He wrote, "You are special. And don't let *anyone* tell you different. I LOVE YOU!!!!" Heavy stuff.

I asked if he minded the way I kept saying I love him. He replied, "No, I don't mind you telling me that you love me. Because you're not the type to say something like that unless you really mean it. And that makes me feel 'Great'. I love you too. O'Tay!!??!! XXXOOO's."

After a while he sent some of his poems. The lines were

beautiful. "Tree carved initials in playful lust. . . ." "The knowledge I seek to be my thirst. . . ." "I heard the star's passing flight. . . ."

A war poem really gave me chills:

> . . . The spilling of blood
> of men where they fell
> Coloring the ground. . . .

He'd only been in jail a few months when I missed my period and took one of those drugstore pregnancy tests. The thing turned yellow and I was hysterical. George and I agreed it was totally ridiculous to have the child.

I didn't know what to do. I couldn't even drive. If my parents found out, they'd freak. They were intelligent people, but not all that understanding about race. If they found out I was carrying George's baby, they'd self-destruct.

My best friend drove me to Planned Parenthood and they confirmed I was pregnant. I told the counselor that I wanted an abortion, and she said, "Okay, but first you have to go home and tell your mom."

I said that was the last thing I was gonna do. She asked for my father's name and I didn't answer. She said, "Okay, you don't have to tell me, but I'd get fired if I didn't ask."

Four days before my fifteenth birthday my sister and her boyfriend picked me up at school after second period—I couldn't skip my math class. We drove to an abortion clinic in a Seattle suburb. It was in a small building and I didn't know exactly where to go, so I walked into an office on the first floor and asked this woman where the medical clinic was, and she totally freaked. She says, "You're not gonna have an abortion, are ya? *That's murder!*" Apparently she pulled this stunt with everybody.

I ran back to the car, crying. My sister's boyfriend said, "Do you want me to tell her off?"

I said, "This is hard enough as it is. Please, just leave her alone."

I finally found the clinic upstairs. They asked how old I was and I said sixteen so I wouldn't need my parents' consent. I paid the money in advance: a hundred and thirty dollars. I've always been good with money.

The doctor numbed my vagina. I was bleeding bad, crying. They put a clamp in, scraped out the fetus with a scalpel, then vacuumed me out. It was the worst pain. I still flinch thinking about it.

My sister's boyfriend let me out of the car at the top of my street and I walked down to my house and went to bed with a cold pack. When my mom came home from work, I told her I'd loft school early 'cause I felt sick, and she wrote me an excuse. I was so relieved. I figured God didn't want her to know.

George gave me moral support on the phone: "How ya feeling? Stay cool, be brave, you can handle it...." But he avoided the subject in his letters. It was like he didn't want any written proof that he was the father. He only ever wrote about it once, three months later, in one of his long-winded lectures about the responsibilities of love.

"The mistake I apoligize for the most," he wrote, "was my inability to provide the proper 'safeguards' that would have prevented the 'situation' that occurred a couple of months ago. I am very, very sorry to have put you thru that. And without me being by your side no less. I pray you will forgive me. That was my fault." And later he paid me back the hundred and thirty dollars. I figured it was as much my fault as his.

I saved his letters from jail, even though he warned me several times to "throw them all away please!" I'm still not a hundred percent sure where he was coming from, but at the time I thought wo were Romeo and Juliet. If it was all a shuck and he never really loved me, he was sure convincing. He wrote, "I thank luck, fate, destiny, and God for you! Also your parents, without whom you would not have been born. See, parents are good for something."

His letters were always full of x's and o's. He ended one of the early ones, "Love you, Love you, Love you, Love you, Love you!!!!" and "I miss, miss, miss, miss, miss you!!!! I LOVE YOU," and another, "I love you!!! V,V,V,V, much."

Some of his letters had a fatherly tone, like he was counseling a delinquent. Now I realize he was playing his role of George the controller, king of kids. He wrote, "I've noticed that you usually start swearing whenever you get real tired. Its also a quality that says you won't take any crap. Just be careful who you say it to. Axe murderers are not known for taking kindly to someone telling them to 'F-off' (smile).''

He gave me a lot of advice like that. I took it seriously, but now I realize it was mostly on the sixth-grade level: ''Don't ever be afraid to say whats on your mind or what you're thinking. By not saying anything you're not only cheating yourself, but me also, out of some idea or comment that you may have. . . . Relationships are the one thing that needs input and communication between the two parties in order to succeed. Plus 'trust'. . . .'' On and on. I reread every word like it was the Ave Maria.

He wrote huge amounts of gossip about our teenage friends. Sometimes he sounded like a child and sometimes like a child psychologist. Even in jail he kept up on who was sleeping with who, who was mad at who, all the little details. He still seemed obsessed with Lynn Brown, his thirteen-year-old friend. He even used me to get in touch with her and fix her up with one of his safe friends. It seemed he mentioned her in every letter. When I got annoyed, he lectured me about jealousy.

He was always into controlling, and sometimes he admitted it. He wrote, ''I'd rather wait until I see Lynn before I would say anything. That way I could control her and watch over how she might react. . . .''

I wrote about a boy who was hitting on me and he replied that I should call him up ''and say to him 'I hear you like me, but I *don't* like you, will *never* like you; and I never want to see or talk to you *ever*—understand'?!! Then just hang up on him. If he come's up to you on the street say the same thing to him, but loudly enough that other people hear.''

After I told him that I'd heard he hadn't seen Wonzel Mobley in three years, he wrote back, ''My family is close in a strange and crazy way. What, you thought all those weird things I say about what my family say's and does was made up?? Heck, I've been trying to get a sit-com based on my family put on T.V.''

A couple of times he admitted that he had a problem about deception. All his friends called him ''Mysterious George,'' but he never gave any explanation except to me.

''I keep a lot of my life secret,'' he wrote. ''That is just the way I've always been.'' Later he wrote, ''I'm a very private person, you know that. Probably too many spy movies while

I was growing up. But that's the way things are with me. Always has been, always will be. Lie's no, evading yes. I'm sorry."

He hinted on the phone that he wanted us to exchange hot letters, but I felt uncomfortable about it and put him off. He wrote, "I still expect a 'fantasy' letter from you. So don't think you can get out of it. (smile) Actually; we should make it a regular feature of our letter's. That way we will be filling a void of mutual 'missing'. (smile) What do you think?"

I told him I'd be too embarrassed. I also thought the idea was totally stupid, but I didn't say so.

After a couple more letters, he wrote, "I'm still waiting on my very kinky letter from you. Remember, I asked you first!! And besides, I'm your boyfriend so how can you be embarrassed??? It should be so long that it takes two stamps to mail it. (smile)"

So I wrote a girlish letter, and he wrote back that it was "very nice indeed! (smile)" and "I LOVE YOU WITH ALL MY HEART!" He enclosed his own fantasy about me. The scene opened on our favorite mall, Bellevue Square. "As we browse in stores," he wrote, "every time we're out of eyesight behind some aisle or rack we stop to kiss and hug each other. At the same time I'm running my hands over your very nice panty clad ass. . . . We continue to go store to store teasing each other."

It was supposed to make me hot, but I couldn't stop giggling. It was so Mercer Island, so *Bellevue*! Shop till you drop, and—oh, by the way, take a little time to grope your girlfriend. . . .

It went on for seven pages, full of explicit sex, oral and otherwise, but kind of repressed in some ways. He wrote about pressing his "manhood" against my "womanhood," my "moist heat," "your excited full breasts pressed to my chest." You could read hotter stuff in *Cosmo*.

But he got all inspired about anal sex, which I thought was only for gays. He wrote, "My hands spread your cheeks so that I can rim your asshole with my tongue." Hey, that was a whole new concept to me! He wrote, "I continue to tongue your ass as my finger goes deeper into you with each stroke." That was about as far as he went. I wasn't exactly insulted, just . . . disinterested.

He turned up the heat in his next "fantasy" letter. There

was a lot of stuff about the scent of candles, warmed baby oil, massages, "your glistening body by candle light." He wrote, "I slowly slip an oiled finger into your asshole and start moving it in and out. . . . You are now so excited that you are moving all around by yourself. I now slip another oiled finger into you and you start to move all the more."

I thought, *Yuck!*

His third fantasy letter was even grosser, if you can imagine. I wondered what was going on, but then I realized he's been in jail for three or four months now, and *that's the kind of sex guys have in jail! That's their only outlet!* So I tried to understand. I was still thrilled that he loved me enough to be so intimate.

After he'd been away about five months, he changed to a more formal tone. He told me he'd fallen from grace and "I wouldn't be in here now if I had been keeping my eyes and heart on Jesus." He warned me that sin is hard to recognize because it's so pleasurable, "but that's what Satan wants us to think. He is very clever at trapping Christians in subtle but dangerous Sins."

He suggested that my friends and I arrange Bible readings and prayer groups at home. "Everyone is searching for answers and hope, and Jesus has both."

As usual, he gave me advice, including a suggestion that I start seeing other guys. I thought, *Huh?* My great love is telling me to cheat? He told me not to miss out on "the fun that can be had at high school." He warned me not to shut down my social life just because we were in love: "That wouldn't make me feel right." He said I should go to games—spelled "game's"—and slumber parties, dances, picnics. He wrote, "You don't have to love the guy in order to go to a dance with him." I wondered, Is he trying to dump me?

I questioned him, and he wrote back that I'd freaked again and "You've got to quit doing that or you'll get an Ulcer or a heart-attack." He repeated that we would get married when I was eighteen. But he warned me to "always have it in the back of the mind that the reality of breaking up can occur." He said we should continue our relationship, "but lets slow down and enjoy the trip."

I thought, What trip? The one where you tell me to go with other guys? The one where you shove two fingers in my bottom? The one where you lecture me like I'm nine years old?

All this time my friends kept telling awful stories about him. I began to realize that so many people couldn't be wrong. What future would I have with a known criminal? I thought about my pregnancy and how he hadn't even bothered to use protection.

After we'd been apart for six months, I thought what a long time that was for a girl my age. I couldn't visit him in jail; you had to be eighteen. While he was gone I'd met some guys who really liked me, and I'd told them, "No, I'm still with George." I was really missing out.

I finally realized it's not gonna work, this guy's too old, he's a major loser. I mean, the letters were great, but all of a sudden I wasn't in love.

He got out of jail and came straight to my house and tapped on the window. I was kinda faking it, like, "Oh, hi. You're out. *Wow!*"

He gave me a big hug and I hugged him back. When he wouldn't let go, I said, "I'm done hugging for now, okay?"

He sat on my bed and I sat across the room. I could tell he got the message. We talked for five hours and he left. He came over a few times after that. I'd give him a big kiss, but nothing else. We didn't talk about breaking up. It was just over.

Except . . . a couple months later the Mobleys were in Hawaii and George threw a party at their house. He took me into a back room and tried to go down on me. It was hard for me because I had fond memories, but I didn't intend to be orally raped. So I shoved him away.

He was like, No biggie, that's okay, that's cool. You couldn't fluster George.

AFTER HIS LATEST release from King County Jail on May 18, 1987, George Walterfield Russell Jr., now twenty-nine years old, returned to the Mobley home on Mercer Island. He'd served seven months, his second-longest sentence to date, but the cops soon learned that he was buying beer for children and steering them toward pot and pills.

He didn't last long at the family home. Five weeks after

his release police received a tip that a squatter was living
in a cramped maintenance room in the Puget Sound Bank
on Mercer Island. When a patrol car checked, George
emerged from the shadows, smiling and talking: "Here I
am. I'm the guy they called you about."

He said he'd just stepped off the bus from Seattle when
he spotted a friend's car in the bank's parking lot. Then he
claimed that he'd ducked behind the building to have a
drink. Finally he admitted using the maintenance room regularly: "I sometimes change clothes in there when I'm on
the island. It's a party room. Lots of kids use it."

He showed the lawmen how he jiggered the lock with a
coin and squeezed through a hole eighteen inches square.
Inside they found a sleeping bag and blankets, neatly folded
clothing, a coat and other garments hanging from nails,
flashlights and candles, adventure books and pornographic
magazines in stacks, canned food, Lean Cuisine wrappers,
music cassettes, toiletries, and a collection of letters from
Laura Green and others.

Asked if he was armed, George produced a Valor brand
butterfly knife. He pleaded guilty to a charge of criminal
trespass and possession of a dangerous weapon. He was
sentenced to five days in jail and ordered to undergo psychological counseling.

George arrived on time for his first session and was given
the behavioral test known as the MMPI—Minnesota Mul-
tiphasic Personality Inventory. The psychologist reported,
"Mr. Russell has already spent 2½ years in jail since 1983
and further jail time at this point does not seem to be the
only or the most appropriate response to the current offense."

After another session the therapist produced a preliminary report for District Judge Suzanne Staples:

> Mr. Russell presented himself initially as a fairly relaxed,
> confident, friendly and outgoing individual. Although he could
> acknowledge having made some "errors of judgment" he

mostly presented himself as the victim of a legal system that was overreacting to his transgressions. He displayed little insight into the underlying attitudes or thought processes that are associated with illegal behavior.

Psychological testing with the MMPI, however, presents a view of Mr. Russell which is much deeper than the rather likeable, superficial image he presents to people initially. People who respond to the test as he did are usually seen as rather self-centered . . . limited in their capacity to form deep interpersonal relationships . . . quite impulsive, demonstrate poor judgment and have little patience or frustration tolerance . . . become bored easily, and seek excitement, often taking risks without considering consequences . . . are often rebellious toward authority figures and may have trouble incorporating the traditional standards and values of society.

Despite the fact that the psychologist had described the classical symptoms of the incurable behavioral defect known as antisocial personality disorder, he recommended treatment. Describing the therapist to a friend, George was critical: "That guy bases his entire approach on crap psychology like *The Road Less Traveled*. That's his Bible. He wants to keep on making his seventy-two bucks an hour from the county, so he says, 'Read this chapter and underline what you think is interesting and we'll talk about it next week.' He keeps telling me how busy he is, but I notice there's never anybody in his office. He told the judge I'm impulsive and easily bored. What a buncha bull."

After a few more sessions the psychologist prepared an encouraging report for the court. The client, he observed, "appears to be making progress. . . . He has been working regularly . . . continuing to reside with his parents . . . no indications of alcohol or drug abuse. . . ."

The Mercer Island Police Department knew better.

Narcissists are more concerned with how they appear than what they feel. Indeed, they deny feelings that contradict the image they seek. Without a sense of limits, they tend to

*"act out" their impulses . . . They see themselves as free to
create their own lifestyles, without societal rules.*

　　　　　　　　　　　　—ALEXANDER LOWEN, M.D.,
　　　　　　　　NARCISSISM: DENIAL OF THE TRUE SELF

In later years the lawmen who'd known George best found
it hard to pinpoint exactly when he escalated from eccentric
nuisance to hardened criminal, or, for that matter, what
caused the metamorphosis. For years his old friend J. C.
Goodman had suspected that George enjoyed a perverted
thrill from breaking into homes, whether there was a financial payoff or not. Now Patrolman Goodman saw the problem worsening.

> Through George's late twenties we had a long string of
> night-time burglaries. On warm nights people would leave
> the sliding door open and the guy would actually walk into
> the bedroom, and there'd be signs that he stood right between
> the two people.
> Every officer in town knew it was George, but there was
> seldom enough evidence to even make an arrest for criminal
> trespass. It reached the point of almost being a joke. Whenever
> we got a burglary report, it was, "Anybody know where
> George is at?" I guess the closest we came to nailing him for
> house-prowling was one night when some people heard a bur-
> glar upstairs. Sergeant Smith tangled with the guy and they
> both fell off the deck and the guy got away. He was black,
> skinny, wiry, the right height and weight, but it was too dark
> for a positive ID.
> There's no doubt in my mind George was our cat burglar.
> George was stealth. He liked the cockiness of walking into
> somebody's bedroom and standing there thinking, I can do
> anything I want to you people. I'm in command. I'm the
> power.
> And I'm not even trying to intimate that George had any
> thoughts of doing physical harm, because I didn't think he did.
> Not at first.

The situation turned more complicated when a dark-
skinned robber broke into a Mercer Island home and tied

up a woman in the bathroom, then assaulted another female a few days later. A newspaper artist's rendition resembled George, but neither victim could make a positive identification. Most of the local cops were convinced that their old mascot was the daytime robber. A few argued that the MO was too dissimilar.

Paranoia spread among families that George had been victimizing for years, some of whom hadn't bothered to report their suspicions to police. His childhood best friend's mother, victim of the silver dollar burglaries, installed an expensive alarm system.

After a third attack by the daytime robber, the latest victim viewed a file photograph and said, "I know George Russell. It definitely wasn't him."

The island's pet criminal was quietly exonerated, but not everyone got the word. Old friends avoided him; parents glared. For fifteen years he'd blamed his problems on the cops, the courts, his accomplices, the phases of the moon, and now he found himself ostracized for three robberies that he didn't commit. It was a bitter pill.

SERGEANT GLENDON BOOTH had spent years trying to understand George Russell, and he found the latest trend highly unnerving.

George used to have some respect for his friends, but now he was ripping 'em off right and left, threatening people, losing his cool. I walked into Denny's when I was working graveyard one night and this little waitress Robyn was in tears. George says, "Oh, hi, Sergeant Booth. How ya doing?"

I said, "How ya doing, Georgie?"

Robyn pipes up, "He stole my money."

I said, "How d'ya know?"

She told me how she'd just counted out her tips in front of her old pal George, twenty-eight bucks, and then put the money in a Crown Royal bag and stuck it in the waiter's station. Soon as she turned her back, it was gone. She said,

"George is the only one that could've taken it. He saw where I put it."

I was really pissed. I thought, Anybody that'd steal from Robyn would steal from the blind. That little girl worked hard for her money and everybody admired her.

I stood George on his head, but nothing dropped out. He's yelling, "It's the dishwasher! I saw him take it."

I knew he'd stashed it someplace. I searched the bushes, even climbed up on the roof. I wanted his ass so bad. But . . . no money.

Robyn was crying, saying something about George was her friend, she'd known him since they were kids. I says, "George, get off this island. Don't you ever come back here."

He says, "You can't tell me what to do."

"Well, George, I've been friendly with you for years, but you've worn out your welcome with me, man. I got no more use for you. I eat in this place. I don't want you in here and *they* don't want you in here."

So he was eighty-sixed out of Denny's, just like he'd been eighty-sixed out of gas stations and the 7-Eleven and the market and a bunch of other places. They handed him a formal letter threatening him with criminal trespass.

There was a high turnover at the Mercer Island Denny's, and George bided his time till the management changed. Then he was welcomed back.

EARLY IN 1988 George landed one of his infrequent jobs, clerking at a Nintendo arcade, and he promptly bought another car, which he soon wrecked. In eight months he skimmed $23,000, and once again he was fired.

He was thirty by now, unwelcome at home, shadowed by cops who'd once been his friends, and finding it harder to survive on the small island. He tried to supplement his income by offering snitching assistance to the Seattle Police Department, just across Lake Washington to the west, but failed to follow through and was dropped from the list.

Most nights he slept in parked cars or Dumpsters. His personal hygiene began to slip. After a court appearance a judge crinkled up her nose and said, "Be sure to shower before you come into my courtroom again."

An old acquaintance noticed that his clothes had taken on a sheen. "You'd see him on Monday in his Ivy League outfit from Nordstrom and a week later he'd still be wearing the same gear. I was embarrassed for the guy, so I didn't comment. And yet he could splash on some cologne and talk himself into a dinner invitation at any home on the island."

For a time he sheltered with friends, drifting from home to home—a weekend, six days, two weeks—before becoming persona non grata, usually because of light fingers. It was in the home of a Mercer Island physician that he became friendly with an important figure in his life, a blond born-again Christian named Tami Grace.

I wasn't quite twenty-one. My weight was down and I had long hair and people said I looked like a movie star. I'd gone with this guy Mike Weisenburgh, "Georgia Mike," off and on, and one night I saw him shake hands with a black guy at Denny's. It kinda blew me away because Mike had redneck tendencies. At the time there was a lot of talk about the Crips and the Bloods. I thought, What's your gig? What *is* your gig? He was the first black I'd seen in our crowd.

Mike told me that his name was George and he was a really nice guy, even though he was in and out of jail for minor stuff. I said, "How old is he?" and Mike said, "Nobody knows. But you see him with all ages of people." He said George was real relaxed about race. The first time they met, Mike was fresh from Georgia, and after they shook hands, Mike had looked down at his hand and said, "Oh, it doesn't rub off?" George just laughed.

A bunch of us got together at somebody's parents' house on Mercer Island, and George was cooking spaghetti. I asked if I could help and he gave me this big friendly smile and said, "That's the nigger's job, hon."

I said, "C'mon, let me help."

He said, "No way! Let the nigger do the work."

He said it so comfortably and naturally that it wasn't offensive. Just a joke—relaxing, disarming.

Turned out he was living there with a doctor's son while
the doctor and his wife were away. Everybody ate and then
we sat in the outdoor hot tub and watched the snowflakes.
After a while I went inside and warmed myself in front of the
fireplace, and the others followed. I'd just finished a course as
a chemical dependency counselor and I couldn't stop talking
about it. The big debate came up: is marijuana bad for you? I
kept telling 'em, "You're damn right it is. . . .''

George took me aside and said, "Not only are you gorgeous,
you're brilliant! And you're interested in the things I'm interested in.''

My roommate and I were known for our parties, and George
started coming around. I saw him at a few other parties and at
the Overlake Denny's in Bellevue. One night he gave me a
back rub—not sexual, just friendly. On my twenty-first birthday, September 6, 1989, he took me dancing at the Black Angus.

That night I found out why he was always so cool. He was
an undercover detective, a nark!

A week or two later he called me at two-thirty one morning
and said he was in King County Jail and needed my help. He
said some cop would be calling and asking questions and I
should tell him we lived together, we split the rent and expenses, and he had a steady job. It was part of a dope sting.

I said sure and went back to sleep.

The phone rang at four A.M. A detective said, "Did you
know George Russell is in jail?''

I gave the right answers and he said George would be released on his personal recognizance—"PR," he called it. A
few months later George put me through the same deal. I
thought it was exciting, being tight with a nark. We became
pals—not deep, confiding pals, but "let's go out and do
something" pals. He'd comfort me when things went bad. He
was the world's greatest feedback listener. We'd go dancing
at the Black Angus, and he'd never make a move on me. How
could you ask for a better pal?

I always woke up a dance floor quick. People constantly
asked me to dance, and I never had to buy a drink. George
and I would go out and dance till late, and he'd stay over with
me and my roommate and sleep on our couch. We were a great
couple. He loved it when I'd wear a black outfit like Kim

Basinger, called me his Kim. He preferred me dressed up. I assumed he felt it upgraded his image. He liked blondes; you seldom saw him with a brunette or redhead. And *never* with a black woman.

George and I would arrive at the Angus about nine, because nothing ever happened till then, and order drinks—a Seagram's Gold cooler or a Sex on the Beach with a splash of Coke for me, and for George a Miller Genuine Draft or a tequila or both. We'd dance till two and go to the Overlake Denny's for breakfast, and then I'd head home and he'd hit the streets with his fellow narks.

We improvised a lot of no-name dances, and we did the limbo, electric slide, the lambada. Our style was very provocative, sexual. We never touched, but you might as well be making love on the dance floor. How could it be bad? We were both born-again Christians, expressing ourselves with the bodies God gave us. There was a power in it. On Wednesday nights the clubs were packed with people who came to watch. I thrived on the attention. It was childish, but I liked the way everybody admired me and my secret cop.

And George was so fascinating. Sometimes he'd pull away and say, "I can't look at you, hon. It's too dangerous."

I did little things to tease him, and he still wouldn't look. I'd dance closer, sexier, but he wouldn't make a move. We danced for five, six hours at a time, sweating, dancing *hard*, and everybody crowded around. What a trip!

After we'd gone dancing about eight times, my friends began asking me, What's the gig between you guys?

"Nothing," I'd say. "We're just good friends."

"Why do you hang out with each other?"

"I like to dance with him. And he wants a pretty girl on his arm. We create an image."

I didn't mention that he also liked to listen to me, hear about my problems with my boyfriends. I was going through some tough times with Mike Weisenburgh. George knew us both, and he was such a comfort.

IMAGE UPGRADES CAN be expensive, and George made another attempt to sell information. To an Eastside Narcotics Task Force officer he described himself as recipient of several Crimestoppers' rewards and hinted that he was on the inside of a big dope operation. When he was told that the elite unit wasn't hiring informants, he made polite inquiry at the Mercer Island police station and was booted out by a deskman with a long memory.

Rebuffed, George began to look toward the Eastside, where 350,000 people shared four hundred square miles of hills and lakes and overpriced real estate nestled between the glacial trough called Lake Washington and the Cascade foothills. The Eastside had its own Silicon Valley, with companies like Microsoft, Boeing Computer Services, Sundstrand, Nintendo of America, Aldus, Advanced Technology Laboratories and Egghead Software thriving in lustrous new buildings on grounds landscaped in fir, madrona and sunbursts of rhododendrons and azaleas.

The centerpiece of the area was a prospering metropolis called Bellevue, just to the northeast of Mercer Island. In the years following World War II, Bellevue had grown from a placid suburb surrounded by berry farms to a mushrooming city with high-rise buildings, credit-card restaurants featuring salmon steak tartare, health food bars serving arugula and radicchio, gaudy nightclubs with Potemkin fronts, and 90,000 citizens with well-worn credit cards. Bellevue housewives, it was said, baited their rat traps with Port Salut and considered it a drought if the Evian truck was late. Sleek women with chihuahuas on their laps steered "Beemers" and Mercedes 450SLs along streets lacking sidewalks, reminiscent of Beverly Hills and Bel Air.

Bumper stickers noted "Honk if you love shopping" and "When the going gets tough, the tough go shopping." A Cartesian variation seemed to encapsulate a psychological insight: "I shop, therefore I am." Twelve million visitors a year, many of them from neighboring Mercer Island, patronized the forty acres known as Bellevue Square, a Galleria-type complex with two hundred shops, valet parking, glass elevators, an art museum, and its own man-made weather system.

Bellevue produced a stream of envious jokes, most of them gleefully reprinted in Seattle newspapers: Name a Bellevue funeral parlor. *Death 'n' Things.* What's the favorite sexual position of a Bellevue woman? *Facing Nordstrom.* What'll a Bellevuite pay thirty-five-thousand dollars for? *Almost anything.* How can you get a hundred Bellevue women in a phone booth? *Stick on a "sale" sign.*

In reality, most citizens of Bellevue were indistinguishable from the citizens of Seattle or Mercer Island or, for that matter, White Plains or Sherman Oaks, but jokes weren't written about typical citizens.

Bellevue, aka Latteland and Blahvue, was also known for liberated young women with money and looks. George Russell coveted both and soon became a familiar sight in the city's nightclubs. The Black Angus was his favorite hangout, but he also patronized other clubs that thrived on the fat paychecks and freewheeling lifestyles of the Eastside's nouveau affluent. The clubs bore catchy names like McClalla's, C. I. Shenanigan's, Zoonie's, Finn McCool's, Cucina! Cucina! They were "in" one week and "out" the next (and sometimes into Chapter Eleven bankruptcy), and catered to hot-eyed young males and nubile young women in an atmosphere of sweat, cologne, sex and din. Some of the clubs were little more than barns, but a few boasted flamboyant decor. In the Saratoga Trunk one could sip exotic drinks in a dungeon, a tiki house with grass roof, a 1957 MG, a log cabin, a heart-shaped booth called "The Love Connection," a library lined with fake books, a huge Pepsi can, a booth formed from glass bottles and another from hotel ashtrays, and a booth that featured erotic drawings and an oversize penis carved from wood. In all the clubs there were theme nights, promotions, two-for-one sales and other gimmicks—"a party every night, so *fun*, a *blast*," as an overstimulated young female observed, adding the key phrase: "You always end up in a group."

* * *

In most of the clubs normal conversation was out of the question. DJs hyped the amps for Paula Abdul's "Opposites Attract," Bobby Brown's "My Prerogative," Janet Jackson's "Miss You Much," top forty tunes by Boy Toy, Mötley Crüe, Whitesnake, Sinéad O'Connor, Whitney Houston, and rap hits like Young M.C.'s "Bust a Move," Bel Biv DeVoe's "Poison," and MC Hammer's "U Can't Touch This." Customers gyrated in line dances like the electric slide, which was performed to Marcia Griffiths's "Electric Boogie" and played at ear-rattling volume. Busboys wore earplugs, waitresses read lips, and females in estrus and predatory males exchanged phone numbers by yelling into one another's ears. Strobes completed the sensory assault.

For years the Bellevue Black Angus, one of a successful chain, had been a sedate family restaurant, with a pleasant bar and a cameo dance floor. Its quiet ambiance attracted the upwardly mobile businessmen of the Eastside, who in turn attracted young women. When undersocialized ethnics from Seattle infiltrated the action, altercations broke out and anal-retentive yuppies shifted their business to Houlihan's or the Saratoga Trunk or C. I. Shenanigan's. Soon the Black Angus became known as a black-and-white meat rack, or, as one realist described it, "a place where overdressed blacks hit on overweight whites." At the time, it was also popular with cross-dressers.

Here in George Russell's latest substitute home there was a programmed pace to the proceedings, with disc jockeys controlling the rhythms of the evening like symphony conductors. An enthusiastic young DJ spilled his secrets:

> Our instruments were videos, cassettes, CDs and records. We had four neon bars over the dance floor and ran 'em in sequence, plus white spotlights that you alternated and a separate unit that flashed colored beams of light, sound-activated. And we had an "alien" in the middle of the unit, a spinning tilting disc that would spray beams of light like a pinwheel.

My five-hour shift was set in stages. You start the music around nine and keep it mellow for a half hour, with the lights turned down and the patter nice and easy. Ten to eleven o'clock is peak time, and you play big hits, maybe three or four in a row, to energize the crowd. You play a lot of vocals, do a lot of talking.

Around eleven you hit 'em with another set of big loud songs, to keep 'em going. At the bottom of each hour after that, starting around eleven-thirty, you do a slow set. You never play slow stuff at the top of an hour because customers have a tendency to look at their watches: "Oh, God, it's eleven o'clock, I should get outa here." You save the slow stuff for the half hour, and then they'll say, "Oh, it's eleven-thirty. Well, I'll just stay till midnight."

So at midnight you hit 'em with another big burst, and they forget to look at their watches 'cause they're so busy dancing and having a good time. They stay another hour till your next set at twelve-thirty.

The whole object is to keep 'em dancing and drinking and spending. Some nights I walk away just tingling. I'll play a set and get the crowd to scream. I'll holler, "Say yeah!" and they'll yell back, "Say yeah!" I'll holler, "Say yeah *yeah*!" and they'll go, "Say yeah *yeah*!" Pretty soon they flock around your booth. There's nothing greater than to pull off a good night.

Sure, you get problems. Some asshole comes up and requests Lynyrd Skynyrd. I'm lucky if I have one Lynyrd Skynyrd record in my whole collection. I mean, this is a top forty club. So I'll say, "I'll try to get to it."

They'll come back and say, "Where is it, man? I gotta leave in five minutes. *Where's my fuckin' song?*" Like I owe it to him and I'm not paying off.

Or they'll say, "My song's next, right?" when you've already got three others cued up.

Drunks are another problem. Girls are hitting on your ass all the time. Or some guy'll get hammered and want to come back and finger your records. It just *wrecks* 'em. That's one reason we have bouncers.

Everyone blinks when the lounge host turns the lights up about one thirty-five, one-forty. I'll play two or three really slow songs so you wind up on a good note and leave happy, with good vibes. I'll grab the mike and say, "Thank you for coming in. It was great having you here this Friday night. Join us here tomorrow night for indoor skiing," dah dah dah. "Drive safe. Have a good evening. Dah dah dah. . . . See you for breakfast at Denny's."

Then the cocktailers collect the drinks and cattleprod the drinkers out of the building. If you bring it off, it's a trip. I can hardly wait to start my next shift.

In the Black Angus, George Russell always sat alongside the DJ booth, buying drinks and jollying the help. The waitresses augmented their bustlines and wore skimpy skirts that revealed pale half-moons of skin at the tops of fishnet stockings. Security men, mostly off-duty Bellevue cops, flexed triceps at the doors. Male customers showed their virility by downing straight shots of the hard stuff—Jack Daniel's, Black Velvet, Johnnie Walker Red, Dewar's, Wild Turkey. Some of the showier drinkers ordered poppers and slammers, which were banged on the bar to make them fizz.

Women emitted clouds of pheromones while demurely nursing five-dollar drinks like Sex on the Beach, made of peach schnapps, vodka, cranberry and orange juice; Smith & Wesson, a blend of Kahlúa, Coke, vodka and cream; and Electric Watermelon, made of vodka, sweet-and-sour mix, 7-Up and the melon liqueur Midori. The most popular libation was Long Island Electric Ice Tea, a mixture of tequila, vodka, gin, rum, Triple Sec, sweet-and-sour mix and a splash of Coke. Inexperienced drinkers became highly suggestible after a few swigs. On busy nights Electric Ice Tea flowed so fast that it was premixed in a tank and dispensed with a nozzle.

Designer drinks were tagged with names appropriate to the sexual atmosphere. The Slow Screw was made of sloe gin, vodka and orange juice; a splash of Southern Comfort turned it into a Slow Comfortable Screw; an extra splash of Galliano converted the Slow Comfortable Screw into a Slow Comfortable Screw Against the Wall, Galliano being a key ingredient of the Harvey Wallbanger. Among the club's clientele, especially the young females sought out by men like George Russell, it was generally believed that a knowledge of these differences separated the true sophisticates from the dweebs.

The ultimate performance drink was the Waterfall. The customer stacked a pair of shot glasses, beer in the upper and peppermint schnapps in the lower, and allowed the beer to trickle into the schnapps as the mix was frantically gulped. Successful completion of this task was another mark of sophistication, but all too often the liquid ended up in the drinker's crotch. Flaming drinks were banned after a customer ignited his mustache on 151-proof Demerara rum and burned the tablecloth.

As inhibitions dissipated in the evening rut, a male would send his target of opportunity a Blow Job—Bailey's Irish Cream and Stolichnaya vodka topped with whipped cream. If the woman was interested, she would "slam" the drink down in one gulp and return a Screamin' Orgasm, a mixture of Amaretto, vodka, Bailey's Irish Cream, and cream. This mating ritual appeared to be one of several adaptations to the noise level.

When time grew short and a solo night loomed ahead, the desperation drink was Rumple Minze, a clear peppermint schnapps from Germany that was usually "slammed" like a shot. Overindulgers in the minty time bomb had been known to circle and fall and grab their partners' legs. Rumple Minze was 100 proof, half alcohol, and as smooth as springwater. It became the key ingredient in George Russell's pharmacopoeia.

Aᴛ FIRST GLANCE the young African-American from Mercer Island looked a little out of place in his Bellevue hangout, a boy in his father's suit. His behavior was recessive and mannerly, aimed at winning friends rather than making conquests, reminiscent of his high school attitude. As always, he smiled broadly and listened patiently to tales of misfortune and woe. Black Angus habitués took to the laid-back regular who seemed eager to be a friend and talked like a young businessman. But at least one female customer was baffled.

I first saw him at the Black Angus when I was twenty-one. He was there every night, came and went by himself. He seemed to know everybody—bartenders, the disc jockey, the waitresses. He'd stand at the door talking with the bouncers while they carded people. He seemed real nice, very different, a fun guy, a host type, very sweet.

My girlfriends and I noticed that he avoided black women. I didn't understand. I dated black men almost exclusively—I like dark features, dark eyes, dark hair, the black look, Mexican, Italian. George was too white for my taste, and I didn't like the way he dressed. I like men in pressed jeans, a neat look, hair arranged and up-to-date. George always wore sloppy jeans, a white shirt, casual, not much jewelry, definitely not *GQ*. He wore that old style of modified 'Fro. He didn't seem to fit in with blacks *or* whites.

He always seemed to be in a good mood, never pissed off at the world like so many of the other guys. He'd give me and my girlfriends a hug or a nudge. We just thought, It's only George. He called us "hon" and we called him "G" or "George of the Jungle" or "Honeybear." He always had a drink in his hand but he never acted drunk. He didn't seem to have any steady girlfriends. A couple of my friends wanted to jump his bones, but he never seemed to take them seriously. It was just a social thing with him; sex wasn't important. He'd flirt but wouldn't follow through. He drove one girl home and sat in her car for three hours, lecturing on her love life. We didn't know what he wanted out of women, but it sure wasn't sex.

We had no idea where he got his money or where he went when he left the club. He was clever about evading personal questions, so we stopped asking. He told somebody he had a girlfriend in L.A. and visited her sometimes. A few assumed he was gay. I just thought he was . . . eccentric. We wondered why we never ran into him anywhere else in Bellevue. I kept telling my friends, "Don't you think it's just a little strange that we don't know anything about the guy except what we see in the club?''

One night he paid for a round of drinks with a hundred-dollar bill, and I said, ''C'mon now, George. What do you do? Where do you work?''

He looked agitated. I asked him again, and he said, ''I'm a cop. I work undercover, in the clubs.''

It made sense. He never took his jacket off even when he was sweating on the dance floor. We figured that's where he kept his gun. For the first time George seemed exciting.

On Hallowe'en night, 1989, George Russell arrived at the Black Angus Hallowe'en party dressed as the Jolly Green Giant: green tights, green shoes, layered leaves, green face, and a leaf on his head. He was a big hit. He took the occasion to introduce his sometime dancing partner Tami Grace to a blue-eyed gamine named Mindy Charley, and then wandered away to call on his constituents. Mindy confided to Tami that she and George had just started living together.

Tami thought, Great. Later she learned that George was annoyed that his two female friends had hit it off so well. It seemed a strange reaction.

Sooner or later when the classic psychopath comes on stage, things will go wrong. . . . Patterns of temporary success or at least stability are followed by strangely brutal and irresponsible behavior, stupid and unnecessary falls from grace for which there can be no rational explanation.

—Alan Harrington,
Psychopaths

Some of Mindy Charley's oldest friends wondered why she hadn't wound up on a mental ward. Her early life was a textbook case of inconsistent signals, loss and disorder, rendering her childishly naïve in some ways and worldly-wise in others. Although she grew into a good-looking woman with a pretty face and figure, she seemed to exude a frangibility similar to Laura Green's. Her harshest expression, reserved for moments of extreme anger, was "Excuse me? *Excuse me?*," spoken in a small voice and accompanied by a narrowing of her dark blue eyes. In confrontations she usually backed down. The word that most of her friends used to describe her was "vulnerable."

When Mindy was three, her father had disowned his family and married the woman next door. Mindy's distraught mother went on analgesic shopping sprees, filling their suburban Seattle home with knickknacks, designer clothes and jewels. Each morning of Mindy's childhood marked the opening curtain on another domestic drama featuring her mother and siblings: ups, downs, praise, criticism, threats of suicide. In one of her more rational moments the mother bought Mindy a black doll, explaining that her own parents had been racially prejudiced and she wanted to break the cycle. Mindy never forgot the kindness, or the message.

From her earliest years the pretty little child tried to find happiness in her dolls, figurines, stuffed animals and other treasures. For the rest of her life she would value her possessions almost as though they were friends. She also loved books. Her role model became the author Laura Ingalls: "She was my idealization. Find a perfect husband, have perfect twins, live an idyllic life." At nine she vowed to a deaf friend that she would grow up and teach the deaf. She thought of it as "my calling." She attended deaf camp and learned sign language. It seemed to come naturally.

At seventeen Mindy married her high school sweetheart. Together they started a housecleaning business, grueling labor but something of their own. Mindy's spirits quickly improved. She developed an explosive laugh and a big grin—"Friends call it my 'perma-smile.'" She perfected her sign language at Bellevue Community College; "I reached the point where I'd dream in sign language. *Wild!*"

She was preparing to enroll at the University of Washington in speech pathology, therapy and advanced sign language when her young husband moved out without warning. She picked up the pieces and went on with her life, as a Laura Ingalls character would have done.

Mindy had been divorced for a year and was working part-time as a clerk when she met an Army veteran named Chris. An adoptee, he'd been raised in a white family. "He had no racial mannerisms," she recalled. "No jive talk or rap. He just happened to have brown skin."

After they dated for two months, Mindy introduced him to her mother. "Oh, my God," the woman moaned. "What about the children?"

Chris proved to be another sad chapter—and expensive. He was a closet alcoholic with a pathological jealous streak, and he was always borrowing money. "He'd come home from work and say, 'How come you wore makeup today?' "

"I'd say, 'I've worn makeup ever since I was sixteen.' "

" 'Well, you shouldn't've worn it today. Who the hell you tryin' to impress?' "

Christmas was Mindy's special season, a rare period of serenity. It was just about the only time of her childhood when her father had made contact, papering over his guilt with toys and presents. Her mother filled the house with porcelain gewgaws, manger sets and a tree that sagged with decorations—"a Winter Wonderland," as Mindy described it later. At Christmastime mother and daughter tried to put aside their grievances. Five years after Mindy had left home for good, she still cherished her Christmas memories. Her own preparations always began in early November.

On Christmas Eve, 1988, Chris came home drunk. After a few more nogs, he started a jealous argument and punched her on the side of the head. Every year she'd put up a six-foot aluminum tree—"metal base, plastic green leaves, white, flocked, beautiful, my own little tradition."

Chris kicked it halfway across the room. Mindy ran to a girlfriend's apartment and made a few battlefield decisions. She could forgive Chris his brutality, his jealous rages, his alcoholism, but she could never forgive him for destroying her Christmas. He'd always wanted to be an actor, so she gave him bus fare to Hollywood. The relationship left her five thousand dollars in debt.

Childhood rigors had given her resilience, and it wasn't long before her perma-smile returned. She found a pleasant job selling greeting cards and began chipping away at her debts. She scrubbed and cleaned and dusted her third-floor apartment till it sparkled, paying special attention to the wicker hutch where she kept her prize set of china, embossed in bluebirds and pink bows, the great treasure of her life. And she enjoyed the warmth and fellowship of old friends. She still had pleasant thoughts about Chris, but who needed such a headache?

On a warm night in early June, 1989, eight months after the breakup, she decided she owed herself a small celebration. The hangover would last for years.

A girlfriend and I went to the Black Angus on Moola Madness night, when they gave you a hundred dollars in play money that you can use to bid for sweatshirts, movie passes, T-shirts, hot tub sessions—silly stuff like that.

Around nine-thirty, we went out on the empty dance floor and did some fun dances, drill team routines we'd learned in high school. We were like, Who cares? Nobody's watching. We did the electric slide, jazz kicks, just having a high old time.

On the way back to our table I noticed this guy reading a newspaper. I thought this was the weirdest thing. He's in a nice club, a waitress is bringing him drinks, a female DJ's spinning the top forty—Bobby Brown, Janet Jackson's *Rhythm Nation* album, Milli Vanilli—and he's reading a *newspaper*? He also had a detective magazine and a textbook.

At one point he got up and asked the DJ a question and

they danced for two minutes, like he'd known her from birth. Then he went back to his paper.

I thought, My God, this guy's a great dancer. Why's he sitting at that table reading?

Well, I'm so open, I'll go up and talk to anybody. If I get bad vibes, I walk. After all those years with my mom, it wasn't easy to hurt *my* feelings.

I slid over to the rail and said, "It's too bad you're wasting all that talent sitting down."

He smiled, real friendly. "A man's gotta keep up on things."

"Why're you reading a paper in a bar?"

He threw his head back and laughed. "Well, there's an article I want to read."

"You come to a bar to read it? You can go to Denny's, you can go to the library, you can go all kinds of places to read. You came *here*? Why?"

He laughed again, and the conversation just rolled along. He introduced himself as George Russell and asked me and my girlfriend to sit down. It was like running into an old friend. We talked politics, religion, race. Some of his buddies came over and we talked about sign language. I told him about my deaf friend in the fourth grade. He seemed very interested, concerned.

I'd never stayed at the Angus later than twelve-thirty, but I ended up going to breakfast with him at Denny's Overlake in Bellevue. I couldn't get enough of his conversation—insatiable. I'd gone almost a year with a guy who couldn't care less about my feelings, and here's somebody who acted thirsty to find out every last detail about me—who I was, what I wanted out of life, my goals, *everything*. He'd be like, "You're kidding! Wow! Tell me more."

I didn't get up to leave till four-thirty. When he walked me to my car, he said, "Mindy, I've never talked to anyone the way I've talked to you." We exchanged phone numbers. I drove home overwhelmed.

I called him at nine-thirty A.M. He was renting an apartment from a married couple in nearby Kirkland, where I lived in the Shawnee Village Apartments. He told me he was looking out the window for the cops 'cause they'd come a few days earlier and taken some of his notebooks.

I said, "Why would they take your notebooks?"

"Well, I watch things and take down notes on everything I see."

"But . . . why?"

"Well, let's just say it's kind of a game I play. I write everything in code. The cops can get all the search warrants they want and come take my notebooks, but they'll never understand a word."

That set off a little alarm. Like what's he *talking* about? The way he put it, he was doing some kind of investigation and they had no right to take his stuff because he wasn't done with it—something like that. We were on the phone for three and a half hours.

We made a date to see *Lethal Weapon* the next day. I picked him up at his place and drove him to my little haven, an abandoned golf course from the thirties, marshland, with an old gravel pit, a forgotten part of nature. The towns on the east side of Lake Washington were getting so crowded, the life was being squeezed out of them. Californians were moving up, and there were new businesses and high rises and condos all along the freeways, but this secret little place of mine was always empty except for the woodpeckers and crows and bright blue Steller's jays. I saved it for special people, special occasions. Like my first day with George.

He was wearing a navy-blue Seattle Police Department cap. A scanner chirped in his back pocket. He wore navy-blue Yale mid-thigh shorts and a white shirt with button-down collar and button pockets and rolled-up long sleeves. He carried himself so well; it was like he had so much power, very proud of who and what he was, like he owned Kirkland and was negotiating for Bellevue and Seattle. Not arrogant, just self-assured. His nails were long and perfect. I thought, A woman would *kill* for nails like his.

He started talking about religion, and I told him this park was a religious experience to me. I said, "It seems to me that God is everywhere, and when I look around and see a place like this—wildlife, wetlands, silence—that's where God is."

George was quiet, pensive. Then he said that what I'd said was probably the closest he could come to agreeing that there was a God. He confessed he was a borderline atheist. He said he found too much that was false in Christian belief and doctrine. Said his doubts were so big that when he wrote "God" in his notes or letters, it was always in lower case. So we were basically in agreement, and that was just about the only time the subject of religion came up between us.

After a while I realized that I'd said a lot about me but I still knew little about him. I said, "Why do you have that scanner? What do you *do?*"

He said, "Well, if I told ya I'd have to kill ya."

I thought he was being flippant, so I said just as flippantly, "Oh? So you're like working for the CIA?"

He laughed. "Well, let's put it this way, hon. I help out on some undercover work."

We walked to an old sand trap. It was early June, a beautiful time in the Northwest. A soft warm wind was blowing through my hair. I thought, What a perfect scene, Jane Austen, the Brontës, "Cristina's World." A girl on the prairie with her long hair flowing back.

I turned and saw him looking at me tenderly, and I said, "I'm scared to get involved with someone right now, George, 'cause I just came from a bad relationship. It was . . . abusive."

He looked aghast. "You're kidding! Did he ever hurt you?"

"He hit me hard one night when he was drunk."

He acted as if he couldn't believe that another human being would do such a thing. He said, "I just can't believe this happened to a girl like you."

He was like pacing, he was so upset. I felt rewarded that such a bright, superior person cared that much.

We sat in the park for about an hour. Then I drove us to the theater in Lynnwood, north of Seattle. Halfway through the movie he took hold of my hand. He was shaking. I thought, Oh, my God, this guy's so genuine. His hand is so soft.

I patted his arm and said, "It's okay, George. I don't bite."

He whispered, "It's been a long time since I've been with somebody I really cared about." He was still shaking—nervous, terrified. To this day, after all that's happened, I don't think he was faking. I think he was scared that he might have stumbled into a real relationship instead of the manipulative-type thing he was used to. I think he thought, This is someone who could like me for what I am. And he found that *very* scary.

After the movie I drove him home and kissed him good-night. We met the next night at the Angus, and I got a look at a new George, the social butterfly. He'd sit with me for five or ten minutes, then jump up. "Gotta talk to my friends for a sec." Then he'd disappear. To me that was as impressive as his scanner and police cap.

I danced with him when he wasn't doing his Mr. Popularity number. I was thinking, This could really work. All I ever wanted was a relationship where I could be secure with the person and yet have my own set of friends, do my own thing— and *no* jealousy. I was already enamored. George drove me home in my car and asked if he could come up. It seemed like the most natural thing in the world. I'd had a couple drinks, but I'd have said yes anyway.

We talked half the night. I confessed that I didn't have much money; I was living off Top Ramen and soup and Hamburger Helper and had a lot of debts. He asked what was my favorite meal, and I said, "Pork chops and creamed corn."

He spent the night in my bed and didn't make a move. I thought, This guy is really a gentleman.

That morning I worked a three-hour shift at the card shop, and when I came home, George was sitting in my living room talking to my old boyfriend Chris. My worst nightmare! Chris was always *so* jealous. He'd struck out in Hollywood, and he'd come to see if I'd take him back. I expected fireworks, but he and George were sitting there laughing and talking like best friends. They parted happily. I thought, George, you are a *miracle*.

That night we looked through my music tapes. I'd made a tape from old albums: the sixties' greatest hits. We were playing the old songs and laughing and he's telling high school memories. We had three hours of nice conversation before I fell asleep on the floor.

I woke up under a blanket. George was asleep on the sofa. I went off to work, and when I got home, I assumed there'd be a note: "I had to go to work. Talk to ya later," something like that. The first thing I saw was a sack of clothes on my dining room table. The second thing was Sasha, his calico cat.

George walked out of the bedroom and gave me a big hug. The place was spotless and dinner was on the dining room table: pork chops and creamed corn.

I'd never invited George to move in, but there he was. It

was fine with me. I didn't know that squatting with friends was one of his oldest habits.

It took me awhile to get used to his hours. When I came home from work in the afternoons, he'd be sleeping or reading a detective magazine or the newspaper. He seemed interested in crime. He borrowed my copies of *Two of a Kind* and *"Son,"* and I never saw them again. He seemed especially interested in the Green River murder case and the forty-nine victims.

Every night at eleven or eleven-thirty he'd disappear. It didn't matter to me; I was in bed by then. Around four-thirty or five, I'd wake up to the smell of sausage, grits and hash browns. The first time he made grits, I said, "No way I'm touching that stuff." He put butter and pepper on it and it was fantastic.

After breakfast I'd crawl back into bed. It was a dream come true. He paid his share of the rent and helped with the bills. Nothing was ever said about money, but sometimes he'd leave a hundred, two hundred dollars. To somebody who was totally broke, it seemed like a fortune.

Pretty soon I realized I'd been in love with him from the beginning. I wanted to learn everything about his family, but he put me off. He told me his real father walked out before he was a year old, and his mom went off to college to make a better life. He said he was sent up the Florida coast to his grandma and his aunts. He told me he was pulled back and forth between five women in a strange house in a strange town, and it was tough on a little kid. He said his mother didn't send for him till she married his stepfather when George was six.

He told me how his mom kept getting better and better teaching positions, and after divorcing Dr. Mobley she became a professor of English and humanities. He said she had a vacation home in the Caribbean. He said he was tight with his mom even though she was now teaching at San Francisco State and married to the university president.

At last he took me to meet his family, and I was impressed. He called Dr. Mobley "Dad" and Mrs. Mobley "Kris" and seemed to admire them. They all seemed warm together, very tight, a lot of joking and kidding around. They called him "Russ." He showed me a postcard from his half-sister, Erika, at Yale, very warm, affectionate. She addressed him as

"Russy!" and signed, " 'Riki' to you always." She suggested ways they could get together and instructed him, "So you're coming next year if I come, right? You'd better!!" The note ended, "Love ya loads."

Whenever Erika hit town, George became the instant big brother. He would borrow my car to pick her up and chauffeur her around. He was the most devoted brother you could imagine. He seemed to want to be tight with his family, even though they were kind of mixed up genetically.

He was also very brotherly toward Kris and Wonzel's son Diron. He was a nice-looking kid, energetic, nine or ten and very bright. We started going to his practices and games. George yelled his head off, gave advice, cheered. Every kid on the team adored him. He talked on their level, got right down in the dirt. Diron would bring his friends home and they'd wrestle with George like he was nine years old himself. He was genuinely, totally loving with kids and family. I couldn't believe it later when I was told he abused some kids on Mercer Island, strong-armed them and took their money. Looking back, I wonder how many George Russells there were. Six? Eight? *More?*

In those first few weeks, I only saw the good George. He had so many big ideas. He planned to write a hit song and was constantly drawing up lists of titles: "Flowers in a Crack," "An Audition of Angels," "Knock Twice Before Leaving," "The Basement of the Top Floor." He wrote short stories. One of his opening paragraphs sounded like it might be a connection to his own life:

Let me start off by saying that I didn't exactly see my quest to completion. I never did get to come face to face with "Ian Merker". Or at least I don't think I did. There are alot of people looking for him in there own way's. I should clear up one issue though. He hasn't commited any crime that would have the police looking for him or anything. Far from it. He's just being sought after. The best way to explain is to tell the story and then you will understand. And if you recognize him from this, and most any one will, tell him to make himself known.

*   *   *

The unfinished works of George Russell! He was always jotting down notes, ideas, jokes, wisecracks. He liked irony and paradox. He wrote, "Owning it, I wondered if I owned their wishes too. Which fearfully gave rise to acknowledging that I might be responsible for their desire's also."

And: "I've never met him and wouldn't know him if I ran over him. But I'd like to try."

And: "If a dog's life is 7 years to man's one, we must ask the questions. 1) If a dog breaks a mirror, does he get 49 years of bad luck?? 2) When a dog chew's his food, does he have to chew it 224 time's per bite?"

It didn't bother me that he wasn't like any man I'd ever known; I saw that as a plus. He didn't talk about love, but he was loving. He gave me a beautiful diamond ring with three stones, said it had been in his family. In the evenings he would drive my car to town and rent me a movie, then say, "I've got a police job to do tonight, Min. Do you mind if I borrow the car? I'll fill the tank at the cop shop."

I had to go to bed anyway. I thought, Who wouldn't say yes to a free tank of gas?

One night I asked how come he didn't own a car, and he explained, "I'm dealing with a bunch of drug handlers. If I had a car I couldn't relate to different aspects of society. It would blow what they believe me to be."

It made sense at the time. I never doubted that he was an undercover cop 'cause he had that scanner and a boot knife and his SPD cap. He told me he sometimes worked with a Mercer Island nark named Tom Kettells. It was exciting to think that my little burgundy Nissan was chasing around on drug cases.

He enjoyed cop humor, the way they joked and teased each other. George got even with one cop by putting a Snickers bar on the front seat of his patrol car, to show he was being laughed at. I thought that was cute.

Our lovemaking was pretty conventional. He refused to wear a condom, said he wanted to give me a baby. He had no problem with impotence. He was very sensitive to my needs, took his time, kissed me slowly, passionately, made me feel like I was the only woman in the world. He satisfied both of us. But I'm such a basic person, so that's not hard to do.

He rarely spent the whole night in my bed. After we made

love, I would fall asleep and he'd tiptoe into the living room to the sofa. One night he shaved his pubic hair with a Bic razor and told me he did it every six months "for hygiene." It wasn't as though he was hairy; he had about three hairs on his chest. He didn't explain those long fingernails, either.

In September, after we'd been together three months, I found a big ugly dildo under my bed. I thought, Oh, my God, why is this thing here? I decided not to mention it.

A couple of weeks later we were making love and he got it out. I told him to put it away; I wanted nothing to do with it. He didn't argue. Two or three weeks later it disappeared into one of his paper bags.

He was neat about his person and his clothes, but I wouldn't call him obsessive. He kept most of his stuff in duffel bags and sacks and knew where everything was. He was very methodical about the laundry. I always folded my kitchen towels in thirds and that seemed to bother him. I'd come home and find them refolded in halves. I thought, What the heck does that mean?

He had a boxful of cassettes and porno paperbacks, like two for ninety-nine cents, kid stuff, no pictures. I flipped out when I found 'em in his stuff. My girlfriend said, "Let's run one of the movies."

It was a 1972-type pornie where the girls wore Famolare shoes with ripple soles and knee-high sox. We ended up laughing 'cause it was so dated.

Well, at least I knew George wasn't running out and buying new pornies on our money. I finally got up the nerve to confront him and he laughed and said he hadn't looked at 'em for years. A few times I came home from work and found them on the VCR, but then they disappeared.

He had some other strange habits, too. Like he couldn't stand for me to go into our bathroom while he was in there. To me it was a joke. I'd pop in while he was taking a shower and jump up on the toilet and say, "Hi!" Or I'd sprinkle cold water over the top. He had a great sense of humor, but not in the bathroom. He began locking the door, even when he was just combing his hair.

The Black Angus had a different promotion every Thursday—Moola Madness, ladies' night, stuff like that—and neither of us wanted to miss out. George insisted that we couldn't leave or arrive together. We'd leave the apartment in my car and I would drop him off at a bus stop on the I-405 overpass in Kirkland. He had the timetables memorized, said buses were his favorite way to travel. From there I'd make the ten-minute drive to the Black Angus and he'd always arrive within a few minutes of me and stash his bag next to the Dumpster at the McDonald's next door. We'd stay four or five hours.

He never exactly explained why we couldn't leave or arrive together; he just mumbled something about his undercover work. He said it was okay if we ran into each other in public, but we couldn't be seen on a date.

One day I was driving along the lake in Kirkland and saw him talking to a woman. Their heads were about two inches apart and he was patting her shoulder. When I called him on it, he explained that her boyfriend was in trouble and she was upset and he was trying to help her out. He said that was one of his responsibilities as a nark.

There were plenty of other mysterious things, but I was too much in love to worry. He'd start the evening in one set of clothes and come home in another. Or I'd drop him at the bus stop and fifteen or twenty minutes later he'd arrive at the Black Angus in a different outfit. I'd say, "George, where did you change?" He had a different explanation every time. After a while he just shrugged me off.

Money was a problem at the Angus. Sometimes he'd come over to my table and slip a five-dollar bill into my pocket and walk away. On most nights I was lucky if we danced one dance together. But George was worth it.

We'd been together less than two months when things changed big time. I didn't know much about boy-girl games and I didn't understand. Breakfast in bed came to a screeching halt. He turned snippy and cold. One day I defrosted the fridge and he asked what I'd done with the stuff inside.

I said, "I put everything on the counter. I sloshed in a few buckets of boiling water, cleaned it up, and put the food back in. Why?"

He said, "There was a piece of foil in there, Min. What did you do with it?"

"What do you mean?"

"I had a piece of acid in there." He sounded like a schoolmaster talking to a bad kid. "I was supposed to take it into King County to have it tested. I did a drug bust last night."

I said, "George, please believe me. I never saw it." He didn't flip out, but his cheek muscles were pulsing.

Then strange things began turning up. I found a hand-tooled turquoise bracelet and a ring hidden in my china creamer. I asked where they came from, and he said it was police evidence and he had to turn it in downtown.

Five bullets and some more bracelets showed up in my wicker hutch. He told me they were mementos of a police job.

One day I was dusting my bookshelf and a double-edged razor blade flipped up and almost hit me in the eye. George said he had no idea where it came from. Two weeks later I reached into my soap basket and cut my finger on another blade. I was so naïve, I didn't suspect what he was using it for.

Sometimes he gave me explicit instructions not to disturb him and went into my spare bedroom for one of his rituals. He would spread a bath towel between two candles and sit cross-legged, and he wouldn't let me see what he was reading. I didn't have the heart to complain about it.

Pretty soon our main contact was the cold little instructions I'd find when I got up to go to work:

Mindy will you fix this shirt. Wake me at five P.M. if I'm not up.

He never signed his notes "love" and he seldom said "please." Whenever I wrote a response, I went out of my way to say "I love you." He didn't reciprocate. Somehow I'd gone from lover to housekeeper. It didn't enter my mind that he was seeing anybody else. If I make a commitment, that's it, and I can't imagine anybody else cheating.

I began hearing disturbing things from friends at the Angus. "George doesn't think of you as a girlfriend. . . ." "You're just a friend. . . ." "You're just roommates. . . ."

I confronted him. "Why are you telling people we're not boyfriend and girlfriend?"

"I'm *not* telling people that, hon. Where do you get those ideas? There's a few girls that I don't tell about us 'cause I'm trying to help them, and if they thought I was living with somebody they wouldn't feel close to me. They'd withhold things, and I couldn't help them out."

So I'd say, "Well, what about your male friends? Why are you putting me down to them?"

"They're pulling your leg."

In the middle of August he began these closed-off moods. After all those years dealing with an upset mother, it was hard on me. I could always tell by the way he held the newspaper whether he would be receptive to conversation. He had the most effective way of closing you out. You could say something to him and it was as if you hadn't opened your mouth. *Total* indifference. It wasn't like he was upset at me or ignoring me. It was like I didn't exist.

I'd get so *upset*. "What have I done? Why are you mad at me?"

Silence. The paper wouldn't even rustle. After an hour or two I'd start to cry. Somehow he knew that silence was the quickest way to hurt me. No, it *wasn't* like talking to a wall. When you talk to the wall, you at least can pretend that the wall's absorbing something. With George there was nothing, no sense that he'd even heard you.

He'd go days like that. I'd say to myself, Okay, fine, it's over. I'd start to go out with my old girlfriends. Then he'd be nice again—for a day or two. It was like he didn't want me, but he didn't want me to be with anybody else.

I decided I had to fight back, and my car was my only weapon. After I cut him off, he developed a pattern. He'd ride the bus home from the clubs at three-thirty or four in the morning, stash his duffel bag in the bushes, walk a mile and a half to the 7-Eleven, buy the paper, then walk back home—exactly the same, night after night. Could it have had something to do with the ongoing cat burglaries in my neighborhood? Thirty or forty of them? But I didn't learn about the burglaries till it was too late.

When I heard him coming in, I would get out of bed and ask, "How'd things go tonight?"

No response.

"George, did you hear me?"

"Yeah," he'd say in this stoic, cold, even voice. Then he would stretch out on the couch with the paper.

I tried to make myself numb. I felt completely screwed over.

We never went anywhere together. At the Black Angus he'd come over to my table and have a drink, but he wasn't *with* me. Or he'd say, "I need the car. Here's an extra five bucks. Have another drink. Catch a ride home."

Just when I thought things would get better, they got worse. If I came through the front door of the club, he slipped out the back. Or he would dance with his favorite blonde and not even acknowledge me. I began to realize that this was the most unhealthy relationship imaginable, worse than the one with my mother or the one with Chris, because George was so cruel. He picked up on my insecurity and used it to dominate me. At last I was beginning to see the pattern. The trouble was, I was still in love.

He went to King County Jail for ten days in September and explained that something had gone wrong on one of the stings. I was still trying to believe his stories, but I was dubious.

My twenty-third birthday came up two days after he was released and I decided that we had to do something together— any old thing, a walk, dancing, whatever. The frustration was getting to where I couldn't handle it.

When I got home from work at five-thirty, he was in one of his closed-off moods, laying on the couch, reading his favorite work: *Crime Scene Search and Physical Evidence Handbook.* I sat in the bedroom till nine-thirty, then came out crying. "Can't you at least say happy birthday? After all the nights when you're out on a job or doing something with your friends? All the nights when I sit home? Why can't we do something tonight?"

He slowly lowered the magazine and looked at me like I was an amoeba or something. He said, "Mindy, you just blew everything. I was gonna take you to dinner and then to the Black Angus. But if you have *that* attitude, forget it." Then he called his old girlfriend in L.A. and talked till I went to bed.

I decided that the only way to live through this nightmare was to treat him like a roommate—you do your thing, I'll do mine, just pay your share. Toward the end of September, when we'd been together for almost four months, he said, "I don't have any money for the rent."

Another shock. I prided myself on making that $425 payment every month, even if it meant skipping meals. I said,

"Excuse me? *Excuse me?* Just what am I supposed to do?"

He said, "Hock the ring I gave you, hon."

I didn't have any choice. I went to Diamond Banque with a couple of friends. The stones were .8, .7 and .4 carats, but one was chipped. We got $330. Later he gave me three or four more rings, said they came from the lost and found at the Black Angus. I hocked them for sixty bucks and we applied it to his back rent.

Then we got the bill for the L.A. call to his old girlfriend, and it was over $100. He wouldn't pay it and I couldn't. When they disconnected my phone, George was like, It's no big deal. Who needs a phone?

I was still going through mood changes—Oh, God, I'm in love with George, I'll make it work. . . . I'd leave him a note saying that I loved him, and he'd reply with some instructions about his laundry. I realized that in three months together he'd never used the word "love." I thought, Why am I bothering? Why am I doing this to myself?

In October he brought an old girlfriend home to stay with us while she was in the process of moving. She was a pretty little thing, a dancer, about sixteen. They acted like they'd been intimate for years. He brings her into my living room, introduces her as his friend Lynn Brown—"hi," "hi!" real jolly. She lifts her long leg over her head and presses it against my wall. I'm going, "Oh, how nice! How talented! *I wish I could do that!*" But I'm thinking, Hey, girl, I'm desperately trying to save a relationship with this guy and you're shoving your crotch against my wall?

I found out later that Lynn used her sexuality to make friends, but she was too young to know that this kind of behavior annoyed females. She pitched her sleeping bag in my spare bedroom and stayed with us for a week. The night George brought her marijuana I just about lost it. I said, "Excuse *me!* She can do whatever she wants, but I will not condone smoking in my apartment."

He said, "Sure, sure." When she left I found some marijuana hidden under a cushion.

By that time I was well aware that he was hiding things from me, lying, running one scam after another. Sometimes it made me angry, but it also made me curious. He always left his royal-blue duffel bag locked with a half-inch silver padlock. He was touchy about that bag; he knew the exact position he left it in. He even knew when his cat Sasha jumped on it.

I opened it with the key from my jewelry box. Inside there was a T-shirt, boat shoes, and about ten little scraps of papers folded in fours. I'd seen him flipping through those papers before but didn't dare ask about them.

On the outside of each piece I found license plate numbers, phone numbers, names, addresses. On the inside there was every bit of information he could get: Social Security numbers, occupations, work schedules, likes, dislikes, kids, pets, et cetera. He'd told me he sometimes traced people for his friends, and I figured it was connected with his police work. But why not keep the information in notebooks? Why these silly little scraps?

By November I knew I was in a desperate situation and had to get out, but I was still in love with him. A part of me wanted to help him, save him, 'cause I had a pretty good idea where he was headed.

Once in a while my sweet George would come back. It was like he was trying to keep me off-balance—bad guy, good guy, but mostly bad guy. He gave me a half-inch round ruby ring in an antique setting, said it belonged to his grandmother in Florida and was worth a lot of money. It touched my heart. I forgot every cruel thing he ever did.

One of my friends worked in a jewelry store, and she said it was corundum, man-made, worth about sixty bucks. I didn't care. To me it was the most valuable ring in the world; I'd sit and stare at it. George knew how I felt, so after our next fight he said he wanted it back. I'd always known he would use it as a weapon, so I'd hidden it under my nightstand.

He stormed into the bedroom, leaning over me, yelling, "Give me my ring now!" He scared hell out of me, so I gave it back. It broke my heart.

Later that night he came home drunk with a white friend. It was four A.M., and they were headed somewhere.

I tried to find out where they were going, but George just walked out the door. I said, "George, excuse me. *Excuse me!*" He turned around and came back in, and I tried to hang on to him to make him realize I needed to talk. That's how low I was.

He shoved me down and jumped on top of me. He stopped strangling me when his friend ran in.

After they left, I looked at myself in the mirror. My neck was black and blue.

I guess I still wasn't low enough. A week or so later he turned abusive again, then went into his shell. I followed him around the house, raving and ranting, telling him we could never save our relationship if we couldn't communicate. He ran into the bathroom. I was wearing Keds and I stuck my foot out and said, "You're not shutting this door on me." He tried to slam it and it hit my foot and popped off the hinges.

He looked shocked. He threw the door open and punched me so hard that I fell backward into the kitchen and slumped against the fridge.

He walked past me and was gone. I could feel the goose egg swelling up on the side of my head. I didn't know what to think. I'd seen hundreds of women hit by men, but only on TV.

About a month before Christmas he was driving me home from the Black Angus around one-thirty on a Thursday morning. I'd had too much to drink, and I was saying, "George, why don't you just leave? Why put me through this? Why can't we just end it and I can get on with my life?"

He didn't answer. By now, I recognized that wall of silence as pure hatred. I said, "Okay, fine, *don't* talk. Let me out!" We were a half block from the apartment complex. "I'll walk. I don't want to be with you another second." Without thinking, I left my purse in my car.

A freezing rain was coming down. My heel broke off in a puddle. I was drenched, sobering up fast. I took off my heels and walked barefoot. When I got home, my car wasn't there and I was locked out.

I banged on my door. No answer. I thought maybe he'd hidden my car and gone inside. He'd pulled that trick before. I sat on my porch, shivering. Every few minutes I knocked again. Inside I could hear the cats going crazy. At three o'clock I used the bushes for a bathroom. I thought, How low can you get? I was crying; my cats were crying.

I knocked every fifteen or twenty minutes, loud enough to be heard inside, soft enough to keep from waking my neighbors. I figured George was on one of his all-night deals. But why hadn't he waited to let me in?

When the sun came up, I was still huddled on the mat against my door so I couldn't be seen from below. I was afraid the neighbors could hear me shaking. The mat was the only warmth I had—no coat, no jacket, no hat, nothing. Windy, crying, freezing.

The manager arrived at eight-thirty—a sweetheart, very fatherly and concerned. I looked like shit when I stumbled into his office. He said, "No problem, my dear," and unlocked my door.

George was reading the paper on the couch. He'd been in there all the time. It was worse than a sock in the face.

I said, "Why didn't you let me in?" He didn't even look up. I said, "What was the point?"

No answer.

I just took a long hot bath.

When I got home the next evening, a car was parked in my spot. I heard a girl screaming, "George. Oh, George!"

I thought, No *way!*

I ran up the three flights of stairs. They were making love on the water bed. I just stood there. They didn't even notice me. I said, "What the hell are you doing?"

He said, "What are *you* doing here?"

She rolls over and says, "Oh, is this the girl you told me about?" They're both stark naked and acting like *I've* got a problem.

I finally broke. I said, "George, you get out of here right now!"

He goes, "Not till you pay me three thousand dollars, hon."

I'm screaming at him, "What are you talking about? Just—get out!"

"No! You pay me for all the rent and everything else. I'm not leaving till then."

The woman pipes up, "You got nothing to worry about, honey. I'm only here for the day. I'm from San Francisco. I'm leaving tomorrow."

Neither of them made a move to dress or get out of the water bed. George said, "Pay back my goddamn money or I'll have you hurt."

I just took off. I didn't know what to do. I called my ex-boyfriend Chris, and he said, "Get over here right now!"

I slept in his living room.

In the morning I called the Mercer Island Police and asked for Officer Kettells; that was the only name I could remember. The dispatcher said he wasn't available. I said I'd been having problems with George Russell and just wanted to talk to someone.

She said, "Oh, everyone's had problems with George. He's harmless."

It made me feel stupid, so I said, "Oh, okay."

Chris drove me home. On the way he told me he was sure that George had stolen his expensive high-top sneakers and asked if I'd mind if he searched the apartment. I said it wasn't a good idea right now. In my heart I still couldn't believe that George would do something like that.

The San Francisco woman was gone and George was asleep on the water bed. He was all apologies. "I was drunk, Min. I made a mistake, it was a one-time thing, I'm sorry, hon. . . ."

We talked it out. No more relationship; from now on we'd strictly be roommates. He would take the spare room and respect my privacy. I thought, I'll live with it. Financially I had no choice.

At five the next morning he served me breakfast in bed. We were lovers again.

Then George and a female friend won the Black Angus "Square Cow Funbar Mexican Super Cruise for Two," from L.A. to Ensenada and back. I wasn't jealous. She was a mutual friend, very nice, and she'd filled out hundreds of tickets and spent a lot of her own money to win.

When they got back from the four-day cruise on December 16, I found a pair of panties in his laundry. George laughed and told me it didn't mean anything. He promised to take me to his mother's vacation home in the Bahamas, but we never got around to it.

Christmas was coming. I knew it didn't mean a thing to George; he hated holidays, and he'd get angry if you even mentioned his birthday. The only holiday he enjoyed was St. Patrick's Day, 'cause everybody partied.

A week before Christmas I unpacked my aluminum tree—the one Chris had knocked down the year before. I just couldn't decide whether to put it up. Christmas meant so much to me, but this year I had no money for gifts, a shaky relationship with George, and my mom and I were hardly speaking. I'd halfway decided to spend my Christmas at work, selling cards.

After a while I said to myself, Hey, Mindy, Christmas is *your* day. It doesn't depend on getting along with others. It's a special, sacred, pleasant, perfect time.

I set my tree on its stand and unwrapped my ornaments one by one. That always had a therapeutic effect on me, calming, rejuvenating. Every ornament had a story. Some went back to when I was a baby. After I turned on the tree lights, I got so inspired I went out and bought a little Christmas village for my bedroom, with tiny people and another little tree.

George looked at the Christmas stuff like it smelled. When I asked him what was wrong, he went into his sulk again. I tried to be understanding. Christmas can be hard on people without a close family. I'd never heard him say a word about his natural father; he was on the outs with the Mobleys (again!), and as far as I could see he had no communication with his mother at San Francisco State—no phone calls, no letters, no cards. Once in a while there'd be a postcard to "Russy" from "Riki," his half-sister Erika, but otherwise . . . George was an orphan.

When I offered a little comfort and love, he turned his back. The same old crap. So we had another fight, and it turned into Custer's Last Stand. I stormed into the kitchen and yelled, "Either pay attention to me or get out!"

The next thing I knew he'd picked up my aluminum tree and speared it at me. He knew all about the fight with Chris the Christmas before and exactly what buttons to push. I was leaning against the counter and the branches brushed my ear. Everything shattered against the wall.

I just kind of fell in a heap. I think I went into shock. My hand touched something; I picked up the remains of a little pipe cleaner candycane that my sister had made for me when she was like two and a half. I scratched my hand on a broken glass ball, a memento of a trip to Disneyland.

I sat there rocking, moaning, "No, no, not again. Please, God, please. Not again." Over and over.

After a while I picked up the candycane and went into the

bedroom and sat on the bed. I thought I was gonna lose control. It was the closest I've ever been to walking down the street to the Fairfax mental hospital and saying, "Put me in those funky clothes."

I must have sat there for an hour. Finally I stopped crying and came out of the bedroom to pick up the pieces.

George was sitting in the middle of the kitchen floor, rocking back and forth, bawling. He looked pathetic . . . haunted. I saw shards of glass in his hair and his shorts and his sneakers. He wasn't wearing a shirt.

He kept saying, "What have I done? *What have I done?*" He cried so loud I raised my finger to my lips and said, "Sshhh!" I thought he would disturb the neighbors.

I didn't touch him or comfort him, but I felt compassion, sympathy. I flashed on the word "schizophrenic," but I didn't know that much about psychiatry.

I went back into the bedroom for a while, and when I came out, he was sitting on the floor, working on two of the broken figurines: a porcelain man in the moon, dipped in velvet, and a penguin bell that my sister had given me the year before. He was trying to glue them together with model cement.

I watched for a few seconds and turned away. At that point I couldn't stand seeing him do something nice. It was too confusing. He repaired every possible piece. I put my tree back up; it was bent, but it was Christmas to me.

The next day George came home and said, "Here, hon. This is for you." He gave me two whale drawings, hand-drawn by a kid at Denny's. He said they were designer drawings, especially for me. Then he gave me a plain gold friendship band, very thin, twelve carats.

I thought, Why does this guy have so much power over me when he acts soft and timid? All I said was "George, why are you doing this?" I hoped maybe I'd see his sensitive side again.

His voice turned brusque. He said, "Well, I'm not proposing or anything, Min, but this is as close as I'll ever get."

A month or two earlier, I'd have fainted with joy. Now I just wondered, What does *this* mean? It sure didn't mean marriage.

In a few days the ring disappeared.

THE MOBLEYS OF Mercer Island dispatched their 1989
newsletter to "Dearest family and friends." It had been
composed by Dr. Mobley's wife Kris in the slightly self-
conscious tone of someone who married into the family.

She noted that "George Russell is living out in Kirkland
in construction as of the last time we talked. He is 32 years
old and is doing quite well on his own. He is single still
and we are also proud of him for achieving this great feat
at last! (I'm talking about being on his own.) Ha!Ha!''

By year's end the cat burglaries in Mindy Charley's neighborhood in Kirkland totaled about sixty. Local police had
no clues or suspects.

Mercer Island officers had known for some time that
George had transferred his operations elsewhere, but they
also knew that he sometimes returned for a midnight prowl
or break-in. It was as though he derived a nostalgic pleasure
from entering homes he'd violated for years, diddling the
same cops, disappearing into the same dark woods and hiding in his forts. As usual, he was almost impossible to
catch.

Sergeant Glendon Booth thought he discerned a worsening trend.

> Most of the years I knew George, he wasn't violent with
> adults. He carried a knife, claimed it was for protection, but it
> was mostly for bluff and for prying into houses and cars.
>
> Now he starts carrying *two* knives. Threatened to slice a
> guy's throat. Slapped a woman in a bar and had to be re-
> strained. Women set him off. You seldom heard of George
> going up against a guy. He usually backed off or claimed he
> was a police officer.
>
> You could see his level of violence was going up. The old
> George would smile and pick your pocket and you'd say,
> "Thanks, George, any time." Now he was becoming more

aggressive. No more kids to push around. Dealing with street people his own age: losers, unemployables.

I'm thinking, Something's gotta give here, something's gonna happen. But in the United States you can't arrest people for what they're *gonna* do. You gotta let 'em do it first.

A YOUNG MAN named Steven Douglas Crandall also detected danger signs, but he'd just met George Russell and was unaware of his history. The streetwise son of law officers, Crandall was raised in a working-class section of South Seattle. He lived by a strict code: "You're loyal to your buddies, you don't rat people out, and what someone else does is their own fuckin' business."

The tall, chunky youth had thoughts of becoming a stand-up comic. He was a few months short of the legal drinking age of twenty-one, but claimed he could drink nine beers without effect. He first met George Russell at a school parking lot and then ran into him at a party for kids, most of them fifteen to eighteen.

George blended in like he knew every kid there. It was obvious he was, ya know, ripped on something. He began this Shakespeare shit: "How art thou? I be George. Forsooth, don't thou comprehendest?"

I didn't comprehendest or pay much attention, ya know? He really didn't seem that cool, just kind of like, ya know, he was like stuck on himself, real verbal, like flashy. Like "I'm bad, I'm hip." Telling the kids, "George never lets you down," and, "You do a favor for me and I'll give it back to you. Ask anybody here." It was kind of like, Believe in me.

He starts rapping about Ted Bundy. Sounded pretty passionate and really fascinated, called Bundy a "star," "a genius guy," "famous," "cool."

He was like, "Bundy created his own fame. No matter what you do, ya know, you'll never be able to say the name Ted Bundy without knowing who he is."

I'm like, What *is* this shit? To me, Bundy was a sick fuckin' bastard and he needed to fuckin' die. But George is saying like, ya know, "There's a lot you can learn from a guy like that."

I said, "Yeah, well, Bundy's right up there with Himmler and Hitler and every other mass murderer. They said they were smart, but yet, ya know, they had to kill everybody to make their life complete."

Then he went off on some woman's book about Bundy—maniacal, raving up and down! "Fuckin' bitch!" "She doesn't know shit." "She's out for a fuckin' dollar." Raving, *raving*. I noticed there were no specifics, nothing. I got the impression it was because the author was a woman. Like, *What right does a woman have to judge one of my heroes?*

After a while I gave him twenty bucks to buy some beer and he tried to rip me off on the change. I said, "Hey, listen, you and me are gonna box for this money." He ignored me, kept blabbing on about how to handle women, blah blah.

I finally had enough. I said, "Look, I'll take my fuckin' beer, I'll take my happy ass outa here, I got no fuckin' time to spend with you, man. I don't like you, you're a punk, you're outa control." I just got in my little car and left.

AT ABOUT THE same time, a woman in her early twenties was invited to the apartment where George was staying and was shocked by what she saw in his bedroom. She told a friend, "He had stacks and stacks of detective magazines, the kind with women being hurt on the cover. He said he thought he could pull off the perfect crime if he just read enough."

EVERY NIGHT G. B. COFFIN, a comely waitress at the Black Angus, found herself becoming increasingly annoyed at the African-Americans who flocked to the club to meet women. It wasn't that she didn't like her job, and it wasn't that she was a racist. She'd grown up among blacks and Asians and other hyphenated Americans, and she'd never given skin color much thought. Then her life went blooey in Oregon and her prison-guard husband was jailed for drugs and armed robbery and she hauled her three children back to her old hometown of Bellevue to take a job waitressing—or, as the occupation was called in the local clubs, "cocktailing."

The twenty-eight-year-old G.B. had worked at El Torito before switching to the Black Angus. From the first night she blended into the operation and enjoyed her coworkers. But she had problems with the club's demographics.

I liked everything about the Black Angus except the loud music and some of the customers. The money was good, from forty to sixty a night. The basic salary was minimum wage: four twenty-five an hour when I was cocktailing and five an hour when I tended bar. The Angus was the only Eastside bar I knew that didn't take a tip credit out of your paycheck or pay you less than the federal minimum. A class operation.

The way the place was laid out, you entered on a flat level and there was a walkway toward the restaurant part with a rail along it, or you could walk down a couple stairs and through a little lobby and there was the bar, all glitter and glass, shelves and bottles, seats for twelve or fifteen, always occupied. They had a bunch of TV monitors, a big screen in the bar area and four little studio screens behind the bar, mostly for music videos. The DJ ran the show. At that time we played a lot of rap music, violent stuff. Some of the customers would hear those songs about offing the pigs and get all amped up. You wondered what they did after they left for the night.

Generally I like to talk to my customers, and generally I'm color-blind, but some of the black guys in the Angus grossed me out. There are high types and low types in all races, and we got the low types. They ogled our cocktailing outfits and did a lot of nudging and pinching. I finally told the manager, "Sam, we're here to serve drinks. We're not here as toys." He just raised his eyebrows. When guys hit on us, I guess we were supposed to shrug it off and walk away.

Some of our customers would say, "I'll take a rum and Coke and your phone number." Very few were sophisticated drinkers. They'd mix Hennessy and Coke, Courvoisier and juice, crème de menthe and Seven. When they wanted a Screw-driver, they'd yell across the room, "Yo, bitch! Gimme a Screw!" I wore a wedding ring, but that didn't slow them down. Believe me, this wasn't the young-exec BMW Micro-soft crowd. Some were barely off welfare, nursing their drinks till they connected with a lounge lizard. We divided the lizards into "clean ones," meaning they never went home with any-body, and "sluts." It was about half and half. We saw black men by the dozens, but almost never a black woman.

The black guys would usually tip pretty lousy unless they were trying to impress a white chick. Some of 'em treated me like I was their slave. "Get it over here, bitch!"

I'd go, Oh, God, and try to keep quiet.

I'd bring the drink, "That's five bucks," and they'd say, "*Five bucks?* You jivin'. How about three twenty-five?"

I'd say, "This isn't a fire sale, sir. Please. I need five dol-lars."

Then they'd get mad and say I was prejudiced.

Sometimes I'd put on a demure little voice and say, "I'm not prejudiced against your race, sir. I'm just prejudiced against *you*."

Long before my trouble with George, I had plenty of prob-lems with our customers. I had drinks thrown at me, a cham-pagne glass, lighted cigarettes. Twice I was tripped when I was carrying a full tray. When one black guy raised his fist, I said, "Go ahead and hit me. It'll be the last thing you do outside of jail." I cut off another man's drunken white girl-friend and he swung at me. I raised my hand just in time. While the bouncers were leading him out, he yelled, "Hey, ho, I'm comin' back for *you*."

You remember people by their drinks. The rum-and-Coke guy. The Dos Equis Dark lady. The Bud Light guy. The vodka-collins-with-a-twist woman. The champagne couple. George was the Miller-Draft-with-a-shot-of-tequila guy. I first noticed him in September, '89, and I was suspicious from the start. One thing you learn in a bar is that people who keep going in and out are usually up to no good. We had a lot of dealers and pimps—up and down, walking around, meeting people, min-gling. I was supersensitive about dealers. Drugs broke up my marriage and changed my husband from a prison officer to an inmate. I'm no goody two-shoes, but when it comes to dope I'm a little irrational, a fanatic.

George came in every night, and I suspected him of dealing right off. Our bouncers and doormen found he kept his beer in the bushes behind McDonald's parking lot, right next door. He'd sneak over and drink it to avoid paying two twenty-five a glass, and then he'd come back inside. The doormen threw his stash away and laughed about it—what a cheap-ass, and so on.

I figured he had more than beer out there. One day a kid about thirteen or fourteen came into the lobby upstairs. George saw him and they left together. It looked like he was dealing to a little kid! That really set me off. Another cocktailer was watching with me. I said, "Well, look at this. Isn't this *special?*"

After that I kept my eyes on him, and he always looked like he was up to something. He smiled too much and he had a big line of bullshit, just like my ex-husband. If you know what to look for, you can spot those psychopaths in minutes. If you don't, they'll make you wish you were dead.

Most people thought George was neat. His friends would say, "Why do you dislike George? He's a good guy."

I'd say, "George is flat-out scum." I thought, Do these people just have blinders on their heads? Can't they see what's going on? Even some of our staff were like, Don't pick on George. For a long time I was the only one around the club who disliked him.

One night he showed up early with two girls, a short blonde and a taller girl with darker hair. They treated him like a king. He set his scanner on the table and the girls watched it. They passed a lot of money back and forth. I thought, Can't they see he's just a sleaze?

I was sure the girls were doing drug things for him. It upset me 'cause they were really young. I thought, Someday this scum's gonna be trying to sell drugs to *my* kids.

So when George went outside I told 'em, "A word of advice from somebody who cares. Don't hang out with this guy. He's trouble."

They kinda giggled. "Oh, no. George is cool. He works with the Seattle narks."

I said, "Yeah? What's he do?"

"He's an agent, an informer."

I knew a lot of cops, and I was pretty sure the Seattle PD didn't use drug peddlers as agents. I said, "I don't think so."

The little blonde said, "You don't understand. He's in here working on dope cases."

I said, "He's got you conned. This scanner isn't for police work; it's for show. You can't even hear it when the music starts. Trust me."

A few nights later George backed me against the wall and said I was pissing him off—"Stay out of my personal life, hon. This is none of your business."

I just laughed.

After that he went out of his way to be aggressive. When we were crowded, he'd brush against me. I'd jerk away and give him a look, and he'd give me that silly smirk. *What're you gonna do about it, bitch? I'm a customer and you're just a waitress. . . .*

Once he came up behind me on the stairs and ran those long fingernails down my back. I whirled around and said, "Don't you ever touch me again."

He said, "What's your problem, bitch? The other women like it."

"Yeah? Well, here's one that doesn't."

A few days later I was talking about George to my pal Carol Beethe at one of the little stand-ups in the Black Angus. Carol came in all the time, sometimes with her boyfriend Tom Jones, sometimes just to see me. She was a really neat person. If the Eastside cocktailers and bartenders ever held a popularity contest, she'd be the unanimous winner. We met when I was working at the El Torito and our crew used to go next door to Shooters, where she worked. I learned a lot just watching her. We talked together, went shopping; our kids played together. When she started bartending at Cucina! Cucina! and I went to the Black Angus, we kept right on being friends.

So I was standing there telling her about George's long fingernails, and I made the motion of scratching her—I talk with my hands a lot—and I look over and he's sitting in a corner staring at both of us. You could tell he knew exactly what we were talking about. After a while, Carol gave me a hug and left.

From then on George made wimpy little insinuations:

"What time you gonna finish tonight? I'll be waiting. . . ."
"Are you gonna be in the parking lot? . . ." Stupid stuff.

Our parking lot *was* a problem. When the DJ flashed the
lights for last call, there was nobody left for the losers to hit
on except cocktailers. You'd hear these frantic remarks on the
way to your car: "I can't live without you. . . ." "I'll *kill* myself. . . ." Oversexed drunks hid in the bushes. It was a scary
situation, and sometimes we escorted each other to our cars.

I told my boss what was happening, and he finally took
George aside and told him it might be a good idea to stay out
of my section, don't talk to G. B. Coffin, don't deal with her—
"Some folks just don't get along." That was okay with me.
Out of the thirty or so tables in the bar, I had about eight. Now
George was somebody else's problem.

Word began to reach me through third parties. "George says
to stop talking about him. . . ." It seemed like I was constantly
on his mind. "George says be nice, be cool. . . ."

I just laughed. I said, "Why should I be nice to somebody
that sells drugs out of our club? And uses kids? That's the
kind of clientele we want to get rid of."

At staff meetings I'd always bring up the subject of banning
him for good. I said, "Look, the guy doesn't spend any money.
He comes in and wanders around." . . . And so on.

The manager says, "We're a public place. As long as he
buys a beer or something, there's nothing we can do."

Sam was afraid of losing our black clientele. He was one of
those people who like to smooth things over. If somebody got
really rank, he'd eighty-six 'em for thirty days and let 'em
back a week or two later. A guy would threaten to kill one of
our people and a few weeks later he's sitting at the bar making
more threats.

Some of those guys were scary, but I wasn't afraid of
George Russell. He always carried a boot knife, so we got
permission from Sam to frisk him when he came in. When
George would make a nasty crack, I'd make one back. And I
didn't whisper, either. Cool George hated to be embarrassed.
People were beginning to laugh at him because of me. I felt
like I was doing a community service.

The Bellevue cops came through a lot, making bar checks,
and I got to know some of them. I figured out a way to help
them clean out the dopers. If I thought somebody was dealing

drugs, I'd ask for his ID, no matter how old he looked. The guy would say, "Hey, I'm forty years old," and I'd say, "Hey, I don't make the rules. Please . . . show me your ID."

Then I'd pass the name and address to my cop friends and they'd put a watch on him. They made several arrests that way. The Bellevue PD had a ride-along plan and I went on patrol with them on my off nights. I sat at their dispatch desk and listened to the calls. It was a blast.

A Mercer Island dispatcher named Terry Orr started coming in, and we became friends. She spotted George and said, "Look out for that one. He's trouble."

I said, "*Tell* me about it."

Terry and I had some nice talks. She told me I should think about becoming a dispatcher. She took me to work with her a couple of times and showed me the Mercer Island routine.

I asked her why she had it in for George and she said he was going around telling people that he worked with the police, but he was really nothing but a little house robber. She punched his name into the computer and it took five minutes to type out his record. And that didn't include the juvenile stuff!

She told me that the last time he was arrested he had the balls to list his occupation as "Seattle police informant."

One night she called me and said there was a warrant out for George for parole violation. She said, "If he shows up, let us know."

He came in with two new blondes and ordered dinner. I called Mercer Island and they made the arrest along with a couple of Bellevue cops. Everyone knew what George thought of black women, so it gave me a special thrill that the warrant was served by a black officer, Sharon Lewis.

Terry and I stood there laughing in his face when Sharon slapped on the handcuffs. He was *pissed*! He was being shown up in front of his groupies.

For sure he knew who'd snitched him off. I didn't care; I was proud of myself.

GOLDEN-HAIRED TAMI Grace was surprised when the cops arrested her dancing partner. George had invited Tami and another young woman to dinner, and they'd been looking forward to overdosing on the lambada, limbo and electric slide. As George was led away, he said, "Enjoy the meal ladies. I'll be back later."

Tami asked, "What's up?"

"No biggie, hon. Just . . . a misunderstanding."

A few minutes later, the waitress named G.B. came over and said, "George won't be coming back. Will you be able to pay the check?"

"Yeah," Tami said. When the food arrived, she pushed it away and went home.

News filtered down that George was sentenced to five days in King County Jail for parole violation, and Tami was surprised all over again. She thought, Parole? For *what*? She decided it was probably part of his undercover work.

Even before the arrest Tami had been concerned about her old dancing partner's morale. He seemed increasingly preoccupied, touchy, remote. She'd always thought that the smiling "Huggybear" would never turn uncool, but it was happening.

Recently she'd spent some time with George and Mindy in the apartment they shared in Kirkland. Tami had been having medical problems plus the usual difficulties with her fiery boyfriend Mike Weisenburgh, and George had invited her to move in for R&R.

As always, he proved a comfort—"much nicer to me than he was to Mindy," Tami recalled later. The women slept in the two bedrooms, George on the couch. He was asleep all day, and they tiptoed around him. Whenever he went into the bathroom or the spare bedroom, he made a big show of locking the door. He never let his blue sports bag out of his sight. One night he lectured them both on why they shouldn't celebrate holidays. Tami wasn't sure if he was kidding, but he sounded serious.

She was baffled by his coldness toward Mindy. "I don't think he even liked her. He couldn't even fake it."

* * *

Toward the end of the one-week stay Mindy confided that she'd once caught George in bed with another woman and found a pair of panties in his laundry. "They weren't yours, Tami?" she implored. "Were they?" Tears welled in her blue eyes.

"No, *no*!" Tami replied. "Mindy, I'm with Mike Weisenburgh. George and I are dancing partners."

Mindy nodded. She said she suspected that George might be involved in cocaine. Tami recalled a glass vial she'd seen him remove from his bag; it was orange with a black lid and resembled a coke container.

Mindy said, "It's all coming together. I've talked to the cops. He's not a nark. He's . . . a crook."

No, *no*, Tami said to herself. Not George. Eccentric, yes. Different, even a little flaky. But no way "Honeybear" could be a criminal.

A week later Tami and Mike assembled with five or six friends to celebrate the couple's latest reconciliation. Tami prepared beef Stroganoff and chocolate fondue and served it in the dining alcove of the new apartment that she shared with another young woman in Bellevue. George ate in a corner by himself. After everyone watched the erotic movie *9½ Weeks*, starring Tami's look-alike, Kim Basinger, she was showing one of her female guests a set of romantic pictures of herself when she noticed George peeking over their shoulders.

"Can I have this?" he asked, pointing to a shot that showed a lean, lithe Tami, cigarette in hand, striking a dancing pose in front of a tree. A shortie nightgown protected her modesty, but the pose was provocative. It had been taken for a boyfriend.

She put George off with a quip and slid the pictures back in the dresser drawer.

A few nights later Tami and her roommate heard scratching noises at a window. Police were called and found no signs of attempted entry.

When the young women came home from work the next day, they noticed that their answering machine had been turned off. Several days later a personal memo somehow transferred itself from the wall to a table. Then a door handle fell off at midnight. The roommates suspected a poltergeist.

A policeman advised them to make a thorough check for missing items. Everything seemed to be in its place, but Tami couldn't find one of her shortie nightgowns.

Then one of her acquaintances from the Black Angus idly mentioned that George Russell had been showing off a set of pictures of half-dressed females, and one of the subjects looked familiar. Tami thought she recognized herself from the description: a rangy young blonde sitting on a futon, bare legs outstretched, wearing a teddy. Like the picture George had admired, this one was sexy but tasteful, the sort of memento a wife might give a husband.

She was still pondering this latest development when Mindy Charley phoned to ask for asylum for the night. She babbled something about a fight and sounded almost hysterical.

A few hours later George called and said he was in the police station. In the background Tami heard him chatting with the cops as though they were old friends. Apparently they were going to escort him back to Mindy's apartment to collect his things and move out.

"Listen, Tami," George told her in a soft voice. "Stay out of this, okay?"

"George," she said, "what happened?"

He said, "Listen to me, hon! *Don't* get involved."

She said, "You're a friend of mine, George. Mindy's a friend of mine. What am I supposed to do?"

He lowered his voice. "I'm warning you," he said. "Butt out. You have no right."

She tried to ask if he was okay, but he was talking to his police pals again. Then the phone went dead.

It WASN'T THE ending that Mindy Charley had expected. Things had been running more smoothly since she and George had begun to separate their lives. He'd been spending most of his time away from the apartment, and the ex-lovers weren't grating on each other's nerves. Another big improvement was the arrival of a young black catalyst named Terry Taylor, a bright, athletic woman who brooked no nonsense from George Russell or anyone else. Mindy was grateful.

We'd always had trouble paying the rent, and I jumped at the chance for my friend Terry to move into our spare bedroom. George didn't seem to mind. Our relationship was over and he wasn't as hipped on controlling every move I made. He was even beginning to listen to me a little bit. I figured another roommate would help with the financial load.

Terry disliked George from the start. She couldn't figure out how I ever connected with a guy like him in the first place— "Girl, don't you know trash when you see it?"

Every time I said a good word about George she got on my case. She made me see things clearly.

She loved the fact that black women put him off; she played on it, drove him nuts. He'd come home and she'd shriek, "Yo, bro, what it *is*? Gimme five, homes!" He *despised* that kind of talk! She'd flop down next to him and he'd get up. She seldom drank, but she kept some wine around for her friends. George would drink it, and she'd tell him off, and he'd leave and stay away for a couple of days. It was a big improvement.

I was already thinking about going out with other guys, and Terry encouraged the idea. She kept telling me, "Hey, check *this* guy out, check *that* guy out." She wanted me to stand up for myself and get away from George. When I felt despondent, she'd say, "Look at yourself! You've got so much going for you." She'd say, "Mindy, I'm gonna kick your butt if you don't start standing up for yourself."

After a while I got the idea. I went dancing at the Black

Angus and dated two or three times. I figured I was on my way out of a bad relationship.

We still owed back rent, because George kept coming up short. When another $425 came due, Terry paid her share, but George made more excuses. In the second week of February, the landlord served eviction papers. The timing was weird. I'd just gone to work as a salesclerk for a Seattle store, with a respectable starting salary and a good future. I was still selling greeting cards part-time and also helping my ex-husband clean houses, digging my way out of debt. At the moment Terry and I had eighty cents between us.

I put out a bunch of phone messages for George and finally got him to call back. He promised to rush over with some money but didn't. He called me at work the next day and told me to meet him at the Black Angus at eight-thirty. I said, "I can't get there. My gas tank's on 'E.'"

He said, "If you want your rent, you better be there."

I called the landlord and said I'd have some money soon. He sounded noncommittal. I borrowed two dollars to buy enough gas to get from Kirkland to Bellevue, the next town over.

I sat in the waiting area till ten-ten. No George. The Saturday night crowd was arriving and the DJ was boosting the amps. I didn't want to be seen. George and I had made enough scenes at the Black Angus. I drove home.

He called me the next day, Sunday. He says, "How come you didn't show last night? I had your money."

I said, "You weren't there when you said you'd be."

"I was there by nine forty-five."

"George, I was *there*. There were maybe fifteen people in the place when I left. You weren't one."

He started his usual line of jive. I just listened. How many times had I heard him spout his lies to me and others? Finally he said, "I'll be at the apartment tonight when you get home from work," and hung up.

I was desperate. We'd had warnings from the landlord, but this was the first time he'd served an actual notice. I wasn't even sure if he would accept the back rent by now. If George stiffed me again, everything Terry and I owned would be thrown on the street.

In desperation I called the Mobley house. Kris answered. I'd been with her and Wonzel ten or twelve times and felt I knew them pretty well. They'd always acted friendly.

I said, "Kris, I don't know where to turn. George isn't paying his share of the rent and I'm being evicted. How do I handle this?"

She told me to take everything George owned and put it in the Dumpster. "And then," she added, "change your locks."

I was in shock. I said, "You know I can't do that."

She said, "Why not?"

"He'd break down the door if I touched his stuff. I can't even move his things around the apartment."

She blew up. That darling little person with the pretty face and the cheerleader's bod—she went . . . *off*! "Mindy, you've got to make a stand! You've got to get him out of your life. He's no good for you. He's no good for *anybody*. . . ."

She talked so fast I could hardly absorb it all. She said, "You've absolutely *got* to free yourself! Don't you know he's been classified as a schizo? . . ."

It was like the poor woman had just been waiting to unload. She said George made their lives hell; Wonzel had tried everything; the cops and the courts tried. Nothing worked. Nothing would *ever* work. And so on . . .

I said something like I couldn't understand how George could be so tight with his mom and so mean to other women.

Kris cut me off. "He won't speak to his mom. They have the *worst* relationship."

I was confused. I started to tell Kris how we had a permanent invitation to visit his mom's winter home in the Bahamas.

Kris is like, "Are you *kidding*? His mother wouldn't let George *near* that place."

Every time I mentioned some other nice thing that George had said about his mother, she'd say, "That's a lie. . . . That's a lie. . . . That's *another* lie. . . ." She said, "The only time he's spoken to his mother since he was sixteen is when Erika tricked him into getting on the phone with her, and he was so angry he wouldn't speak to Erika for hours. He always said his mother ran out on him and she'd never get a second chance."

I could see I'd really touched a nerve. Kris said, "We've tried hard to help him. Wonzel's been so patient. There was a court order that George had to go to counseling. He went three times and wouldn't go back.''

As she talked, she seemed to settle down a little. What's the word—catharsis? The last thing she asked me was to please never tell George that we'd discussed him.

I put the phone down and tried to stop shaking. It was dinnertime; I was home alone; Terry was at her regular Sunday night volleyball game. I was mad 'cause I knew I was gonna lose the apartment that I loved so much *and it wasn't my fault.* It enraged me that I'd allowed something like this to happen.

George arrived at six-thirty with his friend Brian. He was happy-go-lucky. ''Hey, hon, how's it going.'' All lovey-dovey, tried to give me a kiss.

I pulled away. I'm like, ''What about the rent money?''

Then I thought, Oops! You just broke the most important rule: *never* embarrass His Highness in front of his friends. But I was so upset I didn't give a damn.

There was instant fire in his eyes. He said, ''Oh, well, Brian and I, we been out, and now we're gonna talk some more.'' He grabs a fifth of tequila and they start toward the door.

I say, ''Excuse me? I need that rent money. You can either take your stuff and get out, or you can pay up.''

He turns around and says, ''You'll get your money when I come back.''

I go, ''Oh? When's that gonna be?''

''When we finish this bottle.''

I'm thinking, Oh, great. You'll be drunk. But then I remembered, George never really gets drunk.

I refused to back down. I knew I was pushing him, but nobody was gonna make me lose my beautiful apartment after four years. I said, ''When'll you be back?''

He laughed and said, ''I *told* you. When we finish this tequila.''

I lost it. I yelled, ''You awful thing!'' I was crying, screaming. ''You've been using me all this time! If you walk out that door you're taking your stuff with you. *For good!*''

He started down the stairs. I grabbed his duffel bag and his box of porno books and threw them out on the third-floor landing.

George was still headed down the stairs. I picked up the duffel bag and it came open and Chris's missing high-tops fell out. That was the end. I thought, What kind of a person would steal somebody's *shoes*? George had sworn over and over he'd never seen those shoes. I pitched the duffel bag over the edge and it fell ten or fifteen feet to the parking lot.

I swear, George was racing up those stairs before the bag hit the ground. I ran into the apartment and he chased me. His face was a blank; it was like he was on autopilot. He began throwing my things against the walls. Our cat Sasha ran behind my wicker hutch.

He methodically destroyed three shelves of dishes and stuff, every picture on the wall, every videocassette and music tape, everything in my cabinets.

I grabbed at his arms, clawed at him, trying to protect my possessions. It had no effect. There was no comprehension in his eyes, only animal anger—no control at all. The only sound was me screaming for him to stop and him grunting as he tore things up. I tried to jump on his back and he dragged me from room to room. Superhuman! I kept yelling, "Don't touch that. Please, George, *don't touch that!*"

After he was done with the living room and the hallway, he walked past Terry's door and into my bedroom. I had an antique Victorian lamp remake, one of my prized possessions, and he smashed it. He ripped out the phone and threw my mattress across the room and broke my bed. I ran at him again and he slammed me against the wall. When I came to, he was pulling clothes out of my walk-in closet and throwing them on the floor.

I staggered outside. My shoulder and head were throbbing; I could hear my own heartbeat. I yelled, "Please, God, help me! *Anybody help me!*"

I couldn't stop screaming. There were six apartments in my stack and nobody was home.

I finally reached the bottom of the stairs. George's friend Brian stood in front of his car looking dazed. You could still hear George wrecking things up above, an animal growl: "Aaaah aaah *aaargh!*"

I'm crying, "Help me." Brian just stood there.

I ran to another stack and banged on a door. A man opened up, pulled me inside and called Nine-one-one. While he was on the phone, he held my hand, trying to comfort me. I heard him say on the phone, "I don't think she's in any danger, but the guy's still out there."

We waited for the cops—five minutes, ten minutes. In desperation I called the Mobley house to ask what to do next.

I said, "George beat me up."

Wonzel said, "What? Who *is* this?"

I go, "This is Mindy! Your son beat me up. He trashed my apartment. He *hurt* me."

Wonzel said, "Excuse me, but George is *not* my son."

The police arrived in fifteen minutes. I was surprised to find that George hadn't touched my wicker hutch, where I kept my prize china. A little ball of fluff was hiding there, trembling. It was Sasha. Everything else was in pieces. The floor was covered with broken glass.

The cops advised me to get away for the night; George might come back, and Terry was still at her volleyball game. I called Tami Grace and went over there.

I still wanted to talk to Kris, so I dialed the Mobley number again. I almost fell over when George answered the phone. He was like, "Oh, hi, hon"—cool, calm, like he was hearing from an old friend.

I went, "Uh, *uh* . . ."

He said, "Why are you calling here, Min?"

I was totally freaked. I blurted, "Uh, uh . . . nothing." Hearing his voice, so calm, so cold—it was instant terror, like being assaulted all over again. I hung up.

AT SEVEN THE next morning, Monday, February 12, 1990, George Russell was arrested at his family's home on a charge of domestic assault. At a preliminary hearing a judge issued a temporary protection order instructing him to have "no contact, directly or indirectly, in person, in writing, or by phone, personally or through other persons, with Mindy Charley."

After Mindy spent a restless night in Tami Grace's apartment, a doctor diagnosed multiple contusions and a hairline fractured vertebra in her neck. He estimated total medical costs at a thousand dollars. Mindy went home to Shawnee Village Apartments and collapsed on her broken bed.

Later in the morning Terry phoned from work and informed her that George had returned to their apartment around 2 A.M., while Mindy was gone. When Terry ordered him to leave, he reminded her that her name wasn't on the lease. She asked, "What did you do to our place? What did you do to Mindy?"

He replied, "Mindy did that to herself, hon." He pointed out that he'd disturbed nothing of Terry's. After a while, he'd picked up his duffel bag and left.

On Monday night, Mindy twisted and squirmed, pulling her candystriped bedsheet loose at the corners. At 4 A.M. she thought she heard a car door shut.

She gave up on sleep at 7:30 and went down the stairs to her red Nissan. A rear tire had been punctured. There was a Snickers bar on the front seat.

The following morning a paper napkin from McDonald's appeared in her car. She started to crumple it, then noticed George's printing. At the top, four bold underlines stressed "PLEASE READ." He'd written, "Please take care of Sasha. I know she love's you!!"

He professed to be sorry about "that night" and wished he could take it back. He still loved her but guessed that their relationship was over, "as much as I hate that!!!" He claimed that he wouldn't have lost control if she hadn't thrown his bag. She noticed that this scenario deftly displaced the blame from him to her, a favorite technique.

He wrote that he'd visited the abandoned golf course where they'd strolled together the previous June, and it made him wish they could start over—"You can't take the memories of the good times from me. But sadly I can't forget the bad time's either. It hurts me. I can't turn you off like a light switch, nor do I wish too."

The note included a touch of his usual narcissistic philosophy. "We all have problems, even me. I wish I was perfect, but I'm not." She couldn't help thinking, George, George, who the hell ever said you *were?*

He asked her to contact a mutual friend, so they could get together and talk: "I want to hear your voice."

Mindy saw the message as an attempt to soften her testimony at his trial for assault. The tone made her sick, but she followed through on the proposed meeting because she wanted to establish some ground rules. With a few mutual friends, they met in a bar.

"Face this, George," Mindy began. "We're over and done with. Don't contact me in any way, shape or form."

"How about if we run into each other socially?" George asked.

She said she saw no problem.

One of the friends intervened to ask why George had hurt Mindy and trashed her apartment, and once again his reaction made her question his grasp on reality. He spoke of the incident as a harmless prank. "I took some pictures off the wall," he said, "and set 'em on the floor. That's about it."

Mindy said, "Excuse *me?* You broke everything!"

He shook his head. He seemed calm and self-assured as he recited his version. "I was just kinda foolin' around," he explained. "No biggie." She looked deep into his eyes and saw neither anger nor resentment. "Mindy," he was saying in a patient voice, "I'm sorry you got upset. But really, there was nothing much to it."

She picked up her purse, muttered a final "*Excuse me?*" and stalked out. Driving home, she shuddered at the thought that she'd spent nearly eight months of her life with a man who could recast events entirely in terms favorable to himself and recount them in clear, convincing terms. In other words, she said to herself, a lunatic.

She was pleased when a judge extended the protection order for a year. The papers were served on George by his old nemesis, Mercer Island Patrolman Tom Kettells.

Then Mindy heard that he'd moved in with a good-looking young blonde who lived near her own Shawnee Village apartment. She was pleasantly surprised that her main reaction was relief. Her cracked vertebra still throbbed and it would be months before it healed. She figured she was well rid of Mr. George Walterfield Russell Jr.

The gossip hot line soon flashed the news that the blond girlfriend had dumped George for a younger man, and he'd taken refuge with still another young woman. This time he was cementing the relationship with gifts, handing over a ring, pin and necklace. Mindy thought, I wonder how soon he'll tell her to hock them.

She figured he must be pissed. *Totally.* She reread the protection order and hoped it made her safe. By now she'd begun to get the idea that George didn't just dislike her; he disliked the whole female sex. It was small consolation.

STEVE CRANDALL, FUTURE stand-up comic and self-styled high-capacity beer drinker, ran into his sometime booze supplier outside the Black Angus and was treated to an angry lament.

George walked a ways with me, and he was, ya know, kind of pissed off because this girl that he liked was younger than him, ya know, and she liked a guy that was her own age.

I was, "Hey, man, don't sweat it. No big deal. What're ya gonna do, kick his ass?"

George says, "Fuck that. He's just a kid. I'll just whip her ass and fuckin' *do* her." Meaning he'd beat her up and screw her, like a wham, bam, thank you ma'am–type deal. While he's saying these things, he's acting like she's standing in front of him, like he's talking to her instead of me, ya know, making his point. And I was kinda thinking, This guy needs to chill out, ya know? This is like macho to the extreme, a little too tense.

After a while he said he was gonna go up to the Community Center, and I was like, "Hey, shoot some hoops, man! It'll work out steam, ya know?"

George just like, ya know, walked away.

ON A FOGGY evening in March, 1990, G. B. Coffin noticed two young women seated in a far corner of the Black Angus. They acted superior and intense, as though on important business, talking behind their hands and cocking their heads toward the scanner that rested on the table between them.

As the cocktailer watched, George Russell sauntered out of the shadows and the young women began fussing over him. My God, G.B. said to herself, they've mistaken him for the Dalai Lama. She rolled her eyes.

An hour or so later one of her customers confided, "Hey, you better be careful. There's a cop here tonight."

G.B. nodded toward Russell's table and said, "You mean over there?"

"Yeah. He's working undercover."

"No, he's not," she said. "He's a little house robber. He carries that scanner around to make an impression."

Everyone laughed. G.B. thought, Now the jerk's telling people he's a cop. Used to say he's an informer, works "with" the police. God, I can't believe this guy.

For the rest of the evening she kept an eye on him and noticed that he seemed to be watching her in return. As usual, he slid from table to table, hanging out with the DJ and the bouncers, playing his usual role of most favored customer. It riled her blood.

At 1:30 A.M. the overhead lights went on and the clientele ebbed toward the door. As G.B. emptied an ashtray, she felt a presence behind her.

"Stay outa my personal business," George Russell told her in a low voice. "You don't know anything about me."

"I know enough," she said just as softly.

"You don't know shit," he said. "I'll bring some people to tell you about me. I've got references."

She tried not to laugh. "You've got *references?*" she

said. "For being a house robber?" She wasn't frightened. She still regarded him as a wussy manipulator of kids.

"You have no right to say that!" he yelled. "You know nothing about me! I'm legitimate. *I have a real job!*"

The situation struck her as silly, and she started to giggle. "All right," she said softly. "You're legitimate." She just wanted to pick up her tables and go home.

"I'm sick of this bullshit!" he yelled.

"All *right!*" she repeated.

He pointed his long nail. "Goddamn it," he said, "you were told to wait on your tables and mind your own business."

"Oh? By who?"

"The manager."

She tried not to laugh. The only subject she'd discussed with Sam was whether to eighty-six this dickhead for good.

She moved to another table and he followed. "I'm reporting you," he warned.

"Sir," she said firmly, "it's time to go."

"We'll see how long you work here."

She tried to ignore him, but he followed close behind, stabbing the air with his nails. Finally she called to the doorman, "This guy's following me around. I can't do my work."

The doorman touched Russell's arm, but the angry man jerked it away. Another doorman grabbed his other arm and the two men frogwalked him up the short flight of stairs toward the exit.

"You bitch!" he yelled over the rail. "I'll be back for you."

G.B. managed another laugh, but she was beginning to feel uncomfortable. He hung over the rail, pointing and yelling. She'd never seen anyone so angry.

"You're in plenty of fuckin' trouble!" he screamed. She was afraid he would vault the railing. She'd always thought of him as a flake, but this was beyond simple flakiness.

It took five minutes for the men to wrestle him out the front door. As they held him by the arms, he yelled,

"You've had it, bitch! I'm coming back. I'm gonna *kill* you."

She shook her head. The situation had lost any trace of humor. Russell was still making threats outside. She remembered the last months of her marriage, when her husband had threatened her and the three kids, and the family had lived in terror.

She finished her chores, wiping down tables, carrying glassware to the sink, emptying ashtrays, restocking empties. She counted her tickets and checked her credits. After she finished tipping the bartender, she was afraid to walk out on the dark parking lot. It was 2:30 A.M. She asked a bouncer to escort her to her silver blue Mercury Cougar, parked in a far corner. For a change no stage-door Johnnies or Georgies were in sight.

When she reported for work the next night, she learned that Russell had met with the manager. She could just imagine the conversation. In a show of backbone, Sam Tino had told him he was eighty-sixed for two weeks. George had put up a brief argument, then left quietly.

The death threat lingered in G.B.'s mind. After work she asked to be escorted to her car again. She kept thinking, What's he gonna do to me? How can I protect my kids? After a few days, she convinced herself that Russell wasn't man enough to follow through. Then she thought, Yeah, but what if he sends a friend? She told herself that a jerk like him wouldn't have loyal friends. His closest companions were girls who were barely out of high school, using fake ID to get into bars. As for the other black men who frequented the club, they seldom gave him the time of night.

Forget the creep, she told herself. He's not the first guy that threatened you and he won't be the last. Get on with your life. But she couldn't stop thinking that he would be allowed to return in two weeks. What then?

* * *

A few shifts later the easygoing Sam Tino and the rest of the Black Angus crew were relaxing over after-work drinks in the lobby.

G.B. said, "Ya know, Sam, it kills me that a guy like Russell can threaten us and get away with it. Isn't that the kind of scum we're trying to get rid of?"

Another cocktailer said, "He beat up his girlfriend and trashed her apartment."

G.B. turned to the manager. "That's the kind of guy we let back after two weeks? I don't understand."

She was surprised to hear Sam say, "You're right, G.B. T'hell with him."

"Will you remember that tomorrow, Sam?"

"He's outa here for good. I'll tell him when he comes in."

Yeah, sure, she said to herself. Sam was such a pushover. But this time he promised to make it stick.

The day George's original period of exile was scheduled to end, G.B. was standing in the L area below the rail when he strolled through the big front doors like a movie star. A doorman stopped him at the podium and said, "Sorry, George. New rules. It's not two weeks anymore."

George peered over the rail at G.B. For a few seconds they locked stares. Then an assistant manager stepped up and confirmed that the ban was permanent.

As George left, he slammed the doors so hard that everyone was sure they'd broken off their hinges. She heard the two employees discuss making him pay for the damage, but the doorman said, "Let him go. He won't bother us again."

G.B. returned to her cocktailing. It was a relief that the creep was gone for good. Then she wondered, Who's gonna be in my face tonight?

AT SIX-THIRTY ON a chilly Wednesday morning, a week
or so after the latest incident at the Black Angus, Sergeant
Glendon Booth arrived at the Mercer Island police station
and found George Russell reading a book in a cell. Lately
the veteran cop had been thinking a lot about his former
friend.

Through that whole rainy spring a guy'd been slipping into
bedrooms, standing next to women, stealing mementos. It
didn't take a genius to figure who it was. George was living
on the Eastside, but he was acting up on Mercer Island at night.
The risk was low; even when we popped him, he never served
more than a few days. Usually his victims couldn't identify
him—or wouldn't. Nobody wanted to be accused of race prejudice. George knew how to make you feel guilty, make you
feel like a racist. He enjoyed his cat-and-mouse games. We
wanted to bust his ass for good.

Burglars sometimes break into houses for sexual gratifica-
tion, stuff panties in their mouths, crawl through a bedroom
on their hands and knees. George was sneaking in and out,
using his penlight, feeling his power. Sometimes a woman
would see a shadow, hear him go out the door or window.
Sometimes they wouldn't even know he'd been there till they
noticed something missing.

Sitting in the station that morning, working on my second
cup of coffee, I thought back on his record. It seemed like he'd
spent half his adult life in King County Jail, ranging from a
few days for trespassing to a year for felony escape. His juvenile record wasn't much better. God knows how many contacts we'd had with him and how many times he'd been
suspected of a crime.

I had my own theory on what was happening to George. He
used to be a young, handsome, articulate kid, a "pretty boy."
Then he turned eighteen and all his friends were gone. The
bottom dropped out of his life and he couldn't adjust. And
every year it just got worse.

There was family friction, and there were other negative

factors, like the way he tried to outwhite whitey instead of being proud of what he was. Black pride—that's a damn good concept, but what he had was black shame.

So he turns in on himself, and pretty soon he's a grown man with a fourteen-year-old mentality. He was getting flushed down the toilet with age, was losing his ability to seduce young girls, hanging out in joints that he couldn't afford. He'd spent a lifetime using people, and now people were using him. He's putting the make on these good-looking girls, and they're saying, "Hey, Honeybear, how about another round?" But when the bar closed he wasn't Honeybear anymore, he was plain old George, a black guy who talked like a white, and he'd take the bus back to Mercer Island alone. The next thing we knew, we'd get a call about a prowler.

I took a look at the latest arrest report. Same old shit. Early in the morning, this couple woke up and saw a dark shadow in their bedroom, then it was gone. An hour later a citizen spotted him prowling cars on Seventy-second. A K-9 dog named Casey pinned him down in somebody's garage after he outran two officers.

As usual there wasn't enough evidence for a felony charge. George knew our statutes; he'd been studying police procedures since he was shorter than his St. Bernard. The complainants couldn't make a positive ID. It was a typical George Russell situation; we're a day late and a dollar short.

I peeked in his cell. He was beginning to look like a beaten-down old inmate, haggard, dirty. The jailhouse pallor was on his face: sunken cheeks, a burnt-out look.

I thought, Georgie, Georgie, what the hell's happened to you? Don't get me wrong—I didn't feel sympathy. He wanted to make an ass out of every cop in town. I didn't have a *shred* of feeling left for the guy.

Our graveyard officers had been chasing him all night, and now he had to be arraigned. I thought, Here we go again. He'll end up serving a few days and be right back in somebody's bedroom.

I sat him down for a talk, deadly serious. I flat told him he was gonna end up killing somebody. I said, "You go in these houses, George, laying next to these women. What're you doing, jacking off on the floor?"

George always smiles and denies, but this time he was hard.

He said, "You don't have shit on me. You're trying to dump on me. Well, I talked to my lawyer and there isn't a damn thing you can do."

I told him I was gonna ask our district judge to pull his probation.

"Suzanne?" he says. "She's gonna be highly upset that you're doing this." He always acted as if our judges were old friends. Personally, I thought Judge Staples was always too lax on him.

I brought him into court in handcuffs and manacles and left them on. It was ten A.M., March 21, 1990. George was six weeks short of thirty-two. His clothes were torn and he was dirty. I wanted the judge to see him for what he was: a hardened criminal. No more of this smiling and making cracks and calling judges by their first names.

He was arraigned on charges of criminal trespass, obstruction of justice and an outstanding thousand-dollar warrant, and of course he had a story. He said he'd been on his way to visit a friend. At five A.M.! He admitted he'd been using his penlight, but only to keep from being hit by cars as he walked. He admitted he ran, but not to escape arrest. He said he thought Patrolman Kettells was chasing him, and "Tom" had been persecuting him for a long time. Et cetera, et cetera. The same old bullshit. If you knew George, you could recite his alibi before he opened his mouth.

The judge threw out the obstruction charge on a technicality, something to the effect that the officers had hollered "Hey!" instead of calling him by name. She said she didn't agree that George was a danger to the community.

I reminded her that he was a well-known burglar with years of criminal history. I said, "At least twice we've caught him with butcher knives hidden in his shirt sleeves. You mean to tell me he isn't dangerous?" I said, "Look at the trouble he causes our department, up all night chasing him all over the island."

I admit I was pissed off. All the years of aggravation! After a while she told me I was out of order. I got in her face again and it turned pretty hot. She'd never thought much of us cops anyway, treated us like janitors.

George served four days.

TAMI GRACE'S SOMETIME escort Mike Weisenburgh hadn't seen his friend George for several months when they ran into each other at the Mercer Island Denny's. Although he was only twenty, "Georgia Mike" had developed an affinity for bright lights, but he was usually turned away from the clubs for being underage.

George had the solution. "Meet me at Houlihan's tonight," he said. "Go into the men's room, rumple your hair, then walk straight to the bar as though you've been dancing."

The technique worked, and the friends ordered drinks. It developed that George had problems of his own. He'd just been released from jail and needed a bed for a night or two. Mike was living on Mercer Island with his young friends Robert "Robby Bob" Dzurick and Jeff Anderson. He invited George to crash on their couch.

Two weeks later, the newcomer was still in residence. He kept the place stocked with food and beverages and escorted his underage friends into clubs, where he seemed well known. Mike discovered common ground. As they shared a six-pack of Miller Lite, purchased by George at the island 7-Eleven, Mike said, "I got made fun of when I first moved West, so I shucked my Georgia accent. Except every once in a while the red clay comes out a tad bit."

George said, "I had the same problem. Used to say *gree-its*. I was raised near Georgia."

"Where at?" Mike asked.

George said he wasn't sure of the name of the town. He didn't seem eager to pursue the subject.

A month passed, and the three roommates found themselves enjoying the newcomer's company, despite his freaky ways. Mike Weisenburgh didn't know exactly what to make of him.

George was witty and bright, kept us laughing. Played chess, backgammon, cards, anything that required creative thought, mental challenge, I finally figured out where he got so much influence in the clubs. He sucks in with the top dog first, and the others fall into line. Pretty soon he owns the place.

He spent *hours* going through those snips of paper in his pack, studying 'em, writing. He always traveled by bus, said it gave him time to read. He had a bunch of European pornie magazines—brutal, leather and whips, S-M stuff. He kept his things under a table, in duffel bags and paper sacks. He owned maybe two changes of clothes.

We were all interested in sex, but it was a *career* for George. I came home one morning and he was asleep on the floor with a drunken woman. She stayed all day and started cooking salmon. George kept trying to get me and her together. He was *weird* that way. I didn't understand what he got out of watching other people do it, He started rubbing her back, then he says, "Michael gives better massage than me," and he beckons me to take over. I didn't go for it.

We went to one of his girlfriends' house, and me and her ended up sleeping in the same bed while he watched from the couch. So naturally nothing happened.

He was always giving us advice about sex and telling us his own experiences. He said he'd had two and three women at a time and other crazy stuff. He was always telling us how to make it hotter, how to make women do things for you. One time him and a girl were doing it and they cut each other on the neck with a razor blade and sucked each other's blood. He said it was really intense.

I said, "Well, George, whatever turns your crank." But I'm thinking, That's a tad bit far-out for me.

Then he started talking about his latest girlfriend and how a couple girls interfered and messed it up for him. He was really hurt, upset. Almost lost his cool and went sad. I thought he might even cry. Then he starts smacking his fist into his palm. Whack whack—*whack!* Then he's sad again! It was the most emotion I ever saw in him: sad, mad, then sad again, all in a few seconds.

Mike was aware that George's family lived on Mercer Island, but nothing much had been said about them. A Denny's customer passed word that George had been exiled from home for making advances to his stepmother. George bristled when Mike confronted him with the gossip. "Hey, *she* hit on *me*," he claimed.

Mike was sure it was untrue. By now he'd learned that when things went wrong with George, he blamed others. George would hit on anybody, even a buddy's girlfriend, but there was always a lighthearted kiddin'-around quality to it so he could back out if she turned him down.

At a drinking session in Houlihan's, Mike introduced George to a good-looking young redhead named Andrea "Randi" Levine, who was hotly coveted by Mike and several of his friends. At the end of a convivial evening Mike and George dropped Randi off at her Kirkland apartment and drove back home together.

Late the next night Mike answered the phone to hear an enraged Randi yelling that George Russell had just arrived at her place and asked for a lift to Mercer Island.

"What's that guy doing, knocking at *my* door?" she asked. "I got rid of him fast. I told him, 'I don't even *know* you.'"

Mike tried to calm her. "He's just that type of person, Randi. If he meets you, he thinks you're his best friend. I really wouldn't worry about it."

Randi said she certainly *would* worry about it. She lived alone in a neighborhood where there'd been a rash of cat burglaries and intrusions, and she didn't need a strange man violating her privacy late at night.

Mike complained to George, "Hey, man, going to Randi's place—that was uncool."

He acted unconcerned.

"George, listen. Please don't go there without asking me. Okay?"

George said, "I didn't realize it was such a big deal." He didn't seem annoyed.

Nor was Mike annoyed at his drinking buddy. It was just George's way. He was friends with the whole wide world.

* * *

The two ex-southerners visited the clubs nearly every night. Mike suggested that they try the popular Black Angus, but George said he didn't like the management. He said he was eager for the Saratoga Trunk to finish its renovation and reopen as Papagayo's Cantina. It was expected to be the Eastside's top disco, like Nell's in New York or The Palace in L.A.

Night after night George bought drinks and introduced Mike to women. He was full of advice: how to make an impression, how to avoid losers or holdouts, how to score. The new friends shared insider jokes and comments, as when Mike referred to George as "our token nigger." Racial cracks seemed to amuse him. If an African-American came to their table, George would switch gears. "He'd try to lay on the black jive," Mike recalled. "He was a regular chameleon."

After a while Mike began to feel guilty about the relationship. "George wasn't paying any rent at our place, but he was spending a lot of money on me. Where I come from, that's called taking advantage. I asked him where he worked and he said he had a night job. I said, 'Is it legal or illegal?' He just shook his head. Later he made an innuendo about working for the narks. Then I thought, He goes to work at two A.M. He doesn't have a bank account or carry ID, and he deals strictly in cash. He uses an address where he can't be tracked. *He's a crook!*"

The suspicion was reinforced when George showed up with a Smith & Wesson stainless-steel Model 659 pistol. He said he'd bought it from a friend and impressed his roommates by field-stripping the gun in a few minutes. Mike brought out the nine-mm Beretta automatic that a girlfriend had left in his care.

"All us Georgians love guns," he explained later. "That Beretta was a beautiful piece, fit right into your hand. George and me acted like kids about our guns, didn't know any better. We went over to the Bellevue Park 'n' Ride

with two girls and popped some rounds at glass jugs.
George wasn't a very good shot. Later I chilled out and
stopped carrying mine. I realized it was no damn toy.''

Mike owned a bronze 1983 Malibu four-door, "your basic
boring sedan business car." When George asked if he could
borrow it, Mike's inclination was to say no. But he yielded
after George said he just needed to run to the 7-Eleven.

George returned the car at dawn.

A week later the offense was repeated, then again. Mike
became annoyed when George offered the same trite old
explanations: "I had a flat. . . ." "It wouldn't start. . . ."
Mike thought, What the hell's he up to? Robbing bank
machines? Sticking up stores? *In my car?*

The pressure was eased when George began borrowing
roommate Robby Bob Dzurick's old Chevy station wagon.
The bearded, rugged-looking Robby Bob was the kind of
person who would drive a hundred miles out of his way to
help a friend and take offense if he was offered money. He
was glad to lend his car.

No one in the Seattle Police Department knew exactly
how long the skinny young black man had been throwing
his weight around the alleys and storefronts of the area
known to cops as the Cesspool, but late one night his appearance became a matter of record.

By day the neighborhood was a colorful part of downtown Seattle, popular with tourists and filmmakers. It was
described by Seattle *Times* columnist Erik Lacitus as
"ground zero, the place that shapes our perceptions of the
inner city. . . . Not exactly Mr. Rogers' Neighborhood."
The colorful centerpiece was the Pike Place Market, where
farmers and fish peddlers and craftsmen pushed their wares,
and winos scuttled in and out of storefronts. A set of sag-
ging establishments—the Elliott Hotel, Deja Vu topless bar,

Liberty Loan, Turf Bar, Mirror Bar—looked bleached and exposed in the sun.

When the booths and stalls closed at dusk, the neighborhood became the Cesspool, a place where night people went in search of trouble. Disenfranchised Indians passed bottles of Thunderbird, chicken hawks trolled for runaway boys, and dope peddlers drifted into their own special areas: the Latinos in the one hundred block of Pike Street, blacks a block away on Pine, and gang members two blocks east at Third.

At one o'clock on the morning of May 10, 1990, Patrolmen Steve Piccirillo and Jerry Holley, college graduates who combined their interest in sociology with fieldwork as "harness bulls," were just rounding the corner of First and Pike in their Dodge cruiser when they saw a black man patting down a Hispanic male against the side of a tan station wagon.

The black man explained that he'd observed the Hispanic shoving something in his pocket and was just checking him out. Beneath a torrent of words and familiarities, the subtext seemed to be, Hey, Officer, I'm your friend. I was just doing you a favor. . . .

The cops asked for ID, but a hot burglary call sent them scurrying back to their car. As they pulled away, the bespectacled Holley called out, "Listen, we're gonna be back. If you're still here, you've got problems."

En route to the burglary scene Piccirillo, a power lifter with a chiseled Dick Tracy profile, told his partner, "I've seen that guy before." Ten or twelve years earlier in Denny's on Mercer Island, Piccirillo, a college student at the time, had watched as the affable young man visited one table after another, like a politician running for office. He wished he could remember the guy's name.

The two Seattle patrolmen put out word that a black male in a tan station wagon was acting squirrelly in "David Sector" and might be worth a discreet interview. They also warned that he might be armed.

* * *

Three hours later Cecilia "Cecie" Doucet, a handsome blonde who enjoyed police work so much that she signed her Christmas cards with her radio call sign, "3-David-5," was sitting in her cruiser at Second and Pike when she heard the squeal of tires. She looked up and saw an old Chevy Capri station wagon accelerating and braking, a grinning black male at the wheel.

She pulled the car over and approached cautiously. "Right from the start," she reported later, "the guy was so accommodating, syrupy, sweet. Talk talk talk. He answered questions before I even asked them. I asked for his driver's license and he said, 'Oh, gee, Officer, I don't have it on me right now.' I asked for the registration and he already had it out. Called it the redge, like cops do. It listed the owner as Robert Dzurick, with a Mercer Island address. I asked for ID, and he handed me a business card from the Eastside narks and said, 'I'm George Russell, Officer. I'm an agent. I work for you guys.' "

When Doucet asked if he was registered, he didn't seem to know what she was talking about. "That told me plenty," she said later. "Legitimate police agents have proven their reliability, and we register them for legal purposes. When an unregistered guy claims he's an agent or an informer, that usually means he's into a power thing, 'I'm important,' 'I'm a powerful dude,' 'I know people. . . .' More likely he's a two-twenty, which is our Seattle PD shorthand for a psycho."

She wanted to search his person and car but lacked the legal requirement known as "probable cause." She hadn't observed the man in the commission of a crime or even a clear-cut moving violation.

"He was just a guy who was acting weird and needed to be checked," she explained. "So I wrote him for not having a driver's license. But it stuck in my mind that this George Russell was a very bizarre person."

* * *

A week and a half later, at almost exactly the same small hour, a veteran sergeant was cruising his favorite part of Seattle when a minor disturbance caught his eye.

Doug Vandergiessen came from the Dutch-American tulip lands near the Canadian border; with his blondish hair and turned-up nose, he could have passed for Hans Brinker. A powerful man who enjoyed action, he worked the Cesspool by choice. Most of his thirteen years on the job had been spent on the graveyard shift in a one-man car in David Sector. On his first night, he'd been advised to bring reading matter "because you're really gonna get bored," so he'd stocked up on Michener and Jakes. Then he'd encountered the 220 who lived in the bushes by the Public Library, followed by a wino with a Ph.D. in medieval history, car prowlers in shorts and designer shirts, pimps in clouds of cologne, prostitutes, stowaways off Asian ships, smugglers, runaway teenagers featured in the prizewinning documentary *Streetwise*, all of them more fascinating than the characters in books.

He hadn't yet met George Russell.

It was a generic spring night in the Cesspool: cool breezes, stars, light air. Nothing moved on the Sound; the jumbo ferries had made their last runs. I was driving south on Second Avenue toward the station. At three-thirty on a Sunday morning, I wasn't looking to get involved in anything. Cars from King and Queen sectors passed me on their way in; only a few from David Sector were still on the street.

As I passed Pike I saw an '83 Chevy Malibu parked down near First, and some street people milling around. It was nothing unusual; they were always fighting. These things tend to break up and everyone goes their own way, and the temptation is to drive on past.

I turned west on Pike so they'd see my car and break it up. The Malibu started to pull away.

I put my flashers on and rolled down the windows. This clean-cut–looking black guy stopped his car and I said, "What's happening?"

"Oh, nothing," he says. "Those street people were hassling

this guy.'' He nodded toward his passenger. The white kid looked about twenty-one. My impression was they were friends.

I asked, ''Is there any problem?''

''No, no,'' the driver says. ''It's all done. We're outa here. Thanks a lot for stopping.''

The guy drives to Second Avenue and turns south. I continue on to where the street people are still milling around and I call out, ''Are you all taking off?'' I wasn't overly polite; I figured they were troublemakers and I wanted 'em off the street.

When they didn't budge, I got out of the car and said, ''Come on, get outa here. I don't want to see you around anymore.''

One said, ''Hey, Officer, is that guy really a cop?''

I said, ''I don't believe so. I know all the police around here.'' I said to myself, If he was a cop, he'd've told me.

The guy said, ''Well, he said he's a cop.''

''Well, that's no big deal.''

''Then he got out of his car and pulled a gun.''

I says, ''A *gun*?''

''He hit my friend with it.''

I look at this Indian fella and he's bleeding from the side of his head. All of a sudden, I'm thinking, Wow, we got something here.

I make a U-turn back to Second. I spot the car three blocks ahead and get on the radio: ''I'm trying to catch up with a four-door Chevy Malibu, headed south on Second at University. The guy identified himself as a policeman and he's got a gun. Request backup.''

I knew that backup might be slow in coming at that hour, but I was sure somebody from David Sector would show. The guy was accelerating. He runs a couple lights and heads toward the waterfront. He busts another light at Western. I'm closing on him when he runs the light at Alaskan Way, the street that parallels the wharves.

I turn on my lights and siren and make another call for backup. I see red lights about four blocks behind me, so I know help is on the way. The rabbit makes an abrupt right turn across the sidewalk and plows into a chain-link construction fence. By the time I get out of my car he's standing there with his hands in the air.

Now I'm *sure* he has a gun. Otherwise he'd just pull over and wait. Either the gun's hidden or he's ditched it.

I draw down on him. "Don't move! If you move, you're dead."

My backup comes wheeling in. It's Steve Piccirillo and he's already got his gun out. The driver says, "It's cool, it's cool. Everything's fine. My name's George Russell. I'm from Mercer Island."

I say, "Where's the gun?"

"What gun?" He looked hurt that we'd even mention such a thing.

Pitch patted him down and he had an empty left-hand shoulder holster. I put him in cuffs. We checked inside the car and found a scanner and a wallet with IDs for Michael S. Weisenburgh and Robert M. Dzurick. A knife with a five-inch blade was under the seat.

Then one of the backup officers spotted something behind the left front tire. It was a stainless-steel Model 659 with a live round in the chamber and a full clip.

The guy's passenger was still sitting inside. Looked confused and scared, said his name was Mitchell. He said, "I was in a fight up at Pike, and this guy rescued me. Then he kinda ordered me into this car. He had a gun, and being that I really didn't wanna stay there, I went along with him." He said he'd seen this Russell slide the gun under the tire.

I said, "Who's Russell to you?"

Mitchell said he'd never seen the guy before. We took his name and address as a witness and kicked him loose.

By this time three or four police cars were at the scene, but I still didn't think this was any big deal. Pitch told me he'd handled Russell a week or two back and the guy was a cop wanna-be. You run into them all the time; I used to be one myself, worked three years as a volunteer before I got my first police job. I didn't think we were dealing with anything heavy.

We impounded the car and drove back to Pike to take witness statements. The victim had a three-quarter-inch laceration on his face, and his girlfriend was still hysterical. The first thing I did in the station was to write Russell for misdemeanor reckless driving. I could have made it a felony, but my experience is that most traffic felonies don't stick. You write the guy a lesser ticket and you got him.

I thought about citing him for evasion. Under the statute, a police officer has to have his lights and siren on for a substantial time, and the guy has to be running intentionally. Russell said, "I'm sorry, Officer. I didn't know it was you. I thought those Indians were coming after me."

I said, "Bullshit."

He says, "Honest to God, Officer. As soon as I heard your siren, I pulled over."

I could imagine him in court—so believable, so logical. It was like he knew the law to the last semicolon. I asked why he'd identified himself as a police officer, and he said, "How else was I gonna break up the fight?" The good citizen, doing a public service.

He even had an explanation for the gun: "I bought it on the street from a Cuban guy. About a month ago. A hundred and fifty-five bucks. It's just for personal protection. Yeah, it could be stolen, but *I* didn't steal it. *I* bought it."

I could hear that one in court, too. It's no crime to carry a weapon in your car.

The guy had this silky smoothness. Not a drop of sweat. No hard blinking or foot-tapping or sniffing. He said he knew some people in the department and named a couple names. Then he starts saying things like, "Maybe we can work something out."

You hear that all the time, and I have a standard response: "You can take care of that from jail." Sometimes I stop a guy who says he'll give me a big dope dealer. I say, "Call Narcotics in the morning." I'm a patrol cop. I don't make deals.

The more time I spent with this Russell, the more I began to realize something was seriously wrong. Pitch and some of the other officers agreed. No normal person could be this cool, sitting there surrounded by cops, chatting away like I'm Oprah and he's the star guest. He reminded me of Ted Bundy: no emotions, no guilt I said to myself, This guy's got to have his fingers in something else; he's got to be wanted somewhere.

I did a quick search at the computer and basically came up empty. His Seattle record was clean except for a traffic ticket that Cecie Doucet had written a week or two before. I was puzzled.

Then I ran the Smith & Wesson serial number, TBA6798, and the gun came up in King County records as stolen. So I booked him for possession of stolen property. That meant he'd spend the rest of the night in jail.

By the time I was finished typing up the incident report, it was after six A.M. Russell was in a holding cell and I figured he'd be released on low bail or personal recognizance in a few hours. I hated to let it drop there, so I sat down and wrote a memo to our Special Investigations Unit:

PLEASE FIND ENCLOSED A COPY OF A REPORT OF AN INCIDENT THAT OCCURRED ON MONDAY MORNING 5-21-90 IN THE AREA OF 1ST AND PIKE. INFORMATION FROM OTHER D-SECTOR 3RD WATCH OFFICERS REVEALS THAT THIS SUBJECT HAS BEEN HANGING AROUND IN THE AREA FOR SOME TIME NOW, AND HAS BEEN STOPPED OTHER TIMES FOR BEING INVOLVED IN SUSPICIOUS CIRCUMSTANCES, PARTICULARLY CIRCUMSTANCES THAT APPEARED TO BE RELATED TO REPRESENTING HIMSELF AS A POLICE OFFICER. THE SUBJECT IS "COOL," WITH "REASONABLE" EXPLANATIONS FOR EVERYTHING SUSPICIOUS. HE DESERVES SOME ADDITIONAL INVESTIGATION. THANKS.

At my typing speed it was nearly seven A.M. when I finished and an hour later when I got home. I thought, The guys in Intelligence are overloaded, and they're gonna ignore this. It was just something I had to do.

By MIDMORNING GEORGIA Mike was beginning to wonder if his Malibu was gone for good. He and George had driven home from Houlihan's the previous night, and George had asked if he could borrow the car to go back to the club for an hour. The hour had stretched into ten.

Mike called all over Mercer Island and Bellevue, and none of his friends had seen George or the car. Then the phone rang. "Mike," the familiar voice said, "I'm in King County Jail. Everything's cool. I gave two guys a ride and we got stopped. The guys had felony warrants. I explained to the cops, but they took me in anyway."

"Where's my car?" Mike asked.

"Impounded," George said. "They wanted to tow it, but I made 'em put it on a flatbed." He acted as though he'd done his friend a big favor.

Mike clucked in disgust. How many times had George recited these bullshit tales of woe? The bottom line was that the Malibu was in the police storage lot and it would cost a hundred bucks to get it out. If Mike would come up with the money, George said, he would repay him promptly. And oh, yes, the cops had Mike's wallet. George didn't sound as disturbed about the car and wallet as he was about his gun and scanner. He said that the police assholes had taken them as evidence and they wouldn't be returned till after he went to court.

Mike ransomed his car and discovered that the bronze finish was scratched from hood to rear fender. He collected his wallet from a plainclothesman and asked, "What do you know about Russell? He's been living with me and my buddies. What am I dealing with here?"

The detective unfurled a computer printout. "This is just his Mercer Island record. Bellevue's got paper on him. So does Kirkland, Redmond, King County."

Driving home across the I-90 bridge, Mike whispered to himself, "We gotta dump this guy fast."

When George arrived, Mike asked, "Where'd those marks on my car come from?"

George said, "Some black guys scratched it with their knives."

"Listen, man," Mike said in a flat voice, "you can't stay here anymore."

Without a word, George began stuffing his possessions into paper sacks. He picked up his blue duffel bag, donned his Members Only jacket and said "Bye" in a friendly tone. The last time Georgia Mike saw him, he was doing his cool walk down the hill toward his stepfather's house.

SERGEANT DOUG VANDERGIESSEN'S memo was kicked up to Detective Rick Buckland, a soft-spoken Vietnam veteran with a cowpoke's skinny frame, narrow blue-gray eyes, straight blondish hair to his collar, and a freewheeling style more suitable to the open range than the streets of his native Seattle. He'd just returned from two years on assignment to the Drug Enforcement Agency, narrowly missing death in a shoot-out. At forty-three he was living every detective's dream: as a decorated member of the Seattle PD's elite intelligence unit, he picked his own assignments.

To reach this eminence, Buckland had spent twenty-two years in and out of uniform, starting as a patrol cop in the Cesspool, becoming the youngest detective in the department at twenty-five, and progressively working in narcotics, burglary, gang warfare, homicide, juvenile and the police academy. He was one of the detectives who walked into a Chinatown gambling club and found thirteen bodies—the "Wah Mee Massacre," ultimately solved. He helped get to the bottom of a multimillion-dollar fish scam directed from Norway, and he was instrumental in catching computer criminals who bilked Merrill Lynch out of a million and a half dollars.

Among police insiders, Buckland was considered independent by some, stubborn by others. In an office where smoking was discouraged, he persisted with his Winston Ultra lights. "The worst I'll get," he explained to his colleagues, "is ultralight cancer."

An introspective man, he was known for his skill at interrogating criminals, matching their shucking and jiving with his own. His interview reports routinely described body movements. He always pushed his chair a few inches back so he could watch his subject's feet.

"Rick's the kind of a guy that gets involved in an autoerotic hanging and looks up every book and article he can find on the subject," said a sergeant. "He has no pride. He'll phone every psychiatrist in town and say, 'Hey, doc, whattaya make of this profile? Gimme your ideas.' He's a thinker, a loner. He makes connections, solves puzzles. And he doesn't give a damn if he gets credit or not."

Buckland handled every case as though his shield depended on it, including the chippy arrest of George Russell.

Two things caught my eye. One, it bothers me when anyone impersonates a police officer. Two, why did he put that guy in his car and drive him away? Maybe it's nothing, but isn't this going a little far in playing detective? He put the kid in his car under color of law. What was he gonna do with him?

King County confirmed that the gun had been stolen in Kirkland on the night of April 22, a month earlier, along with a mugful of change, two gold chains, three sterling silver rings and two watches. The burglar entered through an unlocked door and the couple didn't know they were hit till they woke up. Intrusions like that always send up a red flag. It takes balls to sneak into somebody's home while they're there—or some kind of weird need. It's like raping a whole household. As with any rape, there's the potential for violence and even death.

I called Mercer Island, and a detective described Russell as a burglar and thief who was almost impossible to catch. I thought, What do we have here? *Super-George?* Mercer Island estimated they'd had forty contacts with him since 1985, and there were contacts in other jurisdictions. But so far he'd steered clear of the Seattle PD.

I wanted to nail him for burglary, but he stuck with his story that he bought the gun from a Cuban named Felix. We tried to get him for "felon in possession," but his only felony conviction was for escape, and it didn't qualify under the statute. The guy is slipping away and I'm getting uneasy.

The printout showed he was under a restraining order for beating up a woman named Mindy Charley. Her address was a few blocks from where the gun was stolen, but I couldn't catch her at home. I checked with King County and learned there'd been nighttime burglaries in the neighborhood—rings, bracelets, coins, minor stuff. The perpetrator was black and used a small flashlight. It looked like he was doing it for souvenirs and trinkets, hidden bags of money, nighttime kicks and mystery, not to make a living. In crimes like this, the loot is often secondary.

I finally located Mindy, and she told me her history with George. Said he always carried a penlight. Very interesting stuff, far beyond the expected. It didn't take a genius to see there was a real problem here and it could only get worse.

Still going from Tinker to Evers, I interviewed Mike Weisenburgh. He told me more of the same. I warned him and Mindy and other detectives that in my opinion this man would seriously reoffend. He's already a one-man crime wave, and there's a good chance he'll escalate, maybe to rape or murder.

I was working completely out of my bailiwick. I only hoped people were paying attention. You don't ordinarily call other departments and say, "Well, this guy's a burglar, but I think he's a potential killer." I ordered George's mug shot and showed it around. I wanted this asshole off the street.

He was released on June 7, after serving eighteen days in King County Jail on old warrants. We couldn't make anything heavier stick. It made me nervous to see him walk.

I kept the case on my desk, waiting for something to happen. In my mind, the only question was when.

As the summer of 1990 approached, G. B. Coffin was finding it hard to drag herself to work. She didn't blame the Black Angus or the other cocktailers or the management; she blamed her life, its texture, the wrong turns, the breaks. She wasn't the type to fob off her responsibility; she tended to assign too much blame to herself, and it made her morose, sad, a mood which she tried not to pass on to her three children.

She thought about her bartender friend Carol Beethe. That poor woman went from one romantic crisis to another: a marriage that was on and off and on and off, a semisteady boyfriend who slept around, various Casanovas and lechers and sex fiends who hit on her every night at the bar, and a few young men whom she hit on herself, sometimes winding up in situations that were awkward for a married woman with two children. And yet . . . Carol was always smiling, always up, one of the happiest women on the Eastside nightclub scene. G.B. wished she had the same good spirits.

Lately she'd been dating a master carpenter whose grip could bend a spike. He talked about their future as though they were already a family. On weekends he took her and the kids hiking and fishing in the Cascades. The only problem was that he had a crazy compulsion about moving to Hawaii. Construction work was slow in Seattle, logging was down, salmon runs were dying; it was time to move on. Every night when G.B. walked across the dark parking lot to her car, she found the idea more tempting.

Three months had passed since the blowup with George Russell. In G.B.'s mind, he'd reverted to his original status: cradle robber, burglar, dope peddler, *wimp*. Death threats were nothing new; she'd had her share, including some serious ones from her convict ex-husband and his cohorts. Compared to them, George Russell was nothing but mouth.

She was more concerned about a customer she thought of as the Bundy Man because of his resemblance to the Northwest's most famous serial killer. He came in frequently, always alone, said the minimum, acted nervous, and ogled cocktailers and female customers. He'd had plenty of opportunity to mix with the women who came to the bar to meet men, a selection that ran from rich wives and respectable professionals to so-called lounge lizards and bar sluts, but he seemed to prefer leering and watching. Like Bundy, he was good-looking, with an aquiline nose, a long face, and a preoccupied air that seemed to suggest a haughty intelligence. He was about six feet tall with a medium build and reddish hair. G.B. didn't know his name; she'd waited on him any number of times, but he'd never identified himself.

The Bundy Man unnerved her and the other cocktailers enough for them to note the license number of his red four-door sedan and enter it in the bar log, just in case.

MINDY CHARLEY HAD been avoiding the Black Angus because she was nervous about running into George. All romantic feelings were gone, but the memory of his face and fists, his cruel tongue and Roman candle temper still poisoned her dreams and made her reluctant to go out at night.

When a friend informed her that George had been banned from the Angus permanently, she realized that the situation was now reversed: it was the one place on the Eastside where she could feel safe. She and some of her old girl-friends began dropping in, and she became friendly with disc jockey Mark McAmmond, a big affable man who worked his toggle switches and controls and lighting board like a concert pianist, controlling the nightclub crowd with virtuoso techniques. Mindy admired skill in any walk of life, and she found herself attracted to the young DJ.

"Thanks for being here on this r-r-rockin' Friday night," Mark would call out in his exciting style. "We're gonna be blastin' into the next hour with Janet Jackson, MC Hammer, and then we'll get some AC-DC on for the folks who love to r-r-rock 'n' roll. So don't go anywhere, fasten your seat belts, and *hold* on. . . ."

Mark seemed to have a sixth sense about the tempo: when to speed it up, when to slow things down. If the crowd needed a jolt, he would play a song like "Shout" by the Isley Brothers, don sunglasses and a silly hat, jump on top of his booth and sync the words, dancing low, danc-ing high, till everyone joined in. Mindy loved the way peo-ple responded to his banter and pyrotechnics. As he explained over a drink one night, disc-jockeying was an art, not a science.

She wasn't bothered by the women who buzzed around

his booth, because he managed to find an excuse to visit her table at the end of each set. Soon they were meeting at Denny's Overlake for coffee, then dating, and by late spring they were lovers. Ever since childhood, resiliency had been her long suit, and the bad memories of George Russell began to fade.

One mid-June evening she stopped at the Black Angus after work and was intercepted by her friend Sean Trumbull, a DJ who doubled as lounge host and cashier. "Look, Mindy," he said, gently taking her arm, "I would rather you didn't come here without Mark."

She was surprised. "Why?" she asked.

Sean said, "It's George. He's been around."

Mindy was confused. A detective named Rick Buckland had told her that George was in jail for assaulting a guy at the Pike Place Market. And anyway, wasn't he permanently banned from the Black Angus?

"He's been pacing up and down our parking lot," Trumbull went on. "The other night he was out there by himself till two-fifteen. Asked me how you were doing."

"Thanks for the *great* news," Mindy said, and trudged back to her car. When she got home, she looked around for a Snickers bar. Nothing that George did would have surprised her; he seemed like an evil force who could walk through walls. Even after Mark arrived, she felt afraid.

It didn't take long to confirm that George was back on the street and hanging out at Papagayo's Cantina, the newest and hottest club on the Eastside. Formerly the Saratoga Trunk, the building had been gutted by an arson fire and remodeled in a flashy Latin motif. The word was that George was picking up bar bills and being treated as an honored guest, with free admission and a reserved table by the DJ's booth. Papagayo's seated five hundred, and there was usually a long line waiting to get in. It seemed that George had already developed enough clout to move his friends inside with a nod. Some customers were under the impression that he was a paid host.

Mindy marveled at his gall. My God, she thought, he gets thrown out of one place and skips to another without missing a beat. Pretty soon he's an insider again. What'll it take to teach people that he's a certified criminal? *A TV special?*

She realized that she would have to avoid Papagayo's. It was unnerving enough that the newly reopened club was only a twenty-minute walk from the Black Angus. She wondered if George was tracking her. Did he watch her apartment at night? Follow her to work? A few states had passed anti-stalking laws, but Washington women were still unprotected.

Once again she prepared to live in fear. But this time she had big strong Mark for protection. They planned marriage. She hoped George would be intimidated.

There was a final item of unfinished legal business between the two former roommates. On June 20 Mindy watched as George was led into court in bright orange overalls to face the domestic violence charge growing from his February rampage. A bailiff explained that he was wearing prison clothes because he was serving a three-day sentence in King County Jail. Mindy was confused; hadn't he just been in jail for something else? Court records confirmed that he'd served eighteen days for a variety of old misdemeanors, then enjoyed two weeks of freedom before returning to serve a short sentence for reckless driving. It was his twenty-fourth incarceration. In and out, Mindy thought, out and in. . . . The flow chart of a wasted life.

The District Court judge lashed into George for his violent behavior, found him guilty of the domestic assault on Mindy, but suspended a ninety-day sentence on condition that he pay $540.96 for the property he'd destroyed.

As the prisoner was being led from the courthouse, he called out in a sweetly musical voice, "Bye, Min. Bye-bye. See ya soon, hon." He sounded like a dear friend. Once again Mindy wondered about his sanity.

DETECTIVE MICHAEL BECKDOLT of the Bellevue Police Department enjoyed his new part-time job at Papagayo's Cantina because "it made me feel like a cop again." By day his title was "Crime Prevention Specialist." After twenty years of service he'd become the department's chief jock and PR man, running sports programs, speaking at schools, handing out awards, dealing with the press. He'd never been a street detective and hadn't worked traffic or patrol since 1981. A thickening man with an endearing lack of pomposity, he enjoyed dealing with people and viewed his weekend work as two nights of enjoying the human comedy, with pay.

The old uniform was a little tight, but it felt good. I was hired to work front-door security, ten-thirty to two-thirty. The scene outside the entrance was usually a melee, a jungle. There was a five-foot painting of a bright colored parrot, a *papagayo*, sitting on a palm tree on the wall above the awning, and underneath there were kids milling around the door, yelling to get in, arguments breaking out, cars honking and gunning their motors. Most Eastside clubs didn't have dress codes, but you couldn't get into Papagayo's unless you wore a shirt and collar—no T-shirts—and that caused a lot of bellyaching at the door.

Bellevue nightclub business was cyclical, but Papagayo's started hot and stayed hot. It attracted all kinds, but mostly upscale young professionals, spending their fat pay from places like Microsoft and Boeing. You seldom saw anyone over thirty-five. There'd be Rolls-Royces and Jags and Porsche Carreras in the preferred parking area. The rest of the lot crawled with Jeeps, pickups, BMWs, Hondas—you name it. Denny's was just to the east, Fred Meyer to the south, The Wherehouse right out in front. They shared a parking lot, hundreds of cars, people coming and going all hours of the night. The club itself was in a big rectangular block with a red stripe around it, like it was gift-wrapped. There was a turret at one corner with a spike on top. It had once been a warehouse, but you'd never know it.

Each night we'd check the parking lot for illegal drinking, pour the stuff out and break the bottles. We weren't concerned if there was screwing in the cars, but we had to make sure the women weren't being brutalized. Our main assignment was to stay visible, show the flag. Juvenile gangs weren't a problem yet, but there were a lot of athletes and studs and plenty of macho friction.

George Russell helped make our evenings go faster. He usually came on the bus, arrived early and stayed late. He'd have a paper sack with a change of shirt. Years back I'd played basketball with him at the Mercer Island Boys Club; he played for the Mercer cops and I played for Bellevue. After that I saw him at places like Charlie's and Houlihan's when I was working security.

George would step outside to cool off from dancing and we'd talk by the front door. "Hey, Mike, how's your hammer hangin'?" Big smile, big handshake, always in a good mood, "Glad to see ya, what can I do for ya?"—everybody's old friend George. We're both talkers; we'd sit there and shoot the shit about police work, officers we knew, basketball, sports— guy talk.

Girls were never far from his mind. He was always talking about how he'd like to have it with this one or that one. He had a thing about a flashy little blonde named Tamara Francis. She was living with a Japanese businessman at the time and driving a white Porsche 930 turbo special slant nose. It was parked out front of Papagayo's almost every night, a prestige symbol, looked like a race car. George wanted to date her big time. Once in a while I saw them talking, but they never left together.

One night there was another knockout in the line. "I heard she works at a topless bar in Seattle," he says. "Man, I gotta meet her."

Next week he told me that him and some other guys took her home and she stripped for 'em.

I thought, What a bullshitter. But I kept quiet. I didn't know what was coming.

PART TWO

MURDER ON THE EASTSIDE

. . . The term regressive necrophilia had been used to describe the insertion of foreign objects into the vagina or anus, something we had observed in cases involving seriously disorganized offenders. We interpreted it as an act that displayed tremendous hostility toward women. . . .

—ROBERT K. RESSLER and TOM SHACHTMAN,
WHOEVER FIGHTS MONSTERS

IT WAS FRIDAY night, June 22, 1990, and a construction worker named Smith Everett McClain was on his way to pick up his friend George Walterfield Russell Jr. George had just been released from the King County Jail, and he was restless. They planned to begin their evening over dinner at Papagayo's Cantina, then improvise. Smitty was driving his high-riding 1989 Toyota 4×4 pickup, extended-cab version, candy-apple red outside and soft gray inside, a dream machine that seemed to glow as it cruised the shaded streets of Mercer Island.

At twenty-six Smith McClain was losing a war with the bottle. His fiancée had wearied of his alcoholic abuse and told him, "I want you to get your stuff and get out." He'd alienated friends and was in danger of losing his job as a construction worker on custom homes. For the time being he was staying in his mother's house on Mercer Island.

No matter how low his morale, Smitty kept his pickup in mint condition. As a former detailer, he was a master of the esoteric art of beautifying cars with carnauba wax and silicon, cotton balls and Q-Tips, and chamois as soft as moss. Friends said he took better care of his red Toyota than he took of himself. Recently he'd cut out two pieces of leftover cream-colored rug and fitted them on the floor to protect the factory carpet. Every few weeks he shampooed the segments and the floor mats. As he said later, "This truck's my baby. I just like it being clean."

Like others in his social circle, Smitty looked forward to evenings with George. In George's company, you never had to wait in line or pay a cover charge. You were treated like a VIP. George was an amateur matchmaker and was generous about fixing Smitty up, once with his own steady girlfriend Kathy. He was a good sport and sometimes told "nigger" jokes in fun. He wasn't reluctant to pick up a check or buy a round. George was Smitty's idea of a good time.

The two young men had more in common than their Mercer Island backgrounds. Both had considered careers in law enforcement, Smitty less seriously than George. After George saw the movie *Lethal Weapon*, he told friends that the plot was based on a case he'd worked with Smitty. He seemed to live in a wishful world of cops and robbers and tried to draw Smitty into his mythology. He kept his nose in his police evidence book, but Smitty doubted that he had the guts to become a cop. Whenever a fight threatened, George would slip away.

His attitude toward women seemed to be a mixture of admiration and contempt. He hinted about a bad experience with females as a child, but provided no details. He professed to admire his sister Erika, in prelaw at Yale, but he also seemed envious of her intelligence and beauty and the attention showered on her by his parents. Whatever the reasons, Smitty got the idea that George was bitter about women.

When they arrived at Papagayo's, the two good friends found that George's longtime pal Lynn Brown had reserved a table behind the red railing that marked the off-limits area for minors. Barely eighteen, the supple Lynn had spent twelve years at the barre and was headed for a career in dance. George told Smitty she'd been one of his best friends for almost six years.

Soon after nine o'clock Lynn and George did a turn on the floor. As she walked off, she was carded and asked to leave. She promised to rejoin her friends across the parking lot at Denny's after Papagayo's closed.

Smitty and George lingered over their Boston clam chowder, chicken strips and cheese bread, then moved to George's favorite table by the disc jockey booth. The DJ was fiddling with a mist-making device; everyone looked forward to an evening of sound, light and fog.

Before the two friends took their seats, George asked Smitty for the keys to his truck. "I can't stay in the bar without a collared shirt," he said. "There's one in my duffel bag."

Smitty hated to give up his truck keys, but he didn't want to alienate his friend. "Don't drive it anyplace," he emphasized.

Hours passed. Smitty drank, danced, talked, drank some more, then began to wonder what happened to George. He decided he was probably doing his thing, wandering from table to table—"in with the in crowd." Smitty looked around and couldn't see him. Someone in the restaurant said, "Oh, George? He's just outside."

The sidewalk entrance provided a direct sight line to the place where Smitty had parked his red pickup. It was two days after the summer solstice, and at forty-eight north latitude the sky still held some light. The truck was gone.

Smitty walked around the lot, drank a beer, then toured the lot again. He was baffled. George had never pulled a trick like this. Smitty hated to be parted from his "baby." It was like losing a loved one.

DETECTIVE MIKE BECKDOLT was working his part-time security job when he saw the young man slump to the curb with his head in his hands.

He just sat there for ten or fifteen minutes, kind of staring, angry, bitching to himself. Definitely looked hammered. When he started getting agitated, I went over and recognized him as somebody I'd seen around. He told me that George Russell borrowed his pickup and hadn't returned it. He wanted me to put out an APB—an all-points bulletin. He was saying, "How the hell am I gonna get home?"

I remembered talking to George earlier, under the awning. The first time was when he came out to take an air break from the dancing, which he did two or three times a night. About an hour later I was with the parking valet, Todd Arviso, and I noticed George coming through the front door again. He spoke to both of us, seemed in a good mood, as talkative as usual. He said he was gonna drive a girl over to her place to pick something up, then kinda winked. It was like saying, I *told* ya. I'm taking her home.

The girl was already twenty or thirty feet away from me, walking into the parking lot. From the back she looked about five-six, stocky, a hundred and thirty, with darkish brown hair, wearing a jacket. She was kinda stumbling, and George caught up and held her arm. I didn't see them get into a car. I thought, George talks to a lot of girls, but this is the first one he's ever left with.

I didn't pay much attention. Multiply this incident by a hundred, and you had a typical night at Papagayo's—young people pairing off, breaking up, arguing, making out in their cars. I was a lot more concerned about a guy that kept trying to pick up women in the parking lot: white male, about twenty-five, well dressed, not bad-looking, in a black Mercedes. He talked to a bunch of women; two or three left with him and came back. I thought there might be some dealing going on, but I got busy and didn't notice him again.

The rest of the shift went pretty quiet till the young guy came out and started bitching about George. He was practically accusing George of stealing his pickup, kept calling him "asshole." I defended George—"I've known him for years. He'd never do a thing like that. . . ." I tried to calm the guy, but he was too upset. I heard somebody call him "Smitty." We walked all over the parking lot and couldn't find his truck.

My shift was over at two-thirty, but I stayed a little extra to help Smitty out. I finally left when he walked toward Denny's.

George and his crowd always went there for breakfast after closing. I figured it was no big deal. George and the pickup would show eventually. There were a dozen things on my mind, but murder wasn't one of them.

AT THE BLACK ANGUS, a mile southeast of Papagayo's Cantina, it had been another busy Friday night. The bartenders dispensed rivers of Blow Jobs, Waterfalls and Slow Comfortable Screws Against the Wall, and so many Electric Ice Teas were ordered that they ran out of premix. Mark McAmmond was off duty; another disc jockey hyped the energy level with frequent playings of "Electric Boogie" and other line dance songs.

Tami Grace and her former boyfriend Mike Weisenburgh sat at a table with Mike's roommates, Robert "Robby Bob" Dzurick and Jeff Anderson and a few other friends. The dinner meeting had been planned as a sort of "Victims of George Russell" reunion, with Mindy Charley as the honored guest, but she didn't show up. Mark had phoned to report that she was sick to her stomach and couldn't make it.

The dinner conversation centered on George's idiosyncrasies. Lately he'd added the FBI and CIA to his list of employers. Someone observed that he'd made an oddball comment: "Have you ever noticed there's never been a black serial killer?"

The convivial diners knew that Mindy was fed up with the subject of George and figured it was just as well she'd stayed home.

Around 11:30 P.M. a former employee left the Black Angus and walked to his car, parked at the rear of the club near a Dumpster and an industrial compactor that served the busy McDonald's restaurant next door. The trash corral was surrounded on three sides by an eight-foot wooden fence, open to the south. Just before reaching his car, the man saw a ponytailed white male standing at the opening and heard what sounded like a couple arguing inside the fence. As he backed out of the parking space, his headlights swept the area, but no one was in sight.

A half hour later a loud brawl developed in the parking lot, and several neighbors in the adjacent Pacific Village condos called 911. A Bellevue police log entry noted: "Caller can hear a female screaming to someone to 'stop it.' " A second caller said there was "lots of screaming and yelling in the lot. . . ."

A male was heard yelling, "You fucking bitch, don't fuck with me."

A condo dweller heard a high-pitched scream that was "very different." Another caller called it "bloodcurdling." A lounge host was alerted and ran outside. A shirtless young man was staggering about the trash area; he claimed that he'd been beaten "for no reason" by a brawny male with long blond hair. Blood seeped from a four-inch pavement burn on the victim's face. The host recognized him as a regular who'd been eighty-sixed earlier. At the first sound of police sirens, the injured man sprinted across 156th Avenue toward a tavern called The Mustard Seed Too and disappeared. Police checked the McDonald's trash corral with their flashlights and left.

At 2 A.M., after a few more altercations, a Pacific Village resident heard a female yell, "Somebody help me. You're hurting me. Stop it. *Stop it.* You'll kill me!"

As her screams died on the night air, an angry male voice exclaimed, "Were you fucking him? *Were you fucking him?*" A car engine turned over, tires squealed, and the area went silent.

It was a typical weekend night in the parking lot.

G. B. Coffin finished her cleanup chores around two-twenty and stepped into the refreshingly cool air with her pal Roxanne Mally, another cocktailer. The Bundy Man had been in again, leering at women before driving off in his red car around midnight. G.B. had worked hard for her forty dollars in salary and fifty-one dollars in tips and was in a hurry to get home to her children. A breeze blew through the dark area where employees kept their cars.

She glanced at the Dumpster and compactor, vaguely defined in black and gray. The chunks of metal always gave her the creeps. She'd seen the compactor chew up garbage and trash. It looked as though it could digest a cow.

She shuddered and hurried toward her car.

Ten minutes later a couple in the Pines Apartments, just north of the Black Angus, heard a clopping noise outside their ground-floor unit. It sounded almost like a horse, but they concluded it was someone running in hard-soled shoes. Both of them reported later that they'd never heard a noise quite like it.

At 3:15 A.M. an off-duty Papagayo's bartender drove through the parking lot to see if his waitress girlfriend was still around. The lights of his black Nissan pickup swept the trash area and picked up nothing unusual.

A mile away in the Overlake Denny's, Smitty McClain was still recounting his sad story to anyone who would listen. He spoke in a rapid, shaky manner and sounded like a bereaved parent.

There was still no sign of George Russell or the candy-apple 4×4, despite the fact that Denny's was his traditional last stop on weekend nights. George's old pal Lynn Brown and her boyfriend, Denny's bartender Hans Johnson, were equally perplexed. George had promised to meet them here for breakfast.

For nearly three hours the friends waited at a front table. Now and then Smitty peered across the lot toward the Papagayo parrot, its slashes of color softened by shadow. There were no pickup trucks in sight and hardly any cars. The wide street in front, usually six lanes of bedlam, was silent except for the rumble of early-morning buses.

As he sobered up, Smitty seemed to become more desperate. He asked Johnson if he'd ever heard of George doing anything so outrageous, and Hans said yes, he had. George had a habit of borrowing cars and keeping them too long, but he always returned them in good condition. Smitty didn't seem cheered by the information.

As the sun rose on a bright June day, he finally accepted the bartender's offer of a ride home. After the ten-mile drive to Mercer Island, Smitty checked his driveway for his "baby" while Hans and Lynn waited. The Toyota wasn't there.

Smitty thanked Hans for the ride, entered his garage and walked past his married sister Shawn, five years older, a bank employee. Exhausted from preparing for a lawn sale in the morning, she and her girlfriend Jill Leslie, a second-grade teacher, were dozing on bunk beds in the garage.

Inside the one-story rambler, Smitty phoned Dr. Wonzel Mobley's home number. A sleepy voice informed him that George wasn't home. Smitty threw up his hands and went to bed.

SHAWN AND JILL had turned in at 2 A.M. The garage was bursting with furniture and other items for the two-day sale, a popular annual event, and the merchandise had to be set out for the eight o'clock opening, when bargain hunters would implode on the quiet street, fighting for parking space and flattening the grass.

At four-thirty Jill had just gone inside the house to shower when the kitchen phone rang. A familiar voice said, "This is George Russell."

Jill recognized her old friend from Mercer Island High. He wanted to know if Smitty was home yet, and she said no. George griped that he'd been searching for his pal all night. The conversation lasted less than a minute.

After the shower Jill learned from Shawn that Smitty had

come home and gone to bed. She peeked into his room and saw that he was asleep.

At 6 A.M. the two women were outside arranging sale items, including the bunk beds they'd slept on. They'd lucked out on the weather. The temperature was in the high fifties and the blue sky was dotted with puffs of cloud. For a change, the forecasts had been right.

The two old friends were trying to decide how to move a big TV console when George Russell pulled up in Smitty's red Toyota. Shawn was surprised. In the dawn activity she hadn't concerned herself about her brother's overnight activities or how he'd managed to get home without his truck. But he was "meticulous to the point of fanaticism" about the 4×4, as she explained later, and it wasn't like him to lend it out.

She marched to the driver's window and said, "What's going on, George? Why do you have my brother's truck?"

George told of chauffeuring someone home and losing track of Smitty. He said that he'd driven eight or ten miles to West Seattle to see if Smitty might be visiting a friend who lived there.

As they spoke, Shawn noticed a reddish orange stain on the front seat, circular, about six inches in diameter. George explained that his passenger had thrown up after eating clam chowder. He parked the truck on the street, and the women asked for help with the TV and a few other items.

As he lent a hand, George grumbled good-naturedly about wasting the whole night looking for Smitty. He seemed his usual self, neat, clean, calm.

Shawn offered him a lift home and he declined with thanks. He exchanged a few reminiscences with Jill about her father, Mercer Island High School's basketball coach, then picked up his duffel bag and ambled down the driveway in his cool walk. Shawn asked if he was sure he didn't want a ride and he said, "No. That's okay." He disappeared in the direction of his home on North Mercer Way.

* * *

Just after 7 A.M. a maintenance man for the Crossroads McDonald's restaurant stepped outside to sweep up. A few cars dotted the parking lot, leftovers from the previous night's action at the Black Angus, just to the north. A Corvette's rear end advised that "Shit happens." An old Jeep plugged "Dukakis." A black '84 Camaro looked fresh from a car wash.

After he'd tidied the parking lot, the workman checked to see if any trash from McDonald's had blown onto Black Angus property during the night. Something caught his eye just inside the opening to the Dumpster, about fifty feet away. He stepped closer. A body lay faceup on the concrete.

BELLEVUE DETECTIVE MARVIN Skeen, a twenty-year cop with a reputation for unflappability, was assigned to "persons crimes" for the weekend. He was forty-four, married with children, and noted for his therapeutically calm manner and understated style. He walked with a rolling gait, as though permanently at sea, and typed with all ten fingers, courtesy of the U.S. Army. The senior man in his unit, he was described by one colleague as "sneaky fast. A lotta fools took him lightly. You can look them up in the penitentiary."

Like most Bellevue detectives, Skeen was a college graduate, holder of a B.S. in police science from Washington State University. He'd caught on with the Bellevue PD when the town was still a bedroom community whose main police problem was juvenile delinquency. "We had a lot of drinking, marijuana and burglaries," he recalled, "and an eccentric chief who sent SWAT teams to the park to enforce the curfew."

It had taken Skeen several years to shake the wheat of eastern Washington from his cuffs and adjust to his upscale environment. "I had a '58 VW bug, and when I drove to work I'd see these Jags and Ferraris and Maseratis and I didn't know what the hell they were. Where I came from, rich folks drove Cads and Lincolns. For my first five or six years in Bellevue, I was a walking case of culture shock.''

The old man of the Bellevue detective unit had just begun to entertain the thought of crawling out of bed when the fire department radio reported "a male body naked, possible DOA. Behind the Black Angus restaurant.''

I was in a good mood. I'd just cleared a bunch of cases and inactivated a few others. In fifteen years as a detective I never was able to clear my case loads completely, and I figured this was as close as I'd ever get.

Driving toward the scene, I counted up in my head: this would be my seventeenth murder case, twelve as the primary investigator. The unsolved cases stuck in my mind. A detective learns by doing the job—get out there and get burned, and don't screw up, 'cause a detective isn't allowed to screw up. But you do, you do. On my first big case I sat on a footstool and fell over backward. The woman says, "Inspector Clouseau!" The worst part is I still haven't solved the case.

A black-and-white patrol car blocked the entrance to the Black Angus parking lot. As I walked toward the trash area, I could make out a body. I wondered why it was just outside the fence instead of inside, where it wouldn't have been so conspicuous. Was somebody trying to make a statement? The day was turning sunny and warm, already sixty-three degrees, and it looked like the victim was sunbathing.

As I got closer, I saw that the radio had her sex wrong, and somebody had taken pains posing her. I'd seen bodies torn apart by animals, a naked body in a tanning booth, a couple of skeletons, a lawyer murdered in his office—all shapes and sizes. But this was the first time I'd ever seen a body that was obviously posed.

Her left foot was crossed over her right ankle. Her hands were crossed on her stomach, left over right. A fir cone was tucked under her hands. Her head was turned a little to the left, and a white plastic lid from a Frito-Lay dip container covered her right eye.

All she wore was a gold choker with a crescent-shaped white pendant and a gold watch with clear stones around the face. Right next to the body was a little pile of debris, as though somebody had swept up but hadn't collected it yet; I figured that was probably where the plastic lid originated. Two brooms were leaning against the wall.

Till you got real close, she looked like a young girl. She was about five-eight, maybe 150 pounds, white, curly light brown hair with a reddish tint, medium length. Her nail polish was shocking pink. She didn't look real beat up, just a little blood on her face and abrasions on her right arm and breast, both hips, knees and feet. There were some scratches on her neck, probably from her own nails where she tried to get her fingers under the necklace as the guy tried to strangle her. Her face was a little off center from being hit, and blood had seeped from a head wound. She looked like she'd been in a minor traffic accident. There was no ID, no clothing; no rings or bracelets with name or initials, no hint of who she was.

My first feelings were a little confused. In some weird way it looked like the killer cared about this woman. He was mocking the cops, maybe, laughing at us, but he also had feelings about the victim. The posing seemed like a statement against females in general, "in your eye," degrading, violent, but there was a restfulness to it. I thought, Maybe he felt sorry for her *after* he killed her, and that's why he laid her out so carefully. It was almost like looking at a body in a coffin. He *wanted* her to be found. The feeling I got was the guy was sending a message, but what the hell was it?

I realized that this was gonna be a hard one. I made a WAG—wild-ass guess—that she'd been dragged around the Dumpster area, not just dropped there. That would explain the abrasions. It wasn't even a SWAG—a scientific wild-ass guess.

While I was waiting for the crime scene investigation van and the medical examiner, I walked around the parking lot, sticking surveyor's tape on anything that looked significant: an earring, a disposable diaper, a silver chain and cross, a beer bottle, some beauty bark, other stuff. Nothing I tagged turned out to be relevant. We ran the license plates of a couple of parked cars. They weren't relevant, either. They were left by people who'd been too drunk to drive home the night before.

The ME said he'd never seen a victim posed like that. He measured the body core temp at eighty-three, placed the time of death at 2:20 to 5:20 A.M. After they took her away, I saw dark red stains at the opening to the industrial trash compactor. A presumptive test for blood was positive.

SMITH MCCLAIN AWOKE to the chatter of the first customers at the lawn sale, and his sister Shawn informed him that his "baby" was parked on the street. He parted a path through the shoppers and was relieved to find that his truck was undamaged. He wondered why a floor mat had been removed and thrown in the back.

When he opened the driver's door he smelled something that he had difficulty describing later: "When I had been hunting before, you can remember vividly when you cut open an animal, what it smells like . . . beyond vomit. Smellwise it was the most violent vomit I had ever smelled, if that. It was beyond awful. It was all over the interior of the truck. All over. . . . I also smelled a faint smell of—like a lemon-scented Lysol, as if someone had tried to clean it up or cover the smell."

Smitty fought a gag reflex and tried to figure things out. Not only had his friend George absconded with his truck, but he'd vomited all over the cab, even on the windshield visors, leaving a thin residue, reddish white. There was a thicker red stain on the driver's seat.

Smitty phoned the Mobleys again. This time he recognized Kris's voice. He knew her slightly: the last time he'd visited the house with George, she'd started talking about George's breakup with a woman named Mindy, but George gave her a shush, and she stopped. Now she seemed a little annoyed as she reported that he still wasn't home. "Please ask him to call," Smitty requested.

He phoned several mutual acquaintances, but no one was helpful. Once again, his elusive friend was among the missing.

* * *

At 11 A.M. George finally phoned from the Northwest shrine of designer clothes known as Bellevue Square and nonchalantly asked if Smitty wanted to go shopping. Smitty said, "What the hell happened last night?"

George went into one of his disjunctive rambles. He said he'd had "the hots" for the blonde with the Porsche 930 but after she agreed to go for a drive with him he didn't want to be seen in the passenger seat of such a nice car so he took her riding in Smitty's truck and he got nervous and drank too much Rumple Minze and threw up his clam chowder. Then he missed connections with Smitty at Papagayo's and the Overlake Denny's and spent the rest of the night trying to find him, including driving all the way to Smitty's friend John Goertzen's place in West Seattle. At the end he sighed and said he was sorry.

Smitty was insulted. This wasn't an alibi or an excuse; it was pure cowshit. Why wouldn't George want to be seen in the white Porsche? He was *always* chasing good-looking women, talking about them, lusting for them like an adolescent. And since when did he start getting sloppy drunk? In their eight-year friendship, he'd seen George drunk once or twice, but he'd never seen him lose control. As for the drive to West Seattle, John Goertzen was Smitty's friend, not George's. How would George even know where John lived? He'd never been there.

Smitty asked a few questions, but George managed to avoid a response. Smitty said, "I don't know what you did to my truck, but I just want to get it cleaned up." George promised to take care of everything—"No problem!" Smitty was disgusted. With George, nothing was ever a problem. He didn't have problems; he *created* them.

Holding his nose, Smitty removed the floor mats and flung them in a corner of the garage. A plastic cup lay on its side on the passenger's side floor; he remembered that George hadn't finished his Boston clam chowder the night before and had asked the waiter for a container. Smitty put towels over the stain on the driver's seat and headed for an exotic car shop next to the Jack in the Box on Mercer Island.

En route the stench was so strong that he had to stop for air. He couldn't understand why white chowder would leave red stains and finally decided that George must be suffering from bleeding ulcers.

He steered the truck into the detailing bay. A worker examined the cab and asked, "Did all hell break loose in your truck last night?"

Smitty said, "Unfortunately. I wasn't in it."

The detailer said that the truck would stink till it was professionally cleaned. Smitty decided to save the expense and do the job himself. He shampooed the inside, vacuumed the floors, washed and waxed the exterior, and swabbed every corner and crack. Most of the blemishes disappeared, but every time he finished rubbing out the stain on the seat, it reappeared. After hours of work, his "baby" took on its old familiar luster, but it still smelled a little like death.

DETECTIVE MARV SKEEN and his partner John Hansen ordered the murder scene videotaped and then chased the victim's body to the King County medical examiner's office in Seattle. Skeen was happy to be working with Hansen, a big, muscular, bravura-voiced veteran who gave the impression of being a detective multiplied by two. A stubborn man, he was famous among Northwest lawmen for reopening and solving a murder case that had been closed for years. Once he was called "the pit bull," but his attitude had softened a little since he'd followed the latest trend among overstressed lawmen and become a born-again Christian.

The two old hands didn't want to miss the slightest bit of evidence before the woman's body went through the sluicings and slicings of a formal autopsy. They watched as technicians doused the crime lab lights and turned on a portable Wood's lamp, producing a phosphorescing "black light.'' Through a built-in magnifying lens, twenty tiny flares came into sight, each marking a length of fiber or other bit of evidence invisible to the naked eye.

Skeen and Hansen used tweezers to pick up the material, including some found on the pubic area and throat. Two small stains on the upper right thigh appeared to be semen; both were swabbed. A final speck of fiber was found on the victim's watch. Skeen bagged and labeled everything.

The detectives donned goggles as the crime lab technicians lasered the body for latent fingerprints. When nothing appeared, the corpse was enclosed in a tent and exposed to fumes of Hard Evidence, a cyanoacrylate ester vapor that reacts with skin chemicals to raise fingerprints. After an hour of ''cooking,'' technicians peeled the hardened substance off the body and examined it with lasers. Again the result was negative.

''We're snake-bit,'' Skeen observed after taking Polaroid pictures of the victim's lopsided face. He was an unpretentious man, brought up in Pullman, Washington, on a remote road that led to a landfill—''Garbage Dump Lane'' to the locals—and he spoke uncluttered English. ''This case,'' he told John Hansen, ''is gonna be a bitch.''

AT THE BLACK Angus the crime scene remained encircled by bright yellow tape. The responsibility for collecting evidence had fallen to a thirty-one-year-old Skeen protégé named Dale Foote, only recently assigned to the Bellevue PD's major crimes unit after being named ''Officer of the Year'' for his feats on patrol. A former baseball star with a Bob Hope nose, a deceptively innocent mien and a powerful physique, Foote was also a born-again Christian, a ''Christer'' to some of his brother officers, and had never been known to swear. Once he lost his temper during a police baseball game, and Detective Mike Beckdolt asked, ''Did you just say 'damn'?''

''No,'' Foote said.

"Well, say it once," Beckdolt said.

"No."

"Well, say 'shit' once."

"No."

"C'mon! Say it once."

"No."

"Say 'piffle.' "

"Piffle."

For all his piety, Foote was also known as an agitator, an imaginative practical joker, and a wordsmith with a fine command of English. But when he took his first look at the body in the parking lot, all that came to his mind was a tersely whispered "Rest in peace."

In his brief career on major crimes, Foote had worked as lead investigator on only one murder, the Valentine's Day strangulation and shooting of a seventy-one-year-old Asian-American woman named Faye Monwai, an unsolved case that still troubled his sleep. Colleagues kept reminding him that cases involving Orientals were seldom cleared, but he refused to give up, even spending two weeks in New York's Chinatown on a lead. The word at headquarters was that he was headed for a brilliant career if he could learn not to pummel himself with his failures. And perhaps learn to say "shit."

Together with Detective Cherie Baker, on loan from another unit, Foote sectioned the Dumpster area into sixteen grids and began vacuuming up evidence, passing the detritus through coarse and fine filters. It was an all-day job that required frequent cleaning of the equipment to keep the contents of one grid from contaminating the next.

As he worked, Foote pondered the posing of the body. It made no more sense to him than it had to Skeen and the others. Obviously the victim had been laid out in the predawn darkness, probably around 4 A.M., a time when most of Bellevue would be deserted. But this Crossroads area was a regular trouble spot that Foote had patrolled as the city's youngest officer, and it never went quiet, least of all on weekends. Neighbors walked dogs, bicycled, jogged; lovers made out in shadows; kids raced hot cars; dope dealers and hookers worked the corners; patrol cars cruised the streets and alleys and poked around the rear ends of stores. And yet the killer had taken time to lay out the body in a stylized manner, within direct eyesight of the Pacific Village condos and other apartment buildings, apparently oblivious to the possibility of being seen.

Foote wondered, Why McDonald's? Why the Black Angus? There were a million safer places to dump a body, including the deep green Cascade forests and the blue depths of Puget Sound and Lake Washington. Did the killer nurse a grudge so strong that it was worth the risk of being spotted? Was he out to cause the neighborhood the maximum grief? It seemed worth considering.

The posing of murder victims was so rare that it wasn't even covered in police academy courses. As far as Foote knew, this was the first such murder in Eastside history, maybe in the whole Northwest.

As he vacuumed the sun-warmed concrete around the industrial compactor, he noticed pink flecks sifting into the clear plastic bag. The color appeared to match the victim's fingernails. He guessed that dried polish had chipped off her nails while she was being dragged toward the machine. He wondered if the killer had tried to stuff her body inside, then given up and posed her in the opening in the fenced area.

Foote took note that the compactor's maw was at shoulder height. The victim had weighed about 150 pounds, a difficult lift for most men. Perhaps, he thought, the hole had been too small. At best, it would have been a tight squeeze, and might have required butchering the body on the spot.

A McDonald's employee explained how the disposal system worked. Trash and garbage were compressed horizontally into a steel container at the rear. When the container was full, it was hoisted onto a truck and dumped at a landfill, contents unseen. The next truck unloaded atop previous loads.

Foote thought, What a handy-dandy way to dispose of a corpse. But of course the machine would be turned off overnight, wouldn't it?

He pressed the button. The compactor clanked into action.

LATE IN THE afternoon Mindy Charley and Mark Mc-Ammond were discussing their wedding plans when a Black Angus employee phoned and said there'd been a murder. They drove to the parking lot, found it taped off, and hurried into the lounge, where Mark's fellow employees filled them in on the case.

Mindy ordered a drink, took a few sips, and turned to her fiancé. "It's George," she said, and started to cry.

"No," Mark said.

"It's *George*!" Mindy said, sniffling. "I *know* it is. He hates women; he hates the Angus. He knew we were getting together here last night with Tami and Mike and Robby Bob and the others. Mark, it's too obvious."

"What was his motive?" Mark asked, dabbing at her tears with his handkerchief.

Mindy said, "Who *ever* knows George's motive? Maybe he just wanted to shut them down for eighty-sixing him."

A lounge host came over and started talking about the effect of the killing on business. People went to nightclubs to relax and play, he said, not to expose themselves to murder. What woman would walk through the parking lot after dark and risk winding up naked and dead with a fir cone tucked in her hands? Without a steady influx of females, the lounge would lose most of its customers. Some of the employees were already making job-hunting calls.

On the way home Mindy elaborated on her theory. "George isn't getting his way with women anymore, Mark.

Somebody said another girlfriend just dumped him. He used to push us around; now he's the one being pushed. George doesn't like that. Look what he did to me.''

Mark said that murder seemed a long reach.

"I've seen a look in his eyes," Mindy said. "When George goes off, he's capable of anything.''

Mark said she was jumping to conclusions.

Mindy said, "I pray to God I am.''

MARVIN SKEEN AND his fellow sleuths faced a sticky problem: the jumping-off point in homicide investigations was usually the victim's identity, and it remained unknown. Several people had viewed the Polaroid pictures of the abused face. A few said they thought they'd seen the woman in the Black Angus. But no one made a positive ID.

It didn't take long for Skeen to learn that the parking lot had served as a bare-knuckle boxing ring from midnight till just after closing time. In the Eastside club culture, brawls were considered part of the summertime rut, and no blame attached to the participants. The first twenty-four hours of Skeen's investigation were spent chasing down combatants and checking their stories. He had slim hopes of finding the killer this way, but he also had to exclude the innocent.

One by one the midnight gladiators were cleared. The silver chain and crucifix, believed to be an important clue when it was found in the parking lot, turned out to belong to one of the losers, as did a shirt button. Most of the fights had consisted of threats, noise, and missed punches.

A Bellevue PD crime analyst named Lynn Zirkle spent the afternoon phoning outlying police departments, hospitals and clinics, checking for missing women and damaged men. The police dispatcher in nearby Kirkland advised her that an officer was working a missing persons case and would report back. The subject turned out to be a white female, twenty-nine, black hair, blue eyes, five-eight, about 125 pounds. The woman had left town, phoned her boyfriend from Detroit, then dropped out of contact. The information was relayed to Skeen, who said it appeared to be of doubtful use.

At 4:37 P.M. Zirkle dispatched a message county-wide:

AT 0723 HRS THIS DATE, THIS DEPARTMENT RECOVERED BODY OF A W/F, APPROX AGE 20'S TO 30'S, LIGHT BROWN HAIR (POSSIBLY BLEACHED), 504 TO 508, TRIM BUILD. VICTIM OF A HOMICIDE. REQUESTING ANY AGENCIES RECEIVING MISSING PERSON COMPLAINTS, WHERE VICTIM IS A POSSIBLE MATCH, TAKE A CASE REGARDLESS OF WHETHER PERSON HAS BEEN MISSING LESS THAN 24 HOURS. PHYSICAL DESCRIPTION OF OUR VICTIM IS SKETCHY AT THIS POINT. FURTHER DETAILS WILL BE FORWARDED AS WE RECEIVE THEM.

G. B. COFFIN TRIED to cheer herself up as she drove toward work. Saturday nights meant wall-to-wall crowds, an oversupply of loudmouths and ass-pinchers, and interminable arguments, scuffles and fights. But Saturday also produced the biggest tips, and she was the sole support of three children. Lately she'd been leaning toward migrating to Hawaii with her master carpenter. Every night as she drove home from the marathon event known as cocktailing, the Aloha State beckoned.

She drove to the rear of the Black Angus and was surprised to find her car blocked from its parking space by a tape bearing the warning "Police Lines—Do Not Cross." A few cops were standing guard, but they weren't saying much.

She hurried inside and learned about the murder. Her fellow workers spoke in hushed voices. Roxanne Mally, her best friend among the cocktailers, looked stunned. She told

G.B. that she'd been shown a picture of the victim and recognized her as a woman who came in now and then. But she hadn't been in lately.

G.B. surveyed the nearly empty restaurant and bar and thought, My God, some nutcase is killing our customers! We'll lose our business.

Immediately her thoughts returned to Hawaii. Sometimes fate had a way of forcing matters, and as far as she was concerned the decision had just been made. Early the previous morning she'd walked within a few feet of the trash corral and could have been a victim herself.

She tried to push the incident from her mind as she served her first customers. Gradually the lounge filled, but despite the disc jockey's histrionics, the evening went flat. Clearly the word was out.

Just before midnight a detective with blue eyes and blondish wavy hair took her aside and identified himself as Marvin Skeen. He asked if she remembered anyone who'd acted in a strange or hostile manner the night before.

"Just the usual kinks," she responded. "No more than any other weekend night."

He showed her a photo of the victim's twisted face. She thought she recognized the woman as an infrequent customer, an Electric Ice Tea drinker. But the picture was so blurry that she couldn't be sure.

Skeen asked, "Did you see this individual last night?"

G.B. took another look and said she didn't think so.

After the detective left, she remembered that the Bundy Man had been in, ogling females and leaving about an hour before closing. She told a policewoman about the strange man and his habits, and turned over the daily bar log with the license number of his red car. The officer seemed grateful for the lead.

For the first time in their off-and-on friendship, Allen Israel was concerned about George Russell's sobriety. They'd known each other since 1988 when both worked at Bellevue Square, George for Nintendo and Allen for a pharmacy. The Israels were an old Mercer Island family, and Allen was home on summer vacation from college in Oregon. He and George had gone nightclubbing several times.

On this first evening after the murder they'd been driven to the trendy new Papagayo's Cantina by a mutual friend, and en route George had asked to stop at a liquor store. He emerged with a bottle of minty, clear Rumple Minze and almost immediately broke the seal.

Before entering the club, George stashed his duffel bag in the car. Israel knew what was inside: a change of shirt, a few books including *Crime Scene Search and Physical Evidence Handbook*, a scanner and listings of police channels, a miniature chess and cribbage board, and the schnapps. Throughout the evening George drank his usual Miller Lite and tequila inside the bar and made frequent excursions to his hundred-proof stash. By the time Israel was ready to leave for home, George was in a state almost never seen by any of his friends. He was drunk.

A summertime employee named Bryce Richert was supposed to collect a seven-dollar cover charge from everyone who entered Papagayo's, but he always waved George Russell through. Toward the end of the evening Richert was surprised when George came out and tossed him an earring—"gaudy, silver, ball-shaped, dangly, a Gypsy-type thing with squiggling things on it," as Richert described it later.

George seemed like a happy drunk. "I scored," he said. "I bagged a babe."

Richert, a prelaw student at Washington State in the wintertime, vaguely remembered seeing George leave with a woman the night before, but there'd been so many comings and goings he couldn't be certain. He often saw George talking to women but couldn't remember ever seeing him leave with one.

George teetered off toward the parking lot.

MARVIN SKEEN, DALE Foote, John Hansen and every available detective and uniformed officer worked through Saturday night and Sunday, chasing false leads and will-of-the-wisps. They lost valuable time determining who the victim was *not*. She was not the woman who was heard screaming during a brawl in the parking lot. She was not the regular who left early with an unknown male and hadn't reached home, or the woman who yelled, "Stop it! You'll kill me," or any of the other females whose voices had interrupted the sleep of nearby residents. Nor was she the rock singer who'd dropped out of sight after a Friday gig in nearby Kirkland, or the seventeen-year-old problem child reported missing by her grandparents.

Leads to the killer's identity were equally unproductive. He wasn't the angry man who yelled "Don't fuck with me!" or any of the other parking lot brawlers. He wasn't the shirtless young male who'd run across the street toward The Mustard Seed Too or any of the numerous male customers who'd come forward voluntarily or been "fingered" by friends or enemies. The detectives soon grew tired of establishing who the victim and murderer weren't, but it was all they had to work on.

New interest was generated late Saturday night, nearly twenty-four hours after the killing, when a Black Angus waitress spotted a couple making love in the ladies' room and alerted her customers. As the pair emerged to loud applause, the man made a threatening gesture at the waitress and muttered something about "putting you in the Dumpster, too." Then he and his partner marched out the front door with what remained of their dignity.

Before detectives could begin to treat the suspicious remark as a serious lead, the offending male returned to the club with a signed letter of apology and an explanation: "The lady and I are engaged." His remark about the Dumpster was attributed to embarrassed anger.

"We keep hearing from hysterical, panicky people," Marv Skeen complained at a strategy session. "They feed us a lot of things they didn't see or hear but imagined they did. But we've gotta check everything."

He wasn't exactly complaining. He enjoyed a reputation as a detail man, patient, meticulous, sometimes even plodding. He knew you could waste time on ninety-nine leads and break the case on the hundredth. It was the way of almost all homicide investigations, except the ones on TV.

An autopsy was performed by Donald T. Reay, M.D., for seventeen years the highly respected chief medical examiner of King County. He provided a few hints about the killer but nothing about the woman's identity. Lying posed just outside the McDonald's trash corral, she hadn't looked especially brutalized, but the autopsy report showed signs of strangulation, a lacerated nose, facial contusions, deep fractures of the skull, a split liver, contusions and abrasions on both breasts, ragged tears by a foreign object that had been rammed into the anus, and indications of rough penetration of the vagina.

Intact spermatozoa were found in the vaginal vault but nowhere else; apparently the killer had ejaculated. She was drug-free, her blood alcohol level 0.14. By Washington State standards, she'd been legally drunk at the time of death, or "drunk and a half," as one detective put it.

With Dr. Reay's guidance, Skeen and John Hansen concluded that the victim had been repeatedly punched in the face, clubbed on the head, raped, throttled with her own choker, and kicked so hard that her liver split against her spinal column. Traces of dirt and foliage suggested an outdoor murder. It appeared that the killer may have spent as long as three or four hours with the body, and that vaginal and anal penetration had taken place after death. The first description was "sadistic necrophile."

After the autopsy a cosmetologist from a private mortuary wiped the bloodstains from the victim's face, applied blusher and makeup, shadowed her hazel eyes, and fluffed up her curly brownish red hair. The detectives saw that she'd been an attractive woman, with a slightly impish look, good teeth, pretty hair and eyes. Even in her death-mask makeup, she gave the impression of someone who'd enjoyed life.

Hansen, a skilled photographer, shot two rolls of color film. The best takes were shown to Black Angus employees, including several workers who'd already looked at Skeen's blurry Polaroids, but the woman's identity remained unknown.

Some of the detectives began to wonder if there was a Bellevue connection at all, apart from the location of the dump site. Any itinerant killer could have utilized the Dumpster and compactor, and much of the club's clientele came from population centers south or west of Lake Washington and the Eastside.

Reviewing the likely scenarios, lead investigator Skeen had a painful thought: given the interval between the earliest possible time of death and the discovery of the body at 7:25 A.M., the murder could have taken place anywhere within a four- or five-hour drive from the Black Angus, a geographical area that would include most of Washington and parts of Oregon and British Columbia.

That's all we need, the old pro said to himself. An international investigation. He had no idea of his own prescience.

LOCAL NEWSPAPERS MISSED the story on Saturday, a day of short staffs. The Sunday edition of the Seattle *Times* covered the murder in two paragraphs, but the Bellevue *Journal American* carried a long article under a page one headline: WOMAN'S BODY FOUND IN BELLEVUE PARKING LOT. The story quoted Black Angus manager Sam Tino as saying, "We're totally in the dark as to what transpired," and ended with a police request for information.

As a result, leads and tips poured in, and the small detective division soon wallowed in paperwork. The persons crimes section consisted of Skeen, Foote and Hansen. Five more investigators worked property crimes, and two were assigned to sex crimes, making ten in all. Even with every hand working the murder, they couldn't keep up.

Smith McClain didn't read the weekend newspapers or listen to newscasts, and he heard nothing about the posed body. He had his truck professionally detailed and the stains went away.

His sister Shawn read about the killing but paid it little mind. The family was busy, planning an intervention aimed at nudging Smitty into an alcoholism program. At the moment his problems with George Russell seemed a low priority.

ON SUNDAY AFTERNOON the straight-arrow Foote rendezvoused with the frazzled partners Skeen and Hansen in the small coffee room adjacent to their office in the basement of Bellevue's City Hall. As they laid plans, Foote flashed back to the original scene at the Black Angus parking lot. Just about every police official in Bellevue had shown up for a peek, including a lieutenant who planted his girlfriend in McDonald's for a box-seat view. Back then, Foote said to himself, it seemed like the whole department would be involved, but it won't be long before the three of us'll be on our own.

Veteran homicide detectives agreed that if a murder case wasn't solved in the first three days, there was a good chance it would never be solved. My gosh, Foote said to himself, two days are gone and we don't even know who the victim is. Things were looking down.

SUNDAY NIGHT ABOUT nine a young woman named Theresa Veary returned to the Eastside from a weekend camping trip and entered her apartment to the unexpected sound of a clock alarm. Clothes were scattered across her roommate's undisturbed bed. The cats meowed for food. Mary Ann Pohlreich wasn't enthusiastic about Theresa's cats, but she'd always been good about feeding them. Theresa wondered where on earth she could be. Mary Ann had a fondness for expensive nightclubs and Electric Ice Teas, but she didn't indulge in lost weekends. On rare occasions she might go home with a new acquaintance, but only to continue partying.

Lately Mary Ann had been a little more footloose than usual. A quick student with a flair for math, she'd bought textbooks for a community college class in computer science, but the semester wouldn't start for another week. She paid her bills on time and had several thousand dollars in a bank. She was between steady jobs, and on Friday she'd taken a day off from her temp job as a telemarketer.

Theresa remembered that Mary Ann had talked about going to Papagayo's Cantina that night. It was a regular haunt. She always arrived before the cover charge went into effect and stayed till closing. Could she be off on a romantic weekend? It was unlikely. Mary Ann had never married, seemed almost asexual, and claimed that she hadn't indulged since a one-night encounter on New Year's Eve, 1989, a year and a half earlier.

As a nightclub habitué, Mary Ann had become skilled at distancing herself from randy males; she always wore a button on her left lapel bearing a message like "I CAN READ YOUR MIND. NO!" She followed her favorite rock group, Boy Toy, to places like Parker's in North Seattle, Pier 70, Papagayo's, Meekers Landing in Kent, and the Black Angus in Lynnwood, often arriving alone. She avoided the Bellevue Black Angus because she wasn't into interracial dating. She had no regular boyfriend but went out three or four nights a week, gracing the bars and dance floors with her good nature and humor. She seldom had to buy a drink.

Theresa Veary thought back on the last few days. When she'd left their Redmond apartment early Friday morning for work, Mary Ann had been asleep and her black '84 Camaro had been in its stall. The energetic Theresa worked two jobs and hadn't returned home till midnight. She presumed that Mary Ann was still at Papagayo's. Predawn on Saturday Theresa got up to go camping in the Cascades with her fiancé and noticed that her roommate's bed hadn't been slept in.

Now it was Sunday night, a day and a half later. Where *was* she?

Theresa fidgeted on her two jobs on Monday, but she didn't want to embarrass her roommate with anxious calls to friends and relatives. Mary Ann's deeply religious parents weren't aware that she smoked or drank. She'd told a sister that she hadn't engaged in sex in seven years.

Besides, what was the worst-case scenario? A lovesick millionaire had flown her to Acapulco? Theresa hadn't read the papers or watched newscasts.

By Tuesday morning she couldn't wait any longer. She knew that it was Mary Ann's habit on Sundays to drive to her hometown of Ravensdale, in South King County, to attend an Assembly of God church with her family. Theresa phoned the home and learned that she hadn't shown up.

Mary Ann's mother said she was about to file a missing persons report.

Theresa checked with Mary Ann's temporary employer, Delta Warranty in Redmond, where she was highly regarded as a phone solicitor, and found that she hadn't called in even though she'd been scheduled to work a few hours on Sunday. Her car stall remained empty.

Theresa talked to a mutual girlfriend and learned that a body had been found behind the Black Angus Saturday morning. A sense of foreboding swept over her. She drove to Papagayo's and spotted Mary Ann's Camaro in the parking lot. She prayed that her missing friend would be inside at the bar, but she wasn't. Theresa called Bellevue police.

At eight-thirty on Tuesday evening Detective Marvin Skeen arrived at the apartment with pictures of a necklace and watch. Theresa recognized them and broke into tears. Like most female roommates, the two women borrowed each other's jewelry. The necklace was Theresa's.

As Skeen asked his gently probing questions, Theresa wished her memory were better. Asked to describe her roommate's personality, she ran off a list of adjectives: "sweet, fun, caring, naïve, innocent," and finished with "trusting—too trusting."

Skeen inquired about Mary Ann's social life, and Theresa informed him that Mary Ann never brought men home. If a male was persistent about sex, she would try to talk him out of it, pretend to pass out, even scream. The New Year's Eve coupling of a year and a half ago had been with a man named Jim, no last name, and Mary Ann had been drunk.

Theresa mentioned Damon, a long-haired man in his twenties who lived on the Eastside. The roommates had met Damon two months earlier at Parker's nightclub in North Seattle, and Mary Ann had spent a few nights at his place and overindulged with him at Papagayo's. The new acquaintances talked a lot on the phone, sometimes for as long as an hour. Lately Mary Ann had complained that

Damon was acting weird, accusing her of wanting his body, which she definitely did not. Theresa had the impression that they'd broken up.

Detective John Hansen drove to Papagayo's and found the black Camaro. Apparently it had been undisturbed in the parking lot for four days and nights, a key clue that had been overlooked while attention was focused on the Black Angus. Clearly Mary Ann Pohlreich had reached her intended destination, but where had she gone from there? And with whom?

Waiting for the tow truck, Hansen scrutinized the buttons pinned to the headliner:

NATIVE CALIFORNIAN
YOU DO THE THINKING, I'LL DO THE DRINKING
WHY BE NORMAL?
I LIKE YOU. CAN I LICK YOUR FACE?

It wasn't hard to imagine a brassy young woman fending off persistent studs by pointing to a button. It probably worked better than reasoning. What male wouldn't shrink at a message like NOT TONIGHT, I'M EXPECTING A HEADACHE, or NO WONDER YOU'RE GOING HOME ALONE. Another button asked WHAT'S YOUR PROBLEM, DICK-FACE?

At headquarters, Hansen took photographs of the car, then ordered it wrapped in a cocoon of evidence tape and impounded.

At eight forty-five on that same Tuesday night, Detectives Jeff Gomes and Earl Barnes, property crimes specialists who were assisting in the homicide investigation, asked Papagayo general manager Frank Boasen for a roster of employees who'd worked Friday night. Boasen provided the names of six waitresses, five bartenders, and five hosts, all of whom had to be interviewed.

The manager mentioned that a few new items had been added to the club's lost and found box on Friday night, including a yellow sweater that had been found on a chair and a nondescript black purse under a corner table. Barnes opened the purse and found two packs of Clorets, a cigarette lighter, a container of hair spray, a few dollars, and a checkbook belonging to Mary Ann Pohlreich. He sealed it in a plastic bag as evidence.

BELLEVUE DETECTIVES, LIKE most lawmen, disliked the drudgery known as canvassing: knocking on doors, stopping citizens in the street, intruding on the private life of anyone who might be helpful in solving the crime. Canvassing was the investigative equivalent of a miner's sifting of ore or a salesman's cold calls; it paid off, but only at the expense of hours of hard work and boredom.

Over the weekend the detectives had abraded their knuckles on the doors of every apartment and condo within sight of the Black Angus, and now they faced the same chore a mile away at Papagayo's. They'd also dug through nearby Dumpsters and trash cans for the dead woman's missing clothes and other clues. It wasn't the perfect way to spend a radiant June day in the Pacific Northwest.

The new canvass quickly turned up a gallery of suspicious characters, including an obnoxious Australian who gave a false name, took umbrage at being questioned by a female officer, and proved to have an assault record in Texas. Overworked detectives encountered other antisocials who refused to open their doors unless they were shown search warrants, plus several angry men who'd been pointed out by neighbors as sexual degenerates or potential killers. The investigators also had to field the usual calls from crazies who claimed that they'd committed the crime or knew who did, and an unexpected call from a practical joker who fingered a transvestite named Carrie as part of a personal campaign of homophobia. Still another anonymous caller provided police with the Kirkland address of "a whole family that's into murder." It proved to be the home of a minister.

While beating up a man in Seattle, a cabdriver had been heard to mutter something like "found dead in the Dumpster behind Black Angus. I killed her and I will kill you, too." He produced a solid alibi for the murder and explained with a sheepish grin that he'd just been mouthing off. A King County Jail inmate bragged that he'd killed a girl on the Eastside; it developed that he was trying to inflate his image to keep from being hassled by other inmates. Checking out such nuisances sidetracked the officers from solid pursuits such as interviewing all the nightclub employees.

Before beginning his latest rounds, Marv Skeen sought out his fellow Bellevue detective Mike Beckdolt, and the parttime security guard recalled the mysterious man who'd driven his black Mercedes in and out of Papagayo's parking lot and picked up several women. Beckdolt said he thought the individual might have been dealing drugs, but there hadn't been probable cause to search his car.

Asked if he'd noted any other suspicious activities on Friday night, the police department's public relations specialist advised, "You should talk to Brad, the doorman, and Todd, the parking valet." Almost as an afterthought, Beckdolt added, "If you want to find out everything about Papagayo's, talk to George Russell."

Skeen penciled the names in his notebook and asked, "Where can I find this guy Russell?"

"At Papagayo's. Just about any night."

Skeen's partner John Hansen interviewed a striking young woman who said she'd arrived at Papagayo's about nine or nine-thirty on Friday night and was immediately escorted to the head of the line by "a black employee she knew only by the name of George." She failed to recognize a photo of Mary Ann Pohlreich. Hansen logged the information, even though it seemed insignificant.

* * *

Other detectives checked out known sex criminals, concentrating on those paroled to the Eastside. They also pursued the lead provided by Mary Ann's roommate Theresa Veary about a young man named Damon who hung out at Parker's nightclub in North Seattle. There was no longer any doubt that Damon had played a role in the victim's life. Her sister Ruth confirmed that Mary Ann had mentioned him and described him as "about twenty-six, with a younger brother."

A composite drawing of Damon was prepared from Theresa Veary's memory. In a flyer, he was described as a "POI"—person of interest. Skeen and Detective Earl Barnes handed out the circulars at Papagayo's, the Black Angus, Charlie's, Pier 70, Parker's, Jungle Jim's and other night spots. The list of Damons grew into a fat file.

Soon Skeen and his colleagues were red-eyed from poring over lists from the Department of Licensing in Olympia, turning up even more Damons, most of them young, footloose and hard to track. The search made the detective nostalgic for his hometown of Pullman, where families were solid, enduring, rooted to one address or one neighborhood. Eastside people seemed in constant flux, seldom available on a first or even a second visit.

"When I first came here," he complained, "you'd pick up a kid and you couldn't get ahold of his mom and dad, 'cause they're holding two jobs. They didn't really want kids; what they wanted was to live in Bellevue. Or you'd look for an adult and find he was in Acapulco for the month. Or Belize."

When the list of Damons finally petered out, Skeen asked for a check of variations like "Damien," "Damian" and "Damion," and dredged up another two dozen. To his eye-weary colleagues, he explained, "Trust me. It's the only lead we got."

Assisted by personnel dragooned from other Bellevue units, the three persons crimes detectives began a profile of Mary Ann Pohlreich and a log of her final hours. The job required interviewing as far away as Forest Grove, Oregon, a six-hour drive from the Eastside. Some of the leads and names came from fifty telephone numbers found in Mary Ann's belongings by members of her family, plus addresses and numbers from her room.

The detectives quickly confirmed that the murdered woman was a fixture at the newly opened Papagayo's Cantina. She wore eyecatching clothes and smoked thin cigarettes. Her nightclub reputation was somewhat at variance from the glowing description provided by her roommate, perhaps because of a behavioral flip-flop when she drank. After one or two Electric Ice Teas, she would attempt to draw attention to herself, sometimes becoming obnoxious. Male regulars considered her a party animal, a "petertease" or "P.T." An ex-boyfriend said she would go home with strangers and even sleep in their beds, but refuse to let them touch her. She seemed to use sex as a game, a tool. On the rare occasions when she engaged in intercourse, she acted bored and mechanical.

The investigators were told that her nightclub style was to importune males for drinks and then leave them. She referred to herself as a "hot mama" and used any means to meet prospects, including bumping into them and saying an elaborate "Well, pardon *me*!" She discussed her drink-cadging techniques with fellow workers and girlfriends and offered to share her knowledge. She seemed to enjoy insulting men, toying with them, goading, discounting their sexuality. It amused her when males drank too much and lost control. One night in a parking lot she told a man named Ken, "Am I going to have to *laugh* at you?"

In the cruel shorthand of the nightclub demimonde, such women were termed "bar sluts." But Mary Ann Pohlreich seemed a different woman by daylight. She was a talented and dependable worker and a superior student. Although she told a friend, "I'm not into black guys," she'd been the legal guardian of a disabled African-American man for years and handled his financial affairs. She admitted to a yen for tall young males, but she was genuinely gregarious and seemed willing to step outside with anyone who asked her, sharing a cigarette or a casual conversation. Lately she'd been drinking more heavily than usual, especially on weekends. She'd admitted to a friend that she'd passed out in a nightclub parking lot and awakened in a strange man's bed. Of course nothing had happened—she hoped.

The detectives learned that the doomed woman had gone to Papagayo's with two male friends for an evening of dancing. When they arrived at eight-thirty, Mary Ann ordered an Electric Ice Tea and began table-hopping, ending up at the bar. After an hour or so her escorts became disenchanted and left.

She spent a long time talking to Terry and Mark, two hail-fellow businessmen whom she'd met at Papagayo's earlier in the week. The big spenders bought Screaming Orgasms and long-stemmed roses for their dates and two or three other women. After a few rounds, Mary Ann kissed Mark on the neck and playfully grabbed his backside. When he didn't respond, she nudged his crotch with her flat-heeled shoe, causing him to snap, "Cool it!" She seemed offended and turned away.

Soon she was seen near the DJ booth talking with a male who was described later as "clean-shaven, six feet tall, large build, dark straight hair, expensively dressed, possibly Hispanic or Mediterranean." The man seemed bored with her, and when she lost her balance and fell, he turned away as though repulsed.

At least five times on the murder night, Mary Ann approached the disc jockey and demanded that he play "U Can't Touch This," by MC Hammer. Busy with his mix of sound, light and fog, the DJ found the woman an annoyance and played the song just twice.

Late in the evening Mary Ann gave one customer the impression that she was looking for a ride home. Bartender Daniel Haller decided that she was drunk and served her a glass of water. Then he got busy, and when he looked up she was gone. The next time she was seen, she had a fir cone in her hands.

NEAR THE END of the first week of investigation, five men were still being carried as persons of interest. One was a distant family member with a long-standing grudge. Skeen met him when he arrived at Sea-Tac airport, detained him on a "chippy warrant," and deleted him from the hot list after a short talk.

Skeen also scratched the obnoxious Australian who'd turned up in a canvass. "The wrong asshole," he explained at a strategy session.

A young black gunman named George Gumbs was known to be operating in the Seattle area; he'd killed a fellow dope dealer in New York and was implicated in a local homicide and rape. Gumbs was known to pick up women outside Bellevue nightclubs, avoiding the cover charge and the high-priced drinks. The lead investigator checked with his Seattle contacts and reported to his lieutenant, "Gumbs is into killing, but not this one."

The fourth POI was Pohlreich's mysterious boyfriend "Damon" and the fifth was the "Mediterranean" man who'd talked to her at Papagayo's. After hundreds of man-hours of investigation, both were still being sought.

On Saturday evening, June 30, 1990, a week after the murder, Bellevue Detective Mike Beckdolt was working security in front of Papagayo's Cantina when George Russell arrived with a male friend. They exchanged greetings, and George expressed regrets about recent events. As he strolled under the striped awning in his cool-dude walk, he said, "I sure hope you catch the guy." Beckdolt remembered later that he seemed sincere.

* * *

Inside the club several plainclothesmen were trying to look inconspicuous, with little success. Detective Jeff Gomes complained, "In this place, anybody over thirty stands out." They'd worked the premises several nights since the murder, interviewing employees and observing from the catwalk.

It had taken only one visit for Gomes and his colleagues to realize that Mike Beckdolt was right about George Russell. The personable young man strolled around the yuppie club like a part owner. The detectives didn't have to search him out; he sidled right over, offering tidbits of gossip and professional advice.

At first it was like having a helper, Gomes said, an "inside man." But after a while, "I wasn't so happy about it. I thought he was deliberately marking us and feeding us contradictory information."

Gomes's partner, Earl Barnes, a property crimes investigator soon to become a lieutenant, couldn't place George at first.

Then the way he spoke and that skinny little head reminded me—Hey, that's the guy I used to play basketball with on Mercer Island! Of course George remembered *me*; there's only five or six black officers in Bellevue.

Whenever Jeff and I walked in, he'd say, "So-and-so's here tonight and he might be worth taking a look at," and "So-and-so's sittin' over there," blah blah blah. We showed him the photos of the victim and he didn't recognize her. Then he changed his mind and said, "Yeah, I think I know her. She mighta come over to our table that night. I mighta talked to her. She was wearing. . . ." Blah blah blah. "Looks like the same kinda buttons." He brought some guys over to look at the picture. He tried to buy us beers and we said no no *no*. He kept pumping us for information. "How close are you to making an arrest? What are you holding back?" After a while he became a pain, a typical wanna-be. They mean well, but they just gum up an investigation.

John Hansen also cased the place, along with his partner Skeen. Among other objectives, they were trying to find the "Mediterranean" man who'd spoken to the victim on the murder night.

Hansen conducted several interviews before noticing that a slender young customer seemed to be eyeballing him. Another officer identified the gawker as a busy informant named George Russell. Offhandedly Hansen asked himself, How deep is this guy gonna try to insert himself?

Skeen was quietly observing the action when the young man named George sidled over and said he had some information. In the high-decibel setting, the lead investigator didn't quite catch the last name. The tipster came across as a little too smooth and verbose. Barflies sometimes produced useful information, but more often they tied police up with tips and rumors that were firmly rooted in gossip, prejudice and gin. Skeen had already worked his way through enough misinformation to fill a couple of police manuals, and there was another stack awaiting attention on his desk.

He listened as the man rattled on about a young dancer who'd accompanied him to Papagayo's last Friday night. He said he thought she might have talked briefly to Mary Ann Pohlreich. Unfortunately the dancer was away on a vacation trip. He scribbled the name Lynn Brown and a phone number on a napkin.

After a while another officer advised Skeen not to waste time on George: "He's bullshit." Always the detail man, Skeen tried to phone Lynn Brown anyway. The number proved to be bad.

THE NEXT DAY, Sunday, the door to Mindy Charley's apartment swung open and George Russell walked in as though he were still in residence. Mindy gaped as three women followed. One was squat, the others scrawny; all looked wan and weary. They appeared to be in their late teens and stared adoringly at George. Mindy thought, Gee, has the charmer fallen this far?

"Hi, Min!" George said, smiling broadly. "We came to get Sasha."

Mindy produced the undersized calico cat and George handed it to one of the girls. "Here, hon," he said. "This is the present I promised." She accepted the animal listlessly. To Mindy, she looked badly in need of a fix.

As George strolled into the living room, Mark Mc-Ammond lifted his powerful bulk from a chair and said with his customary amiability, "Hi, George."

To Mindy, George appeared shocked. She'd seldom seen him off-balance, but his head jerked an inch or two backward. "Oh, uh . . . hey, Mark!" he exclaimed. "How's it goin'?"

He reached under one of the sofa cushions and removed a white baseball cap. "Well," he said, carefully arranging it atop his modified 'Fro, "see ya later." He walked out the door like a Nubian prince, entourage in trail.

EARLY IN THE second week after the killing, Bellevue Detective John Gerber, nicknamed "the rabbi" for his patient counseling of juveniles, sat at his computer to do some catching up. Like most of the footsore investigators, he was running behind on paperwork.

At a midnight strategy meeting, Gerber had been assigned to follow up on Mike Beckdolt's suggestion to talk to the car valet named Todd. After two or three attempts, the persistent plainclothesman had located Todd Arviso, an olive-skinned young man with dark close-cropped hair and a big vocabulary. Gerber typed out one of his typically meticulous reports:

ARVISO responded in a manner consistent with comfort, straight forwardness and truthfulness. R/O [reporting officer] completed a FIR [field interview report] and noted with interest one new potential source of information he mentioned. He said "George" is a regular at Papagayo's & was there Friday the 22nd. George was described as a BM between 25 & 27, medium weight & a short afro, bright teeth and a particularly round face . . . who is always happy/friendly w/others. ARVISO said George borrowed someone's Toyota 4×4 P/U around mid-evening and took a girl away before returning later. He wore tennis shoes, casual pants & a polo shirt that night and there was nothing peculiar about his leaving until later I learned the owner of the truck was upset he stayed away so long. . . .

ARVISO said he worked from 1930 until 0215 that night. He looked at the pictures and said she looks familiar but didn't recall her being there that night. ARVISO said the photos were not of the gal George left with around 2100; that female wore glasses & looked altogether different. ARVISO said the owner of the P/U talked with the officer on duty about his missing truck during the night and he felt the name was "Schmitty."

Gerber, a former schoolteacher, worked back to back with Marvin Skeen in the small detective office and wasn't sure where the lead investigator wanted incoming reports to be filed. Skeen's desk was a buzzard's nest of notes, FIRs, bulletins, credit-card slips and bar bills from Papagayo's and the Black Angus, interdepartmental memos, reports, phone messages and other paper, and for a while he'd asked his colleagues to put incoming material on his chair. Now the chair was piled a foot high. Gerber finally balanced his report atop the overflowing in-box.

Skeen, long on desk work and short on sleep, eventually scanned the report but assigned it no special importance. If the car valet specified that the woman "wore glasses and looked altogether different" from Mary Ann Pohlreich, he was obviously talking about another woman. Hundreds had passed through the club's doors that night.

Nor did Skeen connect the "George" in Gerber's report with the mouthy young man who'd given him a bad phone number at Papagayo's. Both Georges seemed irrelevant, especially since an FBI-trained profiler had suggested that the killer was probably a single white male with a taste for anal sex that he'd developed in the penitentiary.

With characteristic candor, Skeen said later, "That was a good lead in Gerber's report. I should've picked it up." A detective's job, he added ruefully, "is a constant learning experience."

G. B. COFFIN WINCED as she read the headline in the Bellevue *Journal American:* "Police ask for clues in slaying."

It was plain enough that the cops were spinning their wheels. The article included a suggestion from the murdered woman's roommate, Theresa Veary: "Don't go dancing alone."

Gee, thanks, G.B. said to herself. That's great advice, but what about us cocktailers? At the end of each shift, they were being escorted to their cars, but that system couldn't go on forever. She talked to her friend Carol Beethe and learned that the women of Cucina! Cucina! were in a similar state of nerves.

G.B. thought, What a hell of a way to live. On July 12 she left for a new life in Hawaii with her master carpenter and her children.

So the baby says preverbally I'll never be in this position again, ever to experience this kind of pain. And the only way to do that is to never be vulnerable. I'll always be in control, I'll always be vigilant, and I will do unto others before they do unto me.

—DR. KEN MAGID,
MURDER BY NUMBERS, CNN

All four girls agreed: it was a great feeling. "No more classes, no more books, no more teachers' dirty looks. . . ."

They were free at last. They'd just graduated from high school and moved into a condominium across the street from the Crossroads shopping center. They had pocket money, jobs, boyfriends, cars, looks, energy and promising futures.

Barbara "Bobbie" DeGroot felt almost giddy about the months ahead. "We'll have a free summer," she told her three girlfriends. "Work hard, play hard, date who we want, without having to meet their folks. Stay up, smoke, drink. *Party every night!*"

The condo at Villa 156 rented for six hundred dollars a month, and the graduates spent a frenzied two weeks decorating in "garage sale modern": a sailboating picture on the off-white wall, a smoked-glass dining room tabletop, a creaky rattan couch dotted with tan and brown cushions in a bamboo floral pattern, a low coffee table in a light mahogany stain. Roommate Susan Jetley found a dog-eared copy of *The Joy of Sex* at a garage sale; it struck them all as the perfect conversation piece.

"Everything was plain, cheap, simple," Bobbie DeGroot recalled. "We had three bedrooms and a loft, all unfurnished. Our kitchen had the bare essentials: coffeepot, fridge, stove, not one thing more. The one and a half bathrooms were always a mess. We were four young girls. Who the hell cared?"

The vivacious Bobbie was tall and slender, with tousled brown hair and alluringly wide-set eyes that were almost hazel and almost green. Like her roommates, she was busily earning money for college. Jennifer Graves and Sara Amundson worked at Pietro's Pizza. Suzy Jetley waited tables at Chili's Bar and Grill and sold Birkenstock sandals in the Crossroads Mall. Bobbie worked at Winters Formal Wear in Bellevue Square. In the fall she planned to study acrylics and watercolors at the Art Institute of Seattle. But first came the joys of summer . . . and George Walterfield Russell.

It was two-thirty in the morning, and my roommate Jenny and I drove over to Denny's for some coffee. We went up to the counter and said, "Two for smoking," and as we were going to our seats, this guy in the first booth turned around and started talking as if he'd known us forever. Like he made complete eye contact, *locked* on us. It seems eerie now, like he had a compulsion to meet us, a fascination. We'd been in Denny's a lot and he could have noticed us before.

He said, "So, you girls sneakin' out?"

We said we were big girls, we didn't have to sneak.

He sat at our table and started talking about Calvin and Hobbes. He had the comic book and acted like it was the funniest thing in the world. It's about a little boy and his pal, a tiger. He said he'd read every book in the series and didn't think he could survive without Calvin and Hobbes. We talked for an hour he and introduced us to a couple of his friends that were really hammered. Then he snuck our bill and paid it. We wondered why he left the Calvin and Hobbes book behind if he loved it so much.

After that it seemed like we ran into him every night. We rented from Sara's father and we were always having nonstop parties. One night Jenny gave George our number and he phoned the next day. He and his sister Erika and his friend Smitty took Jenny and Suzy and me jet-skiing and then to dinner at Papagayo's. Everybody in the place knew him; it was impressive. He said he used to hang out at the Black Angus but one of the waitresses got in his face and he was boycotting the place. He seemed like such a man-about-town—strong, sophisticated.

We told him and Smitty to visit our condo anytime. We called our place The Metropolis because kids were always walking in and out and crashing on the couch and the floor. I don't remember a night when it was just us four roommates.

George and Smitty came to one of our parties and then another one. Somebody brought up the murder at the Black Angus and Smitty said, "Oh, it's probably a mad boyfriend from eastern Washington."

George said, "No, it's probably a guy from around here."

Smitty and Suzy Jetley took a liking to each other and started dating, but then he disappeared into an alcoholism program. After the second party George dragged in his duffel bag and paper sacks and threw 'em in my room like he lived there. That night he slept on the sofa.

When he didn't leave in a few days, the situation began to worry me. My regular boyfriend Tim was in Europe, but he was coming back in August, and I didn't think he would appreciate George.

After he'd been there a week or so I called my roommates into the front bedroom and shut the door. My girlfriend Kathy was with us. I was, "Listen, guys, this George thing is getting a little bit out of hand. I think he needs to leave."

Dear sweet Jenny was blown away. She was just *affixed* to George and didn't want to think there was anything in the world wrong with him.

I said, "Jenny, that's just it. He's *too* perfect. Something's wrong."

She said, "Oh, come on, Bobbie, ya know? Like, I mean— you're being *silly*." That's the way our happy Jenny talked, in excited little fits and jerks.

I said, "Jenny, listen to me. People wanted to believe Ted Bundy was a great guy. Smooth, *cool*. George is too much like that."

Suzy was like, "I get the same vibes."

Jenny's like, "Bobbie, that kinda stuff only happens in the movies."

I said, "Well, I don't trust him and I don't want him here."

Jenny asked if it was because he was black, and I said, "You know me better than that."

She said, "Then *you* ask him to leave."

So it was kind of stalemate. We went back into the living room and George asked if anybody wanted to walk to the 7-Eleven with him. I thought fast. "Yeah," I said. "I'll go."

I pulled my girlfriend Kathy into the front bedroom and said, "Listen, I'm nervous about being alone with this guy. If we're not back in half an hour, call the police."

Then I said, "No, wait a minute! I'll call you from the 7-Eleven to let you know we're on our way back. And if we're not here in a reasonable time, call the police."

I didn't know exactly why I was afraid of him. I was a little attracted to him, too. It was confusing.

We walked in the dark to the 7-Eleven. I stayed outside and

called Kathy on the pay phone. "Okay," I said, "we're here. We'll be leaving in a minute."

George dawdled on the way home. He didn't hit on me or say anything out of line. He was just a regular, bright, interesting guy. After that point I started to trust him. And maybe get a little more interested.

He started buying groceries for us. Not that we cooked much. Mostly we ate at Denny's. He kept us supplied with tequila, beer, ale, wine coolers, mixes. He kept a bottle of Rumple Minze in the freezer.

At first he slept on the couch or the floor. Sara and Suzy shared the big loft and Jenny had a bedroom in back. I'd brought a double water bed from my parents' house and paid a little extra for the master bedroom. George began to keep his stuff in my room 'cause we didn't want it all over the place. He lived out of duffel bags and sacks.

From the beginning he acted like an older brother. He counseled us, told us to go for it, don't allow ourselves to get frustrated and excited. "You're too tense, hon. Go have sex with someone. It doesn't matter who." He actually preached that!

He had a little portfolio of girls in their teddies, told us he was working with them to make them feel more comfortable about their bodies. We thought, My God, a sex counselor. How lucky can we get! He said he avoided sex himself and praised himself for it. He really adored himself, told us how abstinent he was and how happy it made him.

In the middle of the night one of our rich-kid friends hit on Suzy and she chased him off. Then the guy went to Jenny's bedroom and tried to give her a back rub. George hollered, "Leave her alone!"

After we got back to sleep, the dude went up the ladder to the loft and tried to get into bed with Sara. What a mistake! Sara came from a Norwegian family, ultramoral. She was five-seven, slender, straight dark brown hair to her waist, always wore stretch pants and a shirt, and a lot of guys had made the mistake of hitting on her.

She hollered and George dragged the dickhead down and slammed his head on the living room floor. George said, "I'm gonna sit on this couch and you're gonna sleep on the floor. If you move, I'll kill ya!" *Our protector!*

He did a lot of impressive things like that. If we were with him at Denny's or somewhere else, he checked out guys that approached. If he didn't like their looks, they were outa there quick. It was like having our own pit bull. He insisted on meeting our boyfriends and monitoring our morals. It was kinda fun!

We usually wore short skirts, small tops with tight-fitting short sleeves—typical summer stuff. But one night Sara put on a tight black tank top that she'd borrowed from her friend, the town wanton from Tacoma. They were quite a pair, quiet churchgoing Sara and her friend the bimbo, and they were gonna stroll around Crossroads. George said, "Please, hon, *don't* wear that dress. It's wrong for seventeen years old. You'll send the wrong signals."

When Sara acted hesitant, George said, "Don't you know Mary Ann Pohlreich was dressed like that?"

Sara borrowed a friend's trench coat and put it over her dress. She wore it in Denny's 'cause she was afraid George would walk in. He had us so intimidated! But his signals were mixed, inconsistent. If you get tense, have sex! With anybody! But for God's sake, don't wear a backless dress.

He was the same judgmental way about marijuana. He brought home a Baggie and then criticized us when we smoked. One night we were without a TV 'cause Sara's father had taken it back, and Jenny and I got stoned and pretended to do the evening news. "This just in . . ." "Ten thousand Swedes ran through the weeds. . . ." "And now our Pentagon correspondent, Wolf Blitzer," followed by a long howl. *Very* funny when you're stoned. We were laughing so loud, George lashed into us, made me feel really bad. I said, "Why're you so upset about this? You gave us the marijuana."

He said, "There's a difference between getting stoned to relax and getting stoned to act stupid." He was so disgusted, he left for the night.

I was thinking about it later. What he was really talking about was control. It was okay to be controlled-stoned but not uncontrolled-stone. George never showed emotion. That was uncool. He didn't like us to drink too much and get laid back. He put a limit on our drinking, usually two or three. After we had our limit, he'd hide the bottles. *Control!*

Naturally we wanted to know personal stuff about him, but

he wasn't telling. It became a hobby with us: find out about George! It was a waste of time. Anything personal, he'd say, "That's not relevant, hon." He slept all day and stayed out all night. When he took us dancing, he wore a white shirt and dark pants. When he left at night, he wore dark sweatshirts and dark pants and carried a little flashlight. We wondered why.

Once he was in the shower and Suzy and I looked through his wallet. There was a bunch of business cards and something about a court date and the address of a "Dr. Wonzel Mobley" on Mercer Island. But no ID.

The burning question was his age. We never found out. We asked him and he said, "I don't celebrate birthdays, hon, so it's not an issue." It just made him more mysterious. We knew his friend Smitty was twenty-seven, so we assumed George was twenty-seven, too. Actually he was more like thirty-two.

He let it slip that he was an undercover cop, a nark, told us he did secret jobs like breaking into houses to get evidence. That was great with us. We'd already had a prowler and a killer was loose, and we could use a cop under our roof. He said he was working on the Pohlreich murder and brought home a poster with HELP in big red letters. He told us he was taking it to the clubs and showing it to people to get information. There were two color photographs of the dead lady, and the Bellevue police phone number. He also clipped some newspaper articles and asked what we thought about the killing. He said the cops ought to be looking for a recently divorced businessman.

We hung out a lot with a great kid named Damien Middleton; he'd been president of our class at Interlake and we'd known him since junior high. Damien had a sixth sense about people, and at first he hated George. He told us, "When I look at him, I get the deepest, darkest, most evil feeling I've ever gotten from a person."

We all said, "Oh, Damien!" Later he mellowed about George and they became pretty tight.

One night George and I were walking back from Albertson's supermarket when he goes, "Hey, there's cops at the house. See that car in front?"

I said, "That's not a cop car."

He said, "Yeah. It's unmarked, hon."

"What would they be doing at our place?"

We got a little closer, and he said, "See those guys getting out? That's Earl and Jeff."

I remembered that Suzy and a couple of her friends had been smoking marijuana and I went ahead and yelled, "The police are here.!" They ran around stashing pot under the sofa and spraying with potpourri.

George brought the cops in without knocking and introduced them as Detectives Barnes and Gomes of the Bellevue PD. The girls were shaking. One of the officers took a deep breath and said, "We're not here for that." George acted as though he was part of the operation.

Suzy's girlfriend says in a slurred voice, "Are you guys really cops? I wanna see your badge."

George told her to chill. The cops asked about Damien, where he lived, what kind of car he drove, et cetera, and we answered every question. We found out later they thought the killer was a guy named Damon or Damien, and good old co-operative George had sicced them on Damien Middleton—the nicest, most innocent guy in the world! I guess he was trying to score Brownie points.

The whole incident just made George look more mysterious and interesting to me. I'd always liked black men. I had a black boyfriend in the eighth grade, a very attractive boy, and after that I was involved with another black man and almost married him.

All the black men I'd been attracted to had very nice bodies, including George. Maybe that's what started it. I mean, I was in love with Tim, but I began to like George a lot. And the weather was nice, and we were all so naïve and smoked pot and Camel Lights and listened to 10,000 Maniacs and the Indigo Girls and drank George's Rumple Minze, Bud Dry and Rainier dark ale, margaritas, wine coolers, and—I don't know, it was like a hazy lazy vacation, Fun in the Sun, What I Did Last Summer. *It doesn't count on the record.*

George had been with us two or three weeks when he started napping in my bed. He'd come home and we'd kiss and cuddle. If it got a little heated he'd walk away, or he'd find some escape, some distraction. Or somebody would interrupt us, 'cause there were always so many people in The Metropolis.

I was attracted to him, but he would never let it go too far.

I mean, his actions showed how much he wanted me, but he wouldn't come out and say or do anything about it. Pretty soon it reached a point where I *wanted* to go further with him and he wouldn't let it happen. Then he'd praise himself for his abstinence.

I was beside myself. I knew Tim would flip if he heard about me and George. Tim knew I was attracted to black men and it always drove him crazy. He couldn't understand it. So here I was, in love with Tim and attracted to George and Tim was coming home soon and—I was all mixed up.

One night when things got pretty heated, I said, "George, you and I need to talk."

"So talk!" he said.

I said, "Not here. Too many distractions."

We went over to Denny's before the bar crowd piled in from Papagayo's and I told him, "Look, I already have a boyfriend. He's in France right now, and when he comes back, I have every intention of being with him. He's not gonna like it that you're in our house, and you can't be there when he comes back. I understand you need a place to live right now, that's fine, but you *cannot* be here when Tim comes back."

George said, "That's cool, hon. I'll be gone by then."

So that's where we left it. Pretty soon we were back in bed and he was getting me all excited and backing off. We had a couple of fights. One night he slept under the dining room table, but then he came back to my bed. We had long discussions. He'd tell me to take things the way they are, stop trying to pry into his life and figure him out. His usual double-talk, mystery stuff.

He'd say, "You just don't see what's happening. You just don't understand."

I thought, What's not to understand? I said, "Why do we only go halfway? It isn't fair for you to leave me hanging. It should be all or nothing."

He said, "Okay, then, it'll be nothing." And for a week or two that's what it was. He slept on the couch or on Jenny's floor or up in the loft when nobody was there. I thought he'd never come back to my bed again, but then one night—there he was. Driving me nuts.

A MONTH AFTER Mary Ann Pohlreich was laid to rest, Marv Skeen summed up the status of the case at a strategy session. "We got nothin'," he admitted in his laconic style.

Six detectives remained assigned, a heavy strain on the ten-man division. All three persons crimes investigators—Skeen, Dale Foote and John Hansen—had been trying to find Mary Ann's boyfriend Damon and working on the tip sheets and FIRs that littered Skeen's cubicle.

By now the lead investigator had collected dozens of exhibits to send to the FBI crime lab. "We didn't have a suspect, so it was pretty low priority," he said later. "I hadn't sent anything to the FBI in nine years, so along with the exhibits I sent an old letter I'd used before, just filled in the blanks. The FBI lab guy called me and spent a half hour calling me six different kinds of son of a bitch. I kept saying, 'Well, just tell me how to word it and I'll send you another letter.' He didn't want to hear about it. I told the guys, 'Hey, I've never been called a son of a bitch before.' They just said the guy was probably having a bad day. I said, 'Yeah, we know about bad days, don't we, men?' "

The local media kept up the pressure, and people began buzzing about "The Crossroads Killer" and "The Eastside Bundy." Among its attractions, Bellevue was a shoppers' town, and crime hurt business. Nightclub grosses flattened out at places like Finn McCool's, Zoonies and Cucina! Cucina!, and the lines shrank at the hot-ticket Papagayo's. In an effort to shake its image as an interracial meat rack, the Bellevue Black Angus changed its format from top forty to country and western, but on most nights disc jockeys like Mark McAmmond played to diminished houses. The staff was reduced by attrition as some of the employees followed G. B. Coffin's example and fled.

* * *

On behalf of the police, the local newspapers ran requests for help: POHLREICH CLUES SOUGHT . . . MORE HELP NEEDED ON MURDER CASE . . . POLICE ASK PUBLIC'S HELP TO SOLVE CASE. . . .

To the investigators, the articles were a blessing and a curse. Leads flowed in, but none helped. Seattle police arrested a sex killer, and Skeen rushed across the I-90 bridge to interview him. He had a solid alibi for the night of the Pohlreich case. Skeen also interviewed a fifty-year-old male whom Mary Ann had once branded "faggot," and a younger man who'd bragged about killing a woman, and a female King County Jail inmate who claimed to have key information but at the moment was busy taking off her clothes and stuffing her toilet.

When he wasn't interviewing oddballs or suffocating in paper, Skeen's thoughts kept circling back to Mary Ann's last boyfriend, the elusive Damon. The lead investigator considered himself an expert on men of similar names; he'd already cleared two dozen, including Damien Middleton. But it still looked like the best lead.

SUSAN JOYCE JETLEY, the bluntest of the condo girls, had never been charmed by their nonpaying guest. For one thing, George was such a suck. It was unnatural, unreal. When Sara was stuck for a ride home from work, he paid for a cab to pick her up. He hand-delivered dinner to the shop where Suzy sold sandals. He brought home a flat of nectarines, Sara's favorite fruit. When Bobbie complained that no one sent her flowers, he bought her a bouquet. He cooked gourmet meals, treated his roommates to dinner and movies, helped with the housekeeping, kept his space immaculate, lightened the mood with jokes and wisecracks, and burst into laughter when anyone got off a good line— or a bad one.

At first Suzy had found his behavior inoffensive, but later she realized it was just because she was young and easily impressed. Barely eighteen, she was a tiny china doll with perfect features, light brown hair to her shoulders, blue eyes and a sturdy backbone. She ran cross-country, worked out regularly, and kept her weight below 100. Even when she put on her three-inch heels and bright red lipstick and her favorite business suit, she had the look of a child playing dress-up.

Suzy and her siblings had been transplanted to Bellevue by parents who'd become disenchanted with the theocracy of Utah. In the sixth grade a Mormon Sunday School teacher had asked her, "Don't you want to be a mommy?"

"No," said the child. "I want to be a district attorney." Suzy wasn't sure what a DA did, but it sounded impressive.

A Mormon bishop asked her parents if there was a problem at home; why would their child want to be a district attorney instead of a mother? "My mom went off," Suzy recalled gleefully. "She said, 'If my daughter wants to be a DA, she'll be a goddamned DA!' When I was fifteen, we left Utah for good."

Now that Suzy and her girlfriends had graduated from Interlake High, she planned a storybook summer before leaving for Harvard and studying to become an English professor. She enjoyed wordplay, ironies, twists and one-liners—"Last week I couldn't spell 'architect,' and now I are one." "The flasher was gonna retire, but he's gonna stick it out for another year. . . ."

George was her best audience. He laughed and flashed his perfect teeth and clapped his long fingers in front of his nose. But after a while it began to seem overdone. There's something wrong with this guy, Suzy said to herself. He may be a nark, as he claims, but he's got another agenda.

She retained a cradle Mormon's preoccupation with theology and engaged George in long arguments, quoting biblical passages while the others yawned. One night he made a typical pronouncement to his teenaged acolytes: "Did you know if we were one eighth of an inch closer to the sun, we'd be burned up? One inch farther, we'd freeze? How can anybody doubt that God exists?''

Suzy thought, How *vapid*. And probably untrue. One *eighth?*

When she tried to determine George's religious affiliation, he hesitated and said, ''I'm born-again Christian.''

''I'm a born-again atheist,'' Suzy cracked, ''or maybe . . . a born-again agnostic. I'm not sure.''

They ended up screaming, and he said she ought to be a cop. She wondered where he got *that* idea; she thought he admired the police. He certainly acted like it, slipping two cops into Villa 156 in the middle of a marijuana party.

We girls had the usual spats that summer, resentments, girl stuff, but we'd gotten along pretty well B.G.—before George. Bobbie and I clashed once in a while 'cause she's French and I'm Scottish. Sara and I were tight and slept in the loft. She'd been a reporter on our school paper when I was sports editor. She was very bright, pretty, a little overprotected. Jenny Graves was on her own plane—sweet, cheerful, a model's looks, terrific at singing and drawing. Her parents considered her St. Jenny the First. Once her father got mad at me for something *she* did. He said, ''You're grounded!'' I said, *''You can't ground me!''* Our parents lived close to each other.

Nobody agreed with me, but it didn't take long to realize that George hadn't encountered Bobbie and Jenny by accident. In the first days after we moved in, we'd had a midnight prowler, and Jenny and Bobbie told everybody at Denny's about it. We were really worried for a while. That's one reason we accepted George; he said he was an undercover cop and he'd protect us. Jenny said he was sent from God. George agreed. Later I realized—*George had been our prowler!* George engineered the whole thing!

He had a scanner and a bunch of police numbers and a police hat and a gun. When I saw the gun, I flipped. I said, ''Get that thing out of my house *now!*''

There was a big showdown. He said, ''I'm armed 'cause I'm working on the Mary Ann Pohlreich case.'' He said he'd been in Papagayo's and talked to her the night she was killed, and he was developing information for the cops.

The vote was three against one, so George and the gun stayed. Big tough guy! Then our three kittens got leukemia and the vet said he had to put 'em to sleep. George freaked, said he couldn't handle it. He stayed outside in the car with his face in his hands.

Before long he'd become our resident hero and foremost authority on anything, *everything*. One day my nine-year-old cousin and my little sister were visiting and he gave them money to buy candy. Before they left he said, "If any guy comes on to you and shows you his penis, just laugh hysterically. That disarms 'em." I thought, What an odd thing to say to kids.

I decided that the best thing to do was avoid him. The longer he stayed, the less I liked it. He was superficial. He extracted information without revealing anything about himself. He'd drag that long pinkie nail down my back and I'd jump. Like most Mormons, I don't come from a touchy-feely family. The other girls loved it.

One day he invited us to a barbecue at his home on Mercer Island. All the Mobleys called him Russ. I was surprised at how affectionate he was with his sister Erika—jokey, warm, physical. I thought how my brothers and I weren't like that. I got the feeling that something really bad had happened between George and Kris Mobley; you could see they didn't like each other. He seemed distant and cold with his stepfather, too. It was like the adults were keeping a hawkish eye on him and he was only tight with his sibs.

After a while the phone rang and it was his real mom. He'd bragged about her, how she was a "dean" at San Francisco State. Erika talked to her, but George wouldn't. Flat refused. I went home more puzzled than ever.

Most of his habits were terrible. He showed us how to open a locked sliding door, as if that was important. If we moved any of his things, he'd freak out. He borrowed my books on Ted Bundy and Charles Manson and didn't return them. The things he read—*ugh!* Pornic magazines. The *Enquirer, True Detective,* the *Star.* To me that's not the reading of a rounded person. He was smart, but I noticed that he couldn't spell and his punctuation was bad. It made me wonder just how smart he was. I asked about his schooling, but he wouldn't tell.

He'd stay up all night, read the morning paper between six and six-thirty A.M., and then go to bed. He slept all day in Bobbie's bed, or he'd nap in the loft. One day the lock stuck and he couldn't get out. He freaked and broke a window and went across the roof. Spiderman! He told us he couldn't be enclosed. He never had a key; he had his own ways to get into the house.

After he finished his beauty sleep, he'd go out all night on his undercover cases, then come home and count his money. He always had three hundred dollars on him. Where'd he get it? It seemed like some kind of warning signal, but—of *what*?

Late one night in July we got an eye-opener. Jenny and I drove home from Denny's and saw a Hispanic guy standing in the parking lot by our condo. George was out, Sara was in California on a trip, and Bobbie was folding laundry.

We said, "Hi, what's going on?" and the guy just looked confused, so we went inside and looked out the window. He was standing in front of our garage, staring at our door. Two o'clock in the morning!

I said we ought to call the cops. Jenny said, "Oh, knock it off! You're always overreacting."

It was garbage night and Jenny said she'd take it out. When she came back in, she said the guy was sitting on the curb, and now *she* was scared. I said, "Oh, Jenny, catch a clue!"

Bobbie called Nine-one-one and asked if they could just drive by. Within two minutes George was pounding on the door. He was *pissed*! He burst inside and said, "What the fuck have you guys started? Why did you call the police?" It was the only time we ever heard him curse.

He acted like we were stupid. He said the cops were all over the place, looking for this guy. He said he'd been in a car with a couple of narks and heard the radio call. They were on a sting at a house up at Crossroads. A guy was growing marijuana and they'd been watching him for several days. The guy always took a shower at the same time, and George was supposed to break in and take pictures. He said the cops couldn't go in because it was against the law. He said he was about to make his move when our radio call came in and the cops had to respond to our house and it screwed up their sting.

He got his flashlight and he and Jenny went outside and played Cagney and Lacey, lighting up bushes, running through yards. After things settled down, he disappeared for a while and came back with a Ziploc bag full of fresh green marijuana clippings, ten or twenty grams. Said it was official police evidence. He also had a four-pack of wine coolers that he claimed the cops gave him.

I thought, Hey, George, you left out the part about the tooth fairy, but I figured what's the use? Bobbie was dubious, too; even Jenny. We never saw any cops that night, not the ones we called or the ones who drove George home. If he was a nark, why would he give us all those details? Real narks don't tell their secrets. We smoked the marijuana.

It wasn't hard to figure the whole thing out. The Hispanic guy was obviously delivering pot. George heard our call on his scanner and realized the cops would rain on his deal. It was so transparent. He lost some credibility that night. But not for long.

After a few weeks I noticed that he always seemed to be with good-looking women, usually blondes, not always bright. I attributed his popularity to Jungle Fever—women who wanted a little color in their lives.

Bobbie kept on sleeping in the water bed with him, and Jenny treated him like Richard Gere. Sara came back from her trip and treated him the way she'd always treated him, like a great guy that she never wanted to be alone with. Myself, I treated him just like he deserved. Like diphtheria.

EARLY IN AUGUST George Russell's old dancing partner Tami Grace ran into his latest girlfriend, a small blond-haired woman, in the ladies' room of the Black Angus. The girlfriend said that she'd finally broken up with George and asked, "How come you never warned me about him?"

Tami asked what she meant.

"How come you never told me what kind of person he is?"

Tami wondered what to say. She seldom went dancing with George anymore. It was as though he sensed that she and Mindy and some of his old friends were talking behind his back and putting a lot of things together. She didn't think she'd said anything cruel or unfair, but it didn't take much disloyalty to anger George.

"I don't know what you're talking about," Tami said after a hesitation. "I got involved in George's relationship with Mindy a long time ago, and I learned my lesson. I stay out now. George's women are *his* gig."

The woman said, "What's between you and George, anyway?"

Tami said, "I'm a pretty girl on his arm. That's what's between us. We have *no* other relationship." It was the truth.

Now that the first murder has occurred, in subsequent crimes the life stresses that preceded the first one may not need to be present. Now that he's over the line, the murderer usually and more conspicuously plans his future crimes. The first one may have had some of the earmarks of spontaneity. The next victim will in all likelihood be more carefully sought out, the murder more expertly done and displaying more violence to the victim than was evident in the first crime. And the lonely boy from the nonnurturing home has become a serial killer.

—ROBERT K. RESSLER and TOM SHACHTMAN,
WHOEVER FIGHTS MONSTERS

Bobbie DeGroot's world-traveling boyfriend Tim Ogle returned from Europe on Tuesday, August 7. She reminded George of his promise to move out. He said he would switch to Jenny's bedroom and sleep on the floor. Bobbie said that wasn't good enough.

"I intended to tell Tim everything," Bobbie recalled, "but one of his pals had already informed him that some black guy was sleeping in my bed."

Tim was enraged. In a long talk in the Villa 156 living room that night, Bobbie carefully explained that George was the condo's protector and big brother. There'd been some innocent cuddling and back rubbing, but no sex. He'd slept in her big water bed when she was at work, but he kept weird hours, so it wasn't a problem.

As they spoke, Bobbie realized that her words were both true and false. She had no memory of intercourse with George, but sometimes they'd drunk Rumple Minze till she passed out. George always assured her later that he hadn't taken advantage. She hoped he wasn't lying.

She cast nervous glances at the front door as she and her boyfriend talked things out, but George didn't show. Before Tim left, he made it plain that he wasn't as annoyed at the nonpaying boarder as he was at Bobbie herself. "It's *you*," he told her. "This is *your* fault. And it's up to you to resolve the problem."

Bobbie thought, You're absolutely right. That was one of the things she loved about Tim; he saw things clearly. Damn you, George Russell, she said to herself. You're outa here for *good*.

O**N THE NEXT** night, Wednesday, August 8, Tami Grace, her roommate and several others went dancing at the Black Angus and then to the nearby Denny's for postmidnight coffee. When they arrived, George Russell was sitting in the nonsmoking area with several teenagers. He sidled over to her group but turned sideways to her. She picked up on the snub and said, "George, what is your kick?"

He said, "You know what it is." He showed no expression.

"No!" Tami blurted out. She definitely did *not* know. "What is your *kick*?"

He didn't answer. When one of her friends asked what was up, George said, "Tami knows. She mouthed off to my girlfriend about me. I thought I could trust her, but I can't."

Tami was exasperated. She thought, He's so *touchy*.

"Fine, George," she said. "Play your game. I don't care."

He turned to walk back to his table. She started to follow but asked herself, What's the use? He has such rabbit ears. He's just looking for an excuse to cut off our friendship. But *why*?

Shortly after 3 A.M. she left for home, still concerned about her old dance partner. She glanced at the nonsmoking section and saw that he was gone. She wondered why he was turning so mean, especially toward good friends. He was such a *different* George.

About an hour later three East Bellevue boys who were tenting in a backyard heard a howl like a cat in pain. It came from the direction of a house occupied by a cocktail waitress and her two young daughters. The woman's name was Carol Marie Beethe.

SHORTLY AFTER SUNUP Dale Foote logged in at the detectives' office. Seven weeks had passed since the murder of Mary Ann Pohlreich, and his friend and mentor Marv Skeen was still playing catch-up. Foote was in line to handle the next murder case even though his desk was cluttered with a dozen other assignments that had fallen to him since Pohlreich. The third persons crimes investigator, John Hansen, was working a tangled arson murder.

Around 10 A.M. the phone rang and a lieutenant asked Foote to report to the scene of a suicide in a quiet neighborhood. The young detective ran to his car.

When I got there, Lieutenant Dave Morrison came up to my car and said, "This is a homicide, Dale. This woman didn't kill herself. You'll see when you get inside." I thought, Well, if it's a murder, it's my turn in the barrel.

We walked past a man and two young girls—the ex-husband and two daughters. He wasn't living there anymore and had working casts on both arms after a fall on the job. Everybody was crying, comforting and hugging each other.

Officer Mike Elliott took me to the bedroom door. I stepped

inside and stopped short. There was blood on the floor. A clock-radio played softly. I saw a small color TV on a dresser. A naked body lay diagonally on a king-size bed. I took a closer look and went numb. No way in this world I expected to walk in on something like that, now or ever. There's a million ways to kill somebody, but to do to a body what he'd done—I couldn't make sense of it. I almost went into shock. I figured the best thing I could do was just stand around for a few seconds and take my mind out of gear. Then I took a deep breath and looked back.

The woman's crotch faced the bedroom door. Her legs were spread and bent at the knees, almost touching at the heels. I thought, No way this positioning is accidental. The killer wanted you to walk in and be hit with the sight. A shotgun barrel was inserted into her body.

I'm thinking, My God, did he pull the trigger? What would a shotgun do if it were fired inside a woman? What am I supposed to see here?

I'm looking for her insides everywhere, but then I'm thinking: Hey, there's just a few blood smears on the walls and ceiling. So I realized the gun hadn't been fired. It was a prop. The guy had bunched up the covers and rested the gun butt on them so that the barrel went straight into her vagina, no angle.

She had on red high heels, nothing else. A teddy nightgown with spaghetti straps was laid out nice and neat. Looked like he intended to dress the body but changed his mind. Her panties were bunched up to one side and her head was covered by a large blue pillow. I figured it was to hide her face, or to suffocate her, or to quiet her death rattles, which could've gone on for a long time while he was doing his thing.

I saw all this in seconds. Then I backed out of the house and told our shift supervisor, Lieutenant Ed Mott, "Round up the troops. We need everybody out here."

He called in the whole detective division, crime lab equipment, the medical examiner. We started making assignments, got a search warrant for the house over the phone, called the prosecutor and told him what we had.

I started the on-scene investigation. One of the patrol officers told me that the woman was Carol Beethe. Her daughter Kelly had gotten up around eight-thirty and found the door to her mother's bedroom closed and locked, which surprised her because it was never locked. She went outside to the sliding glass door and found it open. She looked inside and saw her mother on the bed. She went to the phone and called her dad, Paul Beethe, a few miles away. He got there in ten minutes and took a quick look and figured she'd killed herself. He called us to report the suicide.

Paul said he'd talked to Carol on the phone the night before and she hadn't sounded depressed or upset. She had a good job, her bills were paid, and she was looking forward to a three-week scuba-diving trip to the Caribbean with her boyfriend, Tom Jones.

Officer Steve Cercone advised me that one of the daughters had seen something suspicious during the night. I isolated the two kids in a neighbor's house. I thought, What an awful thing to have to do. Their world's just collapsed and I've got to ask them a bunch of questions about their dead mom.

Jamie was nine. She was crying; you could see this was over her head. The older sister, Kelly, was thirteen. She sounded calm and controlled; I figured it was from shock. "Kelly," I said, "I want you to tell me what happened, right from the beginning."

She was amazing. She was old enough and smart enough to know that her mom and dad had some problems and her mom's lifestyle wasn't like a lot of other moms'. We talked in the house and then we took a little walk together on the sidewalk.

She said she'd been awake in her room about four-thirty when she heard someone walking along the hallway. She raised up on one elbow and looked out the door from her top bunk and saw the silhouette of a man holding a flashlight with a yellowish beam. She figured it was her mother's boyfriend, Tom Jones. She knew that her mom was also seeing a guy who worked at the Factoria Keg and another guy named Dave, but Jones was the only person who entered the house late at night. He was about the right size, slender, maybe five-ten.

Kelly said the boyfriend poked the light in each room. She looked out the window for Jones's Corvette and didn't see it. She called out, "Mom?" but there was no answer. Kelly was real tired. She'd been up late talking to her own boyfriend through the window. She said she fell back to sleep and didn't get up till she found her mother's body.

After we talked, I had the feeling she was traumatized and holding out, unintentionally. I felt that in such a small house, she'd've heard more than she was telling me. I had a feeling she was suppressing something, and when she's forty or fifty years old she's gonna be sitting down with some counselor and she'll remember more. I think her main thought in the middle of the night was, Whoever's with my mom, it's okay. It's probably Tom, nothing new. Her mother was free and easy about sex. It was her lifestyle and her choice.

A FIVE-MAN TEAM, including Foote and his videotaping colleague Jeff Gomes, began the official examination of the murder scene at 11:21 A.M. They found that the sliding glass door to the side yard had been propped open and the curtain draped over the door handle to let in more air on the warm August night. A box fan was spinning at the threshold.

The furnishings were basic, minimal. A small dresser was on the south wall next to a knickknack stand covered with stuffed animals. Women's clothes hung from a wardrobe rack. The clock-radio and a telephone were on a bedside nightstand along with a jar of aloe sun lotion, a music cassette, papers, bills, and a telephone answering machine. There was a matching nightstand on the other side of the bed and a larger dresser on the north wall. Some of the drawers were half open. A rifle leaned against the nearby wall.

The yard was surrounded by a six-foot cedar fence. A maple tree grew just outside the open door, and the family dog, an eight-year-old Lab named Roxie, was enclosed in a small area and acted calm. It appeared that the killer had entered through the glass door, then left the same way after taking time to poke his flashlight into the interior of the house and lock the bedroom door.

* * *

The medical examiner measured the room temperature at 70 degrees and the victim's core body temperature at 81. The woman was deeply tanned. Foote lifted the pillow that had been placed over her face and shoulders and saw that her head was tightly wrapped in several thicknesses of plastic from Bakker's dry cleaners. He unwound the material and realized that he'd seen Carol Beethe when he was a patrolman making bar checks. She was a bartender or waitress; he wasn't sure where she'd worked.

The killer had struck her repeatedly on the left side of the head. The weapon sliced her left ear and left thirteen distinctive Y shapes about two inches long; they almost suggested a cattle brand. Defensive wounds indicated that she'd been killed quickly but not instantly. One blow had almost severed the little finger. A big purplish bruise defaced her left biceps; it looked like a human bite. There were blood smears on the body, bed and floor, and spatters on ceiling and walls.

In police parlance, Carol Beethe had been "blitzed," overpowered so ferociously that she never had a chance. Foote was sure she'd been asleep when the attack began. An autopsy showed that two ribs on her left side had been broken and shoved into the chest cavity, and there were deep bruises on her right side. Apparently she'd been kicked before being violated postmortem with the gun and whatever else.

As Foote bagged evidence and made notes, he grew more astonished by the degree of rage shown by the killer. He thought, This is the angriest that any human being can ever be. It reminded him of the gulping, frenzied, screaming tantrum of a six-month-old in his crib. Foote couldn't imagine what the poor victim could have done to bring on such a murderous outburst.

He removed the gun slowly and measured the depth of penetration: five and a half inches. The weapon was cocked but unloaded. It was a Savage .22 long rifle over a twenty-gauge shotgun, the type of combination weapon used for small game. The armament matched the victim's decor; she was originally from Montana, and two cowboy hats hung on the wall. She had two rings on the ring finger of her right hand and another on the little finger, but the fingers of her left hand were bare.

After the room had been dusted for prints, vacuumed for trace evidence and videotaped inch by inch, Foote stepped back and tried to make sense out of what he'd seen. As lead investigator, he needed a feel for the killer. But no matter how hard he tried, he couldn't imagine what kind of person would inflict such cruelty on a fellow human being and then hang around to pose his victim as though he were playing dolls.

"To me he wasn't like a psychotic who's gonna dismember the body and do some crazy thing," Foote explained later. "He wasn't just some nut. This killing took thought, imagination, improvisation. He spent a long time and gave the scene a lot of attention. He was a guy who did things a certain way, just right. No, the word 'crazy' never came to my mind. The word for this was 'evil.' "

As OFFICERS ASSEMBLED in the neighborhood to begin another canvass, the canvass began coming to them. "Her boyfriends showed up all day," Foote recalled. "Some were from nearby, some from elsewhere. Two or three admitted they were in love with her; they were upset, crying. Other guys were just a pain in the backside. Every one had something to tell us, and as each one approached, I'm thinking, Who *is* this guy? What's his connection? Is he just a looky-loo, or does he know something useful? It wasted a lot of our time."

A picture emerged of an intelligent and likable woman with highly complex needs, the most pressing of which was companionship, both physical and social. At an even 100 pounds, she stood an inch above five feet and wore heels to boost her height. She was usually seen in tight stone-washed jeans and T-shirts that accentuated her good figure. At thirty-six she worked out regularly at the Eastside Athletic Club and spent hours baking in tanning parlors. She was attractive, with tightly curled blond hair, bright eyes and a patrician nose, slightly elongated, and skilled at hair and makeup. She adorned herself with jewelry, including a family-heirloom diamond ring and a gold chain and opal pendant bearing the phrase "No. 1 Mom."

Friends described her as spirited, outgoing, flirtatious, forgiving, happy. Lately she'd been grieving over the loss of a sister to cancer. She was described as a good mother, attentive and firm, who frequently bemoaned the fact that she had too little time for her daughters. When men stayed over, she warned them, "Remember, you're outa here before the kids wake up."

She slept lightly and at odd hours. Friends from the nightclub business would see a light in her bedroom and drop in at three or four in the morning. Sometimes she shopped for groceries at 5 A.M. She socialized in the restaurants and clubs where she earned her living. She enjoyed trendy places like Papagayo's and Zoonie's, but drank little. She would take a hit or two on a marijuana cigarette, but she shunned pills.

Neighbors said that she was overly generous, a soft touch, yet always seemed to have money. She stored as much as seven hundred dollars in Crown Royal drawstring bags and lately had complained that small amounts were disappearing while she slept. No one was surprised; there'd been cat burglaries in the neighborhood. Detectives determined that five or six of the purple velvet bags appeared to be missing from the opened drawers of her large dresser.

A few close friends admitted that they routinely borrowed her credit card to make big-ticket purchases and paid her back monthly, interest free. She also lent cash. Paul Beethe, a tall, good-looking man who seemed crushed by his ex-wife's death, confirmed that she'd owned the combination rifle-shotgun for years and had taken the .22 rifle, standing against the wall, as collateral on a loan. She usually kept both weapons under her bed.

Like many female bartenders, Carol Beethe was described as verbal and quick, a virtuoso of the put-down. She called people "sweetheart" or "honey" but knew how to handle abusive customers and incompetent colleagues. She enjoyed a big personal following. At Giuseppe's, where she'd once worked the bar, and on her present job at Cucina! Cucina!, she was known as "sweet but tough."

Seattle *Times* reporter Nancy Montgomery summed her up: "Carol Marie Beethe lived the same way as thousands of Bellevue women. She was divorced, worked hard to support herself and her two daughters, and struggled with romantic relationships."

Her early history was tragic and might have had something to do with her preoccupation with sex. Allegations of child molestation had split her family when she was small. At twenty she'd married Beethe, a Butte construction worker, and they'd migrated to Bellevue in 1977. They were divorced in 1987 after a long separation, although they remained close.

A friend explained, "Carol didn't think she could be happy without a man; she had to be *with* someone. And of course that meant sex." She enjoyed telephone sex and was an adventurous risk taker. A police report noted:

Carol was described as addicted to sex and would try anything concerning sex at least once and more if she enjoyed it. One of the neighbors told us that he could hear her scream from across the street when she was having an orgasm. She liked to have sex with three or more [and] with any combination of genders. She had a lesbian affair on at least two occasions. She pestered ––––– into helping her fulfill a fantasy that she had of being home alone asleep at night and being made romantic love to by a stranger who broke into her home. ––––– went to a bar and talked a black man into fulfilling her dream which he did. He got a black man to do it to make Carol upset since he knew that she didn't like blacks. Carol went along with it so as not to offend the man. . . .

Carol had sexual relations with at least eight men within the last three years. She was very conscious about who came to her home and it didn't matter if they were male or female.

She'd also had affairs with several neighbors. As Dale Foote discovered, she had the rare ability to network her lovers. "I couldn't imagine anybody who could put competing males at ease together," said Foote, "but she did it."

Foote and his colleagues painstakingly reconstructed her final evening. She'd come home from work at 7 P.M. and fixed dinner for her daughters. For a few hours she studied a book on scuba diving for her upcoming trip to the Caribbean. At 9 P.M. she phoned her mother in Montana and took two incoming calls during the conversation. The second interruption proved lengthy, and Carol told her mother she would call back.

Thirty minutes after midnight, while her daughters were asleep, Carol had driven to the south end of Bellevue to pay a call on one of her part-time boyfriends, a bartender, and drank pop with him till the restaurant closed at 2:15. A half hour later one of the teenage tenters in her neighborhood saw her pull into her driveway as though she were in a hurry and slam the car door. The boy guessed that she was upset or anxious. She disappeared through the front door and a light went on in her bedroom. She wasn't seen alive again.

AT THE OUTSET of his investigation Dale Foote got one of the worst breaks that could befall a detective, whether young and green like himself or as experienced as his hero, Marv Skeen. A perfect suspect fell into his lap.

While Skeen beat the bushes for "Damon," Foote quickly decided that Tom Jones was the Beethe killer. Jones, a businessman by day and Lothario at night, was Carol's steadiest boyfriend, although each dated others.

He'd been pressuring her to remortgage her house so he could invest in the stock market. There was tension between the lovers and also between Jones and Paul Beethe, who instinctively disliked each other.

A close friend reported that Carol "had a mouth" and sometimes used it to disparage Jones and his sexuality. He was said to be a hard worker, humorous, well rounded, sarcastic, self-centered, sensitive about his penis size, and sometimes overly enthusiastic in his lovemaking. A former girlfriend offered the opinion that she'd long considered him a potential killer. Recently he'd received a bouquet of black roses from Carol Beethe and another woman after they'd learned he was bedding them both. The angry pair had included a card showing an assortment of bare back-sides and a message: "You're the biggest asshole of all." One of the betrayed women had scrawled, "Make me bigger, baby," Jones's favorite line in bed. The irate women had the roses hand-delivered to his office.

Dale Foote also learned that Jones would show up drunk at Carol's house at two and three in the morning and start arguments. He had previous arrests for DWI and domestic assault. He drove a dark blue Corvette, and on the murder night a similar car had been spotted in the neighborhood by the sharp-eyed boys in the tent. He'd been scheduled to meet Carol at 6:05 A.M. for a tanning session and didn't show up, suggesting that he knew she was dead. He was the only one of her known lovers who hadn't rushed to the murder scene the next day, and he remained missing and unaccounted for till midnight.

When Jones finally surfaced, he explained that he'd gone to Papagayo's with another girlfriend and had just learned of Carol's death. He appeared drunk when his rights were read and acted "hinky" during a three-hour interrogation, crying and hyperventilating and exclaiming that he "couldn't have done it." He pounded his fists on the table when he was told that Carol had been seeing several other men. He had no clear-cut alibi for the time of the murder and refused to take a polygraph test or provide bite impressions. At one point he made what Foote considered a tacit admission of guilt, claiming that he might have had a "blackout, or "spaced out," but the statement wasn't strong enough to justify an arrest.

What a shame, the detective said to himself as he released his No. 1 suspect at 3:15 A.M. This guy looks guilty as heck. Now the problem was to dig up the evidence.

Foote wished he had time to work exclusively on Jones, but such specialization wasn't in the job description of real-life detectives. He had to interview the dead woman's friends and arrange counseling for her bereaved children. He had to comb the Beethe yard for evidence; Detective John Gerber had already found bent grass that suggested the killer had fled over a back fence. Houses on both sides of Beethe's street had to be canvassed, and employees of Cucina! Cucina! and other clubs were already being interviewed. Dozens of items of evidence still had to be tagged, bagged and sent to the FBI, a tedious task that had nearly given Marv Skeen tendinitis. In larger departments such chores were handled by technicians, but in Bellevue the lead investigators did everything.

On the night after the murder, Foote catnapped for an hour at his desk and then dug into his paperwork. One of his first jobs was to send a bulletin to "All Washington Law Enforcement Agencies" and to nine local jewelers and pawnshops, describing jewelry that appeared to be missing from Carol Beethe's bedroom. Dutifully he typed in laborious descriptions obtained from her insurance carrier, ending with a description: "one lady's 14 karat yellow gold two ring diamond bridal set. Set contains one round cut center diamond measuring 5.58 mm in diameter. Also contains 2 full cut diamond melee weighing .07 carats total."

It was the kind of detail work that made detectives yearn for their days on a beat.

A FEW DAYS after the Beethe killing, G. B. Coffin learned of the loss of her friend. Black Angus waitress Roxanne Mally called Hawaii to break the news and told her that the other waitresses were terrified.

G.B. tried to steady her voice. "She was one of my best friends," she said softly. "We babysat each other's kids."

Roxanne said she wondered if Carol might have irritated one of her customers into killing her.

"Never!" G.B. said. "She was the total pro, *years* of experience. When I worked next door, we used to drop in just to watch her work. She could ease a three-hundred-pound drunk out the door and make him think it was his idea. It was an education to watch her."

The friends agreed that a monster was targeting the women of the Eastside bars, and G.B. felt relieved that she'd put miles of ocean between herself and the killing grounds. She would miss Carol; they'd planned to get together on her first return visit to the mainland.

For days G.B. brooded about the loss and wondered what would happen to Jamie and Kelly, the children. She heard that Cucina! Cucina! had raised $7,000 for them, a nice gesture. She was suspicious of Carol's friend Tom Jones. Some of the other waitresses called them "the champagne couple" because of their favorite drink, but G.B. thought of him as a jerk. He'd come in without Carol a few times and put the moves on her with his eyes. She couldn't pin down what was wrong, but he was . . . different. That son of a bitch, she said to herself, I hope they're checking him good. She thought about tipping her friends on the Bellevue PD but held her fire. If they were any good, they were on to him anyway.

A rogue's gallery of creeps and weirdos and maniacs paraded through her mind, but she didn't give George Russell a thought. She still regarded him as "a little house robber.'' She'd seen too many like him in her years of cocktailing. A dweeb like George wouldn't have the guts to kill.

A FULL WEEK passed without tangible evidence against Tom Jones. Lead investigator Dale Foote assembled the known facts in an affidavit for a search warrant. The judge was impressed with the circumstantial case and asked the deputy prosecutor, ''Why hasn't this man been charged with murder?''

A search of Jones's car and dwelling revealed nothing. The detectives interviewed his ex-wife, his fellow employees, drinking companions, bedmates and friends. He was obviously a carefree young stud with a garish lifestyle, but there was no proof he was a murderer.

In the Pohlreich case, Marv Skeen had also assembled ''a big pile of nothin','' as he put it, and everyone in Bellevue was becoming edgy. In Eastside nightclubs, dancers performed the electric slide while looking over their shoulders. At the end of each shift bouncers walked waitresses to their cars and watched till their taillights disappeared. Foote told Skeen, ''I've never seen the night people this scared. It's amazing how many lives this is affecting. It's all they talk about.''

In the heat of mid-August, arguments broke out over whether to assign more manpower to chase Foote's favorite quarry Jones or Skeen's favorite quarry ''Damon,'' and whether the Pohlreich and Beethe killings were connected, and what the body posing signified, and a dozen other debatable issues. Foote, Skeen and Hansen remained convinced that Jones had murdered Beethe and another man had killed Pohlreich, and that there was no connection. Their opinion was reinforced by the same Seattle PD profiler who'd earlier suggested that the Pohlreich killer was a white male between twenty-five and forty. The veteran

Hansen spelled out the majority position: "In the Pohlreich posing, it was almost like there was remorse—the hands folded across the stomach, the fir cone in her hand, a plastic lid hiding her eye, her head turned away. It looked like a rape that got out of hand and the guy ended up killing her, then felt bad and took her to a place where he knew she'd be found and laid her out in a peaceful way.

"The other case is entirely different. Whoever killed Carol Beethe acted from pure rage, extreme *personal* rage, a desire to shock and humiliate and degrade. So where's the connection?"

Most members of the division agreed with the three persons crimes detectives, but their immediate superior, Lieutenant Mark Ericks, ordered them to keep open minds and continue to look for new leads.

One morning a yelling match developed in the coffee room where the task force met to compare notes. As Hansen related later, "I'd been arguing that we should bear down on Tom Jones, because if the killer's not him, then we've got a stranger, and if it's a stranger, we're in deep doo-doo. Dale Foote agreed, and Mark Ericks accused him of having tunnel vision and bawled him out in front of everybody. It was 'Hey, I told you to do this!' and 'Now I'm telling you to do that!—a very autocratic display. At the time Mark was having some personal problems, and he was under a lot of pressure from the top. Later he was man enough to apologize."

After the show of bellicosity, Detective Dennis Dingfield, one of the most energetic investigators on the case, joked that it was unfair for Ericks to cuss Foote out "because Dale can't cuss back. It's unfair labor relations!"

The strain was worsened by a rancorous note from the lieutenant to Foote that became widely circulated. Ericks complained that too many officers were slipping into his office to gawk at "crime scene photos of our murder victim, autopsy photos, and the crime scene video recording, while I'm not around." He reminded Foote that "this is my office," and "I don't prowl your locker and desk, and you don't have any right to do that to mine. If I have to put the big Steve Fay dead bolts on everything, I will."

At thirty-one Dale Foote was a man of pride and sensitivity, and he tried not to show his discomfort over the personal attack. It was true that he was in a vulnerable position. He was working his second unsolved homicide, and he was "O-for-two" in the terminology of his favorite sport. And he was getting nowhere, despite the close cooperation of Skeen, Hansen and fellow detectives like Jeff Gomes, Earl Barnes and Dingfield.

As he admitted later, "The stress was beyond comprehension, beyond description. I don't verbalize my feelings, so I kept it in, but I couldn't shake the memory of what I saw in Carol Beethe's room or the frustration over not catching her killer. I couldn't just take my family out to dinner and forget about it. My phones rang all the time. I'd wake up in the middle of the night and couldn't get back to sleep. I took the PC home on weekends to catch up on my reports. I'd walk in, say hi to my wife and kids, and disappear. There were hundreds of decisions to make, and half the time I was just feeling my way. I ended up chasing ghosts and wasting time. It took me awhile to gain enough maturity to learn that wasting time is the nature of the job."

BOBBIE DEGROOT HAD elbowed George Russell out of Villa 156, but the expulsion didn't take. "I'm so softhearted," she complained. "After I kicked him out, we ran into him and he looked so forlorn. Somebody told us that a week after Carol Beethe was murdered, George got real drunk at Denny's Overlake and started banging his head against the wall. Then he slapped a girl and they called the Bellevue cops. He wasn't doing too great on his own.

"I felt so bad about him. When I saw him, I said, 'I'm sorry you had to leave.' I told him I missed having him around, and he gave me a nice hug and said he understood.''

A few nights later Jenny Graves brought George to the condo for a drink of Rumple Minze, and he turned on the charm for hours.

''I took him aside and tried to make him see the problem,'' Bobbie recalled, ''but he just didn't get it. I told him it wasn't only that he bugged my boyfriend. I told him that I liked it when he was real affectionate with me, caring, showing that he likes me very much, and then he'd turn around and wouldn't want to be even *near* me, wouldn't want me to even *touch* him. I told him I couldn't handle that.''

Sometime after midnight George was still talking, and she dozed off. When she awoke in the morning, he was asleep in her bed. She wondered what it would take to get rid of him for good, and how much more of this nonsense Tim would take.

One soppy summer evening George said he had to go on a ''treasure hunt'' and asked Bobbie to drive him to Mercer Island. Her '65 Mustang had been breaking down twice a month, and she didn't want to drive that far. George said the trip was important; some people owed him money and they'd stashed it in the woods. Bobbie said it was a weird way to repay a debt. George said he needed the money for a trip to San Diego and a visit to his mom, the university dean in San Francisco.

''We took a couple of friends,'' Bobbie recalled. ''We drove up a dead-end street to a little wooded area—houses on one side, woods on the other. George said that Mercer kids hung out there to drink. He repeated the directions out loud: 'Ten yards in, four yards to the left, two yards back. . . .' We went into the woods and he came out about a minute and a half later with a damp sack. He clapped his hands and said, 'Oh, I *love* it when somebody gives me perfect directions.' ''

Back at the condo George emptied the sack on a newspaper on the floor and the girls helped him count 108 silver dollars and smaller change. He also flashed a roll of hundred-dollar bills.

Jenny took Bobbie aside and confided that George's trip to San Diego was only a cover, that he'd been involved in a bad drug bust and the cops were making him go to jail to cover their asses. His lawyer had managed to defer the sentence till September 4, and George intended to report to jail on September 14 and claim he'd misread the court papers.

Bobbie thought, If he's going to jail, why does he need so much money? She thought about asking him, but it was the sort of question he always ignored.

In the kitchen George was preparing a gourmet dinner. Two pictures of the murdered Mary Ann Pohlreich looked down from a poster he'd taped to the kitchen wall. A newspaper picture of Carol Beethe and several articles about the case were on the counter and the refrigerator door. As he busied himself with the food, Bobbie hopped up on the counter and sat.

"I wish they'd catch that guy," she mused.

George said, "Hon, I can't believe how stupid the cops are. How *dumb!*"

Bobbie asked what he meant.

"They still haven't solved these cases," he said. He held up one of the newspaper clippings. "It's basic crime detection. Did you read this, hon? Look at the similarities between the two women—same hairstyle, same length and color, same age more or less, same backgrounds. They both hung around bars and picked up men. Can't the cops see the connection?"

He sounded like an employee griping about his employer. He cited the unsolved murder of an elderly Asian-American woman. "Of course that was another killer," he said. "I know, because the MO is different. But the cops probably think it's the same guy. They couldn't find their dicks in the dark with two hands."

* * *

After dinner Tim Ogle arrived and George left. She was grateful that he made himself scarce at such times, but it was plain that Tim was still unhappy about the living arrangements. They argued in her bedroom till dawn. "I keep kicking him out and Jenny keeps bringing him back," she told her boyfriend. "Or he comes in through the garage door or the loft or my bedroom window. He doesn't care about locks. He has three different ways of getting in."

Tim was still grumbling when he left for work in the morning. Bobbie walked him to the front door and kissed him good-bye, then looked up and saw George smirking in the loft. She got the impression that he was challenging her to dump Tim. In your dreams, she said to herself.

An hour later Tim phoned. "I'm sorry," he said, "but I don't think this thing is working." He sounded upset. "I can't go on like this."

"Please," Bobbie begged him, "give me another chance. I promise. I'll get rid of him." When he hung up, she was on the verge of hysteria.

I had to go in and open the store. I was out of control. I started screaming at the top of my lungs, throwing things, swearing. It was awful.

Jenny ran into my bedroom and tried to console me. Sara and Suzy came in. Then George stuck his nose in the door.

Suzy went off. She said, "George, this is none of your goddamn business! Just stay outside!"

George grabbed her wrist and told her she was overreacting. She said, "You're stupid!" and slammed the door on him.

My roommates wound up screaming at each other and fighting about *my* problem, and I just couldn't take it. I yelled, "Will you all please *shut up*?"

I ran into the bathroom and sat on the floor. Jenny tried to calm me down. I had twenty minutes to get to Winters Formal Wear, and I was a wreck.

As soon as I opened the store, I called George. I said, "Get your clothes, get your stuff, and get out! I want you *gone*! I'm off work at six o'clock and you better be out by the time I get there or I'm calling the police."

He said, 'Hey, lighten up, hon! Why didn't you say that a long time ago?''

I said, ''I did. *About twelve times!*''

When I got home that night, he was gone. The next I heard, he was staying at the Motel 6 in Totem Lake, near Kirkland. I wondered why he hadn't just gone back to his folks on Mercer Island.

I hated myself for it, but I began missing him right away.

A FEW EVENINGS later Steve Crandall, the youthful student of standup comedy, was getting off a bus near the Crossroads Mall when he spotted someone he'd been trying to avoid. The shortchange artist George Russell came rushing over as though he had important matters to discuss.

I seen him and he's like, ''Hey, what's going on? Long time no see. What you been up to?'' And I told him, ''I was up in Hawaii doing my thing and everything like that and working and everything.''

I asked him what he was doing and he really didn't give me an answer. We got to talking and I asked him again, ''Well, where are you working? What you doing?'' ya know, and he sort of like, he said, ''Well, hey, man, check this out,'' ya know, and he pulled out a diamond ring, and he's like, ''Thirty bucks.''

I spent a lot of time on the streets when I grew up, in a neighborhood where, ya know, people sold things left and right—phones, cable boxes, drugs, jewelry, coats, shoes and such. He set it on my pinkie finger like, ya know, about halfway, and I looked at it, and I remember it was like a gold band, kind of thin, had like one bigger stone in the middle and two smaller stones kind of offset on the sides. Looked like a cheesy little engagement ring. And I looked at it and he said, ''Thirty bucks,'' and I said, ''No, man, that's okay.''

And he said, ''Twenty bucks,'' and I said no, and he said, ''Come on, man. Twenty bucks.'' I had money in my pocket, but I said, ''I ain't got the money on me right now. Let me take it, I'll pay you back.''

That was kind of a way to get ridda him, kinda like you let him know I really had no money, ya know, and, umm, so that was the last I saw of him. Never asked for a phone number, never had a phone number of his, never called him, he never called me. That was the extent of our brief acquaintance—not a friend, just someone I knew, someone I seen once or twice and that was about it.

WITH THE LABOR Day weekend only a few days away, two months had passed since the Pohlreich murder, and Marvin Skeen had finally reached the bottom of his in-box. He'd checked out a long list of Damons and still hadn't found the one who'd been seeing Mary Ann Pohlreich before her death. His protégé and friend Dale Foote had just as little to show for three weeks of footslogging on the Beethe murder. Neither investigator could dispute the headline in the Bellevue *Journal American*: POLICE LACK MOTIVE, SUSPECT IN WOMAN'S SLAYING. TV and radio stations were trumpeting the lack of progress. In the full glare of publicity, the three-man persons crimes unit of the Bellevue PD was falling on its face.

In desperation, Skeen reached out with a lengthy teletype message to "Nationwide Law Enforcement Agencies." In it, he described the murders in all their necrophilic horror and added, "These two cases have some striking similarities but no positive link has been established between them."

The leads that arrived didn't appear to be worth the price of an out-of-town trip, especially since the detective division had already overspent its budget. Skeen didn't know where to turn.

Then he got a break, or so it appeared. One of Damon Stoddard's acquaintances in nearby Redmond, home of the software giant Microsoft, recognized him from a composite picture in a newspaper and called 911.

Skeen talked to the twenty-two-year-old Stoddard in the

Bellevue police station. The suspect looked at the composite and commented, "That's sure as hell me." Skeen felt a letdown. Killers weren't usually so cooperative.

Damon told Skeen that he'd met Mary Ann at Parker's nightclub in Seattle, as the dead woman's roommate had recalled, and later ran into her at Papagayo's Cantina and Pier 70 on nights when her favorite rock group, Boy Toy, was playing. They shared a few hours but never had a date. Stoddard claimed that Mary Ann pestered him with phone calls and called him an asshole. Since he hadn't felt attracted to her, he wasn't concerned when she dropped from sight. He'd heard nothing about her murder and appeared shocked.

Skeen quickly realized that he had the right Damon but the wrong suspect. He arranged for the young man to provide hair and saliva samples and added him to the list of the innocent.

O N THAT SAME Thursday night, August 30, an excited group convened in George Russell's motel room and began drinking and toking and laying plans for a big Labor Day weekend trip to Vancouver, British Columbia, starting the next morning. The trip was George's idea, and he was underwriting expenses. He explained that he wanted a fling with his good friends before leaving for a job in San Diego; he called it "our last bash of the summer." He invited the condo girls and two young women he'd recently met at Denny's Overlake and told them to bring their boyfriends and their cars, since he lacked wheels of his own. He assured the eighteen-year-olds that they could drink legally in Vancouver bars. When someone inquired about his own social plans, he said he intended to find himself a prostitute: "Those Canadian hookers are clean. They get AIDS tests and it's legal and they're just perfect." None of his friends were surprised. George constantly put down monogamous relationships and marriage, but he'd never seemed prejudiced against sex.

Bobbie DeGroot had to work over the holiday weekend, but she couldn't resist the motel party along with five or six others. She was the only condo roommate present: Jenny Graves was at a wedding, Sara Amundson planned to join the group in the morning, and Suzy Jetley, George's constant detractor, had been left off the guest list.

A few minutes after 10 P.M. George left the smoky motel room and returned a short time later with wine coolers and snacks from the nearby Larry's Market. The group drank and talked and watched TV till after midnight, when George and Bobbie reverted to an old habit and began exchanging hugs and kisses on one of the double beds.

As usual, George broke off the interlude. He jumped up and said, "I've got to meet somebody." He gave the impression that he was going on a stakeout and donned his working outfit: dark slacks, dark blue baseball cap, and a navy-blue Interlake Saints sweatshirt that was on permanent loan from Jenny Graves. Worn inside out, it was solid dark. He also took his pocket flashlight with the narrow beam, another part of his usual nighttime gear.

Around 3:30 A.M., when most of the partygoers were sleeping or nodding off, George slipped out the door.

LIEUTENANT BOB HAYS, public information officer for the Bellevue Fire Department, awoke at his home shortly after 5 A.M., donned a bicycle suit for his usual thirteen-mile ride with his wife Patricia, and put out their dog, Demitasse. He'd barely shut the door when the black sheltie-cocker burst into a rare defense mode, an uninterrupted spasm of barks so sharp and forceful that, as Hays explained later, "you wait to see if she'll pass out or quit first."

He stepped onto the deck and noticed that Demitasse was squared off toward the backyard. It was dark except for a dull glow from the street. He peered downhill past some small ponds and made out the silhouette of a man who was holding something light in color—a shirt, a bag, or perhaps a pillowcase.

Hays yelled and the man ran. By the time the fireman reached the bottom of his deck steps, no one was in sight. As he sprinted across his big yard, he thought he heard something thud against his back fence. It appeared that the prowler had stepped on a truck tire and vaulted into a neighbor's bean patch. Hays heard a brushing sound and saw a dark shadow, insubstantial, with the merest suggestion of a light patch in the middle. The apparition faded in the darkness.

Still in his sweatpants and untied tennis shoes, the fire lieutenant ran inside and dialed 911. A patrol officer from the King County Police Department arrived at 5:43, probed the backyard shadows with her six-cell flashlight, and left at 6:01, promising to file a report. It was clear that the intruder had been frightened off before he could make entry.

Hays was pleased to see that his basement tenant, Andrea "Randi" Levine, an attractive auburn-haired woman with many admirers, was apparently undisturbed by the commotion. In his role as landlord and Mr. Fixit, Hays had reconnected her TV the night before; she'd accidentally knocked the plug loose while rearranging heavy furniture. He figured she was sleeping in or perhaps had gone away for the Labor Day weekend. Her '71 Datsun pickup was parked in front of the house, but she could have left with someone else.

Later in the morning he knocked on her door to tell her about the prowler. When there was no answer, he let himself into the apartment. He checked the purse on the kitchen counter and noticed that her keys were gone. He wasn't worried. Randi was an independent, resourceful woman.

The backyard chase was the latest in a series of unsettling incidents in this relatively new Kingsgate area, a middle-class suburban neighborhood less than a mile through the woods from the Totem Lake Motel 6 and a short walk from Mindy Charley's apartment. There'd been burglaries and prowlings and a high level of suspicion and anger. Randi Levine, who lived with two cats, had taken to sleeping with a baseball bat after complaining to friends that someone was stealing her mementos and money.

A few days before this latest prowling she'd phoned Hays predawn and asked, "Bob, were you just outside my bedroom window?"

"No," said the sleepy firefighter.

"Somebody was there. Demitasse was barking at him." Randi said she was too frightened to get out of bed and call police.

Hays had dressed quickly and looked around, but there was no one in sight. A neighbor reported later that she thought she'd heard two males talking outside Randi's sliding door.

Hays had discussed the problem with his uneasy tenant and promised that he and Patricia would keep their door unlocked at night so Randi could run upstairs for help. She'd been nervous enough about the one-bedroom apartment ever since learning that Bob's mother had died there, and when the Hayses were away on vacation, she sometimes called neighbors and complained about noises in the night.

Apart from her skittishness, Randi Levine had always come across to Bob and Patty as a normal young woman. She was twenty-four, hardworking, responsible, but with an unfortunate tendency to select her boyfriends for looks. Now and then they heard her talking loudly in the apartment below and got the impression she was berating someone on the phone. She'd recently told Patty that she was trying to become less involved with men. It had been four or five months since the Hayses had seen a male enter or leave her apartment. Whatever her sex life, Randi Levine was definitely not promiscuous.

ABOUT 6:30 ON Friday morning, an hour or so after the prowling incident at nearby Kingsgate, George Russell returned to his room at Motel 6 with takeout breakfasts for his friends. Four hours later he checked out, and everyone piled into Damien Middleton's green Volvo station wagon for the drive up Interstate 5.

George paid in advance for a double room at the Vancouver TraveLodge. For most of the revelers, the minivacation passed in a blur. Some ate Chinese food, checked out the bright lights of Robsonstrasse and strolled through Stanley Park, and others sipped drinks in the room and zoned out on TV. The gracious host had laid in a stock of bottled beverages before hitting the streets and connecting with twin prostitutes, introducing one of them to his companions before taking her to dinner. Michelle was eighteen at most, with long blond hair and brown roots. She wore a miniskirt, halter and jacket, and George treated her like a celebrity.

At 2 A.M. he climbed to a nightclub roof and deflated a plastic beer bottle that was part of an advertisement. He offered it to Damien for his college dorm room.

None of the companions could remember seeing their friend and guru in better spirits. He'd always seemed happiest around people half his age. On the streets of Vancouver he shared some of his insights into human behavior. Paul Reid, one of the entourage, recalled, "There's a couple walking towards us and we'd look at them and we'd see how synchronized their gait was in walking, and George would say, 'Well, if they are synchronized they're agreeing with each other. If they start to break their sync, then the eye contact is also broken. . . .' And he started talking about, 'Well, you can also tell people's moods by how they smoke their cigarettes and how they flick the ashes or how they put them out. If they put them out and grind them in, that means they're irritated or something.' "

George explained the subtle signals of prostitution and then took Damien Middleton on a field trip to the cobblestoned streets of Gastown, a vintage area dedicated to food, drink, nightlife, and the extraction of cash from tourists.

"Every little mannerism that they would do would signify a different thing," the eighteen-year-old Middleton recalled, "and it was really weird. Like we were walking down the street . . . and he'd say, 'Now watch this, this girl's gonna flip her hair,' and she would. And then a car would stop and he'd say, 'Now watch. She's gonna cross her legs,' and she would. Then somebody would get out of the car and George would go, 'Now watch this. She's gonna bend down to the car window,' and she would. And he said that the mannerisms up there were different than they were down in the States."

The tired travelers returned to Bellevue early Sunday evening. Dropped off at the condo, George jerked open the garage door and carried his gear inside. Jenny and Bobbie gave him big hugs while Suzy Jetley climbed to the loft to avoid the welcoming ceremonies. Lately she'd been finding her unwanted roommate harder than ever to take.

All summer long he'd been jabbering about the murders, giving the impression he had the inside track. Whenever he walked in the house, he'd start in again, laying out the newspaper articles and talking about the stupid cops. He'd worked out some kind of anagram with the victims' initials, made a connection between these killings and some killings in California, or maybe with the Bundy killings—I'm not sure. I heard him explaining, but it sounded like his typical bullshit. He still dropped big hints about Damien. *Our* Damien! He would borrow Damien's long trench coat and wear it for days and then hint that Damien was involved in the killings.

He showed us pictures of the dead women that he'd cut out of the papers, and he said, "Listen to me, guys. One man killed 'em both."

He had another major theme: that the dead girls were skanky sluts. They used men, and he had no sympathy for whores like that. He said they dumped men and deserved what they got.

He said that his girlfriend Mindy once brought home a man when she and George were living together. He spoke poorly of her and said she'd tried to beat him up. He said whenever they'd get in a fight she'd dress up fit to kill and prowl the nightclubs to make him jealous. I wondered if that was what made him so angry at women. It had to be something.

AT 11:23 ON the morning of the next day, Monday, September 3, a man called 911. He sounded excited. As he spoke, a whimpering female voice could be heard in the background.

What are you reporting?
Umm . . . fatality.
A what?
Murder.
A murder?
I believe so. We've got a tenant in our basement and I just found her body.
Okay, let me transfer you over to the medics. Just a moment . . .

The female voice in the background broke into sobs as the medics' operator came on the line:

Call?
Yeah. This is Bob Hays, Bellevue Fire Department.
Yeah. Hi, Bob.
Hi. I've got a fatality in my basement.
Okay. What's the address there?
13315 122nd Place N.E., Kirkland.
Okay, Bob, and what type of . . .
Well, it's our renter, and it appears she's been dead for a few days.
Do you think natural?

No. Uh, it doesn't look that way . . .

Okay, we'll be right on over.

Okay. Umm, you can save the lights and siren 'cause there's nothing to do.

Bob Hays had spent the weekend installing motion detector lights, and he'd peeked into Randi Levine's basement apartment several times, but nothing appeared to be disturbed. On Monday morning Patty Hays noticed that one of Randi's cats was acting hungry. She couldn't find the other. Mrs. Hays was surprised to see that no food or water had been left out for Sambo and Missy.

Then she picked up an odor. Her first impression was that a cat had hemorrhaged or died. She entered Randi's bedroom to check. The TV was on. She noticed disheveled bedding and a bloodstained pillow on the floor. She pulled the sheet back six or eight inches and saw long auburn hair and a bare shoulder. She screamed and ran outside.

At first all she could say was "Randi, Randi . . ." Then she said, "Come!" and led Bob to the bedroom door. When he saw what had been done to the body, he grabbed his hysterical wife and called 911 from the garage phone.

Detective Larry J. Petersen of the King County Police Department arrived at 1 P.M. He was another old pro, seventeen years a cop, quiet and solid, with a radio announcer's resonant voice, a trial lawyer's memory, and an engineer's tendency to work a case in a straight line. Rick Buckland, the Seattle PD supersleuth who'd crossed paths with George Russell five months earlier, had once said of Petersen, "If I die under mysterious circumstances, Larry's the one I'd want on the case."

Petersen was too busy to keep score, but he'd worked some seventy murders as lead investigator and assisted on three hundred more. At fifty-two he was approaching retirement. An astute observer said of him, "Larry clears his cases, but he also covers his ass. He's a go-to-work lunch pail type of guy—open collar, short-sleeve shirts. He's also a great interviewer who can outcon the worst sociopath."

In retrospect, the biggest break of Petersen's career was the fact that he'd missed out on the hunt for the Green River killer. He'd been on vacation the week the famous case broke. Eight years later, despite the creation of a task force and tens of thousands of investigative man-hours, the body count stood at forty-nine. The case had stained reputations, frustrated good cops, helped burn out detectives, and remained unsolved. Through great good luck, Petersen never became involved.

At the Levine death scene a patrol sergeant named Carol Cummings reported that the house was secured and no one had been permitted to disturb the body. Petersen went into the small bedroom and felt a fetid rush of déjà vu. Seven years earlier he'd worked the case of a murder victim with two fresh trout around her neck, ground sausage on her chest, and a wine bottle cupped in her hands. In his twelve years as a major crimes detective, it was the only posed corpse he'd seen.

This posing was even more startling. Under a white comforter with reddish gray stripes, the naked body of a small-breasted, firmly built woman was spread-eagled diagonally across the four-poster bed, heels about three feet apart. One arm rested on a blue pillow. Her hairdo looked recent; her long nails were neatly manicured; her toenails bore an iridescent purplish polish. Part of her brain seeped out. Her mouth was stuffed with a white plastic vibrator. Under her left forearm was a hardbound copy of *More Joy of Sex: A Lovemaking Companion to the Joy of Sex.*

Her body had been violated from her scalp to the soles of her feet with small, neat stab wounds, some not much deeper than nicks. To Petersen's experienced eye, they appeared to have been made after death in a practice known as piquerism, an uncommon necrophilic perversion. It appeared that the assailant might have begun a bloody game of tic-tac-toe on the right breast. Some of the wounds were arranged in straight lines, some in indistinct patterns. The rough shape of a hand was outlined by eighteen or twenty cuts on the woman's thigh just below the pubic area. There was a circular "piquer" on the other thigh.

Petersen looked around the room and saw an aluminum baseball bat on the floor between the bed and a window. It appeared unstained. A pair of panty hose lay bunched up on the floor. A clock radio and a copy of Stephen King's *Misery* rested on a small chest next to the bed. A lacquered Oriental fan with a wild-horse motif covered four feet of wall. A man's hat hung on a peg in one corner, a baseball cap in the other. The wallpaper depicted a series of intertwined mimosa leaves. Spots of blood were visible in arcs, as though sprayed in a fine mist. Petersen realized that the blood must have spun off the murder weapon as it was jerked up and down.

Spots on the floor resembled dried semen. Petersen ordered a swatch cut out and frozen, along with the panty hose. His fellow King County detective Wayne Slater poked holes in a small cardboard box and strung several wires to make a cradle. Petersen lifted the vibrator with forceps and suspended it inside. The same laborious process was repeated with the baseball bat. The evidence was rushed to the crime lab in Seattle.

The detectives found several handwritten notes and perused them for leads. Someone had written, "I love you Randi; only you (ha)(not funny). . . . This looks like a suicide note. It's not. But it is pitiful. . . . P.S., I cried!" The detective ordered the note checked for fingerprints; sometimes the lovelorn became stalkers.

They found an unmailed letter to "Brent." Randi had written, "Surprised? Well, I guess we did it this time, didn't we? I really can't believe all that has happened between us, can you? I loved you so much at one time. I really don't know what happened. Maybe if we had slept together it might have helped. . . ."

It appeared that Randi had been under strain. Brent had sent her a funny card and scribbled, "Hey baby I thought you might enjoy a good laugh in the middle of all your stress."

The victim's datebook was a little out of date:

July 5	Kathleen coming over! Clean up house!!
July 9	Movie w/Wade
July 10	Concert w/Ray
July 13	Rehearsal & dinner
Aug 27	Lunch w/Sam
Aug 28	Lunch w/Paul

Petersen sighed. Who was Kathleen? Who were Wade, Ray, Sam, Paul? Each would have to be located and interviewed. He shot several rolls of 35-mm photographs, mostly of the body, then ordered the scene videotaped. An evidence technician said it appeared that the killer had wiped down the room or worn gloves, another bad augury for the investigation. It was easier to deal with amateurs.

The detective bagged the victim's hands and checked out the rest of the apartment. A dry towel hung on a bathroom rack. A few dirty dishes were stacked up, but otherwise the kitchen gleamed. There were no table knives, bread knives, paring knives, utility knives, butcher knives—no knives of any type. It looked as though the killer had known something about evidence. If he'd used a knife from the kitchen in his frenzy of piquerism, the remaining pieces in the set could be used to identify or trace the weapon. By taking every knife, he'd improved his odds. Petersen realized that he was up against a formidable opponent.

He rewound the victim's telephone recording machine for clues to the date and time of the murder. There were increasingly anxious messages from Business Service Center, where Randi worked as a secretary. A man named Brent, presumably the one in her unmailed letter, phoned about "the camping trip." Another male voice asked, "Why aren't you home yet?" A female said, "We're worried aboutcha." A man asked, "Are you screening your calls?" and Mel said, "Yo, female, please call. I'm worried and so is everyone else. We don't know where you are. . . . Have a great weekend."

A final message from Business Service Center helped firm up the date of the killing. "It's about four o'clock Friday afternoon," a woman's voice said, "and we're getting really concerned about you. Could you please call somebody? . . ." Then the tape ran out. So Randi Levine had died before Friday afternoon.

An interview with Patty and Bob Hays confirmed that the fire lieutenant had seen an intruder's silhouette. Apparently he'd entered the apartment through the garage—it was usually propped open for the cats—and slipped away in the predawn blackness after completing his stabbing agenda.

The lawmen faced an imposing assignment—canvassing for suspects, interviewing persons of interest like Brent and Mel and other male friends, fine-combing the body and the apartment for trace evidence, reconstructing the victim's final days and hours—but at least they had a starting point. In police parlance, Bob Hays's shadowy intruder "looked good for it." Who was he? Petersen theorized that he might have been someone close to Randi Levine, perhaps a past or present lover or someone she'd spurned. To the detective, the crime showed extraordinary rage.

"We're not dealing with somebody who's just killing for the hell of it," the lead investigator told a colleague. "He's venting a frustration. Find the frustration, find the killer." The tested formula had worked for him before.

Petersen was in his King County police office at sunup the next day, "working on paper," when he took a call from Leslie S. Levine of Merritt Island, Florida. Randi's father sounded both outraged and crushed. A retired Boeing executive, he dictated names, addresses and phone numbers of his only daughter's friends and said he was en route to Seattle.

He named Kathleen Del Mar as Randi's best friend and told the detective how to reach her in the rustic town of North Bend, twenty miles east in the Cascades foothills. Petersen phoned and soon found out where the copy of *More Joy of Sex* had come from. Kathleen had given it to Randi as a joke a year earlier. The detective asked her to meet him at the murder house to go through the victim's effects. Sometimes friends made connections that others missed.

After Petersen hung up he rushed to the medical examiner's office and went over the body with black light and tweezers, just as Skeen, Hansen and Foote had scavenged the bodies of Mary Ann Pohlreich and Carol Beethe. At the formal autopsy, there were few surprises. Andrea Levine had been the victim of a "blitz" attack, with death caused by "blunt impact injuries to the head [and] fractures of vault and base of skull. . . ." Her back bore three long scratches, apparently made with a knife or a fingernail. There were three substantial stab wounds in the anal area and a total of 231 piquer wounds on the body, including seven in the sole of the right foot and nine in the left.

Petersen and his partner Wayne Slater tried to reconstruct the dead woman's life and final hours. Interviewing Kathleen Del Mar and other close friends, they learned that she'd been an Air Force "brat," five-five, weighed 132 pounds, with brown eyes and long coppery hair. The friends described her as "a class act," a vibrant young woman who enjoyed the outdoors, old Jeeps, parties, beer, show horses and the Seattle Mariners baseball team. She'd joked that "horses are the only people I can trust." She was neat, tomboyish, quiet, and sometimes a little unsure of herself, but after a few drinks she could be mildly flirtatious. Her key chain carried a metal tag with the inapt description "Bitch on wheels." She was a high school drop-out and was studying for her GED. She got a kick out of sending funny cards to friends: "Attention employees: due to the AIDS epidemic, ass-kissing will be temporarily discontinued. . . ." "When I woke up this morning, I had one nerve left, and now you're getting on it. . . ." One of her favorite cards showed a fat man exposing his backside on a bench and was captioned, "Say no to crack."

Lately she'd complained to friends that someone had been prowling her place at night. The evening before her death she'd met her on-again boyfriend, Brent Carlson, at a restaurant, and discussed going camping in the nearby San Juan Islands over the weekend. They'd decided to put off a decision till the next day. She'd driven home alone just after 10 P.M. and wasn't seen again till Patty Hays stumbled on her body four days later.

KATHLEEN DEL MAR, an animated young secretary, had known the Levines when they lived in the Seattle suburb of Kirkland, before Les retired and moved his family four thousand miles in search of the sun. The twenty-three-year-old Kathleen was as outraged as the blood relatives and eager to help.

She expected to be upset by the mandatory visit to the murder room, maybe even traumatized, but someone had to select the burial clothes. Besides, Detective Petersen had said he needed her expertise at the crime scene. It never occurred to her to say no. She and Randi were tight. Friends said if you knew one, you knew the other. They'd once been roommates, so close that they celebrated their birthdays together.

My mother and fiancé drove to the house with me, but the cops made me go inside by myself to minimize contamination. It was so unreal. Larry Petersen was nice, but the whole thing pissed me off. Fingerprint stuff—black powder, silver powder—was smeared over everything, even on the dishes in the sink.

The cops couldn't handle Randi's cats. We arranged that my mother would take them home. Oh, it freaked me out, comforting Missy and Sambo—"You poor cats. You know what happened. You've been locked in here with her for three days"—and looking into their eyes and knowing that they knew, and they were just terrified. Randi only had Missy for a year, but she'd had Sambo for seven. And he's a one-person cat. She called him Sweet Pea.

I'd asked the cops to make sure everything was covered in the bedroom, but they didn't. That really pissed me off, because I figured I'd been her best friend for almost nine years—and those guys don't think to cover up her blood?

At the last minute they covered her bed with her big white robe. There were pieces of carpet cut out, and Randi had this big fan with wild horses that I'd given her, and it was spattered with blood.

I didn't know what to do about her burial clothes. I mean, I picked out her favorite dress, the one she looked the most beautiful in, and I'm like, Well, what do you do for someone that's being buried? Do you pick out a bra and panties? I mean, I didn't *know*.

So I picked out everything—matching shoes, even earrings. It felt weird going into her negligee drawer. I was trying not to look at her bed and stuff. I was pretty much numb at this point. And then Larry Petersen wanted me to go through her jewelry, and that's when I said, "Well, her amethyst ring is missing." And right then he called the coroner to find out if an amethyst ring had been found on her fingers, and they said no.

I told 'em Randi would *never* have given that ring away. It was like a part of her. If it was gone, then somebody's ripped it off her finger. I only hoped they caught the son of a bitch.

ON WEDNESDAY, WHILE the body of Andrea Levine was being prepared for burial, the apartment of George Russell's old dancing partner Tami Grace received an unwanted visitor.

I was at a baby shower, but my two roommates were home when George showed up at the window. Nicole already felt funny about him. I'd pointed him out a few weeks earlier at Denny's, and she took one look and said, "I don't like that man. He's bad. There's something seriously wrong with him."

We'd been living in Villa 156 since April, but we had no inkling he'd moved in with those four young girls. Actually, we were in 656 and they were in 664; that's how close we were. I'd seen him on the street a few times and ducked. I had bad vibes about what he might do.

An hour or so before I got home from the baby shower, Nicole looked up and saw George peering through the window. He banged on the front door and then on the back. Then he tried three windows. By the time he reached the garage door, Nicole and Laurie decided this wasn't funny anymore and called Nine-one-one. The cops came, but he was gone.

When I got home I freaked. I remembered how George beat up Mindy, and I called the Bellevue cops. They sent a detective over and he asked, "Why would Mr. Russell want to get in here?"

I said, "I don't know. He's playing a game with me. I don't know how to handle it. He claims to be a nark."

The detective made a phone call, then told us, "Narcotics never heard of him."

I mentioned the gym bag George always carried, and the scanner, and he made some notes.

Later I went to the Black Angus, and Mindy was standing by Mark's DJ booth, looking over the dance floor. She had a copy of the Bellevue *Journal American*'s story: ANOTHER EASTSIDE WOMAN SLAIN. It had a King County police spokesman saying that the three murders weren't connected.

I said, "Mindy, you won't believe this! George tried to get into my house."

She goes, "You're kidding!"

"I wish."

She was, "I wouldn't doubt that George is the killer."

"I wouldn't either," I said.

"It makes sense. He hangs out at Papagayo's and he hates the Black Angus. He's conniving enough to leave a body there, ruin business."

I told Mindy that I'd heard that George once tried to barge into Randi Levine's house and really pissed her off.

Mindy put her hand over her mouth. "Oh, my God!" she said. "You don't suppose he's killing women he's had a problem with? *Do you?*"

I was so scared I went straight home and locked my doors.

LATER THAT NIGHT a twenty-one-year-old woman with the euphonious name of Dacia Jubinville dropped into Denny's Overlake, hoping she would run into her new friend George Russell. The mother of two small children, she was tall, slender, with light brown hair. She was described by a friend as "composed, very within herself, maybe a little standoffish."

She'd met George at the Black Angus, where he seemed involved in the security operation. He'd told her, "I just help people." She'd seen him peel off a hundred-dollar bill for a stranger in need. He didn't discuss his private life, and Dacia wasn't the type to pry. As far as she was concerned, he was a great date—until the Labor Day weekend.

He'd stood her up without as much as a phone call. It was so unlike him. She'd wondered if he had a sudden change of plans—a family emergency, an accident. He usually ran on time.

When he finally strolled into Denny's, he acted pleased to see her. He explained that he'd had to go to Canada over the weekend. Then he smiled and handed her a ladies' ring. "With my apologies, hon," he said. The ring was gold with an oval amethyst. He said he'd picked it up on his trip. The gift didn't look expensive, but Dacia appreciated the gesture.

He suggested that they go out the next night, in her car, as always. She agreed to meet him at Denny's.

ON THE THIRD morning after the finding of the Levine body, Detective Marv Skeen was sitting in his cubicle and wondering where to turn. An interdepartmental strategy session on linkage was set for later in the day, and he didn't look forward to it. He'd always made it a habit to avoid such talkathons, and, besides, he had nothing new to report.

He looked down the narrow corridor and saw Dale Foote looking surprisingly alert for someone who wasn't getting much sleep. Skeen still agreed with his protégé and others that Tom Jones was the Beethe murderer, but the evidence was weak, and Jones had been acting more and more like an aggrieved, innocent man. The conscientious Foote was churning out pages of neat reports on his PC and running down leads and taking it as a personal insult that he hadn't yet solved the case. Lately he and Skeen had been thinking about the fire lieutenant Bob Hays. Why had he paid so much attention to Andrea Levine's apartment over the Labor Day weekend? Was the story about the 5 A.M. prowler a fiction to mislead police? It was just another *WAG*—wild-ass guess.

Skeen's phone rang at 8:30 A.M., and he was pleased to hear Rick Buckland's voice. He knew of the Seattle detective's exploits and considered himself lucky to have worked several cases with him.

Buckland said, "Hey, Marv, I might have something for you to look at. A guy named George Walterfield Russell Junior was posing as a cop over here. He had a gun that was stolen ten blocks from Andrea Levine's apartment. We think he was doing cat burglaries in her neighborhood. Used to live nearby with a girl named Mindy. I talked to her. He beat her up and acted squirrelly."

Skeen's instinct was to discount such tips. On hot murder cases, every cop had a favorite suspect and wanted to solve the case and get the promotion. But Buckland was different. He didn't seem to have an ego, and he never called with half-ass ideas. He worked hard and had a brain like a computer. That was what the Seattle PD had assigned him to do for a living: *intelligence.*

On the other hand, Skeen was still convinced of the Tom Jones connection. He tried to remember if he'd ever talked to a George Russell. Oh, yeah, he said to himself, he's the wanna-be that hangs out at Papagayo's. Typical petty thief. Came up with a woman's phone number that turned out to be bad.

"Rick," Skeen said, "why don't you get in touch with Larry Petersen? He's got the Levine case. And come to our strategy meeting today. It's at the Maple Valley precinct at one o'clock."

Buckland said it was off his turf, but he'd be there.

So WERE TWENTY other investigators from eight police jurisdictions, including the state attorney general's office. The ramrod was Captain T. Michael Nault, head of the Major Investigations Section of the King County Police, another cerebral cop, one of the few who'd survived the Green River investigation with enhanced reputations. Nault had become nationally respected as an expert on serial murder and lectured at the FBI Academy in Quantico, Virginia.

The suburban substation was packed on this Thursday, September 6, and every agency wanted to discuss its own unsolved cases. Seattle had an uncaught ax murderer and a burglar who repeatedly used a felt-tip pen to write, "The killer is back." Rural Snohomish County, just to the north, had a fresh strangulation and a body that was found along a highway. Nearby Redmond, home of Microsoft, had a missing woman whose car had been abandoned in Seattle. Tacoma had another round of prostitute slayings, a recurring Northwest problem since Green River days. Bellevue had Pohlreich and Beethe, and King County had Levine. It took awhile to shake out the extraneous cases and get down to the central subject: the Eastside murders and whether they were connected.

Rick Buckland already suspected that the common thread was George Russell.

Captain Nault advised us that the press was waiting outside, very interested, wanted to make this a serial murder case. He said the last thing we needed was the media jumping up and down over a serial murderer when there's no positive evidence one way or the other. He didn't say that these murders weren't connected; he simply said we shouldn't be giving that impression in public. He didn't want the investigation bogged down in false leads and hysteria.

Everybody agreed not to tag the guy "The Eastside Killer" or "The Crossroads Killer." Names like that scare people, and then the case gets larger than life and the killer becomes a hero in his own mind, and maybe he goes out and kills more.

I stood up and asked if there'd been any car prowls in the murder neighborhoods by a suspected black male. And had anybody reported nighttime burglaries while the people were in the house? Some of the guys looked at me like I was crazy. They didn't know what I'd learned about Russell's habits four months ago.

Somebody said they'd had a ton of car prowls.

Somebody else said, "Around the time of the Beethe killing, an older couple woke up with a black male in their home."

I asked if the intruder used a little flashlight. The answer was yes. I said to myself, *Hello, George.* After that I just listened.

The Bellevue people were saying that Levine and Pohlreich might have been killed by the same guy, but they were solid that Tom Jones did Beethe.

After the meeting I talked with a few of the others. I said Jones looked unlikely to me. These killings were off the wall. In crimes like these, you look at *everybody*. Let's say Jones was madder'n hell at Carol, fully intended to do away with her. Well, he knew the house well; he'd *lived* there. Why does he bring in the flashlight? And is he gonna do all this shit with the kids there? Kids who know him well?

I said it had to be a nut, somebody like Russell. I said, Look at his lifestyle: living with teenagers, hiding stuff in the woods, sleeping all day and creeping all night, pistol-whipping, dropping tin, beating up women. Is this a logical suspect or what?

I argued that these were serial murders even if we couldn't say so to the press. I said, "Look at the similarities. The posing. The time spent with the bodies. Trying to hide the faces. Degradation. The age and type of victims. The type of places where they hung out. The method of killing."

I said, "Think of this mathematically. If you don't have a serial murderer, then you've got two or three different psychopaths working the same area at the same time. How many times do you see cases like this in ten years, let alone three of 'em in a few months?"

I suggested that somebody should interview Mindy Charley; then they'd get a real feel for George—his violence, his weird habits.

I realized there was natural human ego involved, territorial pride, so I kept my head down and my hand out. The Bellevue guys agreed somebody should interview Russell and promised to bring him in.

I figured, Now we're on track.

W ITH THE BEST intentions, police spokesmen dutifully flimflammed the press. After covering the strategy session from the hallway, reporter Christopher Jarvis quoted Nault in the Bellevue *Journal American:* "There's no way I can make a case to you that we probably have a serial killer."

Bellevue Lieutenant Mark Ericks was quoted to the effect that if a serial killer were in action, "We'd be saying that loud and clear."

Jarvis knew better. One day earlier the newspaper had run his story, EASTSIDE MURDERS LINKED?, strongly suggesting that a serial murderer was at work. He'd covered the cases from the beginning and saw the clear commonality, but he dutifully reported the deceptive remarks. It was his obligation as a journalist to quote his subjects accurately.

SEATTLE PATROL SERGEANT Doug Vandergiessen wasn't enthusiastic about taking business calls at home, but this one was a pleasant surprise. Detective Rick Buckland brought him up-to-date on George Russell, ending with the news that the man Vandergiessen had flagged for the intelligence unit had become a hot suspect in Bellevue's triple killings.

"It's hush-hush right now," Buckland warned.

Vandergiessen thought about all the tips he'd turned in through the years and how it was like dropping pebbles down a well. "Honey," he told his wife, "remember the day I didn't get home till eight in the morning? The guy with the gun? Well, it looks like he's a serial killer."

For a patrol cop, it was almost like winning the lottery.

SHORTLY AFTER THE Maple Valley meeting, Detective Mike Beckdolt, in his own words, "finally woke up from my sleep." Eleven weeks had passed since the crime prevention specialist and part-time security guard had watched George Russell escort a wobbly woman across Papagayo's parking lot. The incident had signified nothing at the time or later. Nor had he given any thought to the angry young man named Smitty who'd staggered around the parking lot looking for his truck.

> I was very removed from the murder cases, talking to kids about drugs and stuff, setting up sports events, making speeches—my usual job. Right after the Maple Valley meeting, Marv Skeen came up to me and said, "Hey, Mike, we're looking at an old friend of yours in the murders."

I asked who.

He said, "George Russell."

My whole brain lit up! I went, "Holy shit!" I tried to collect my thoughts.

"Marv," I said, "did you know George left Papagayo's that night with a woman?"

He said, "No."

"Yeah! In somebody's truck. He didn't bring it back at closing time. I helped the owner look for it."

"We need that truck," Marv said. "What was the guy's name?"

I couldn't remember. I said, "I don't know if I ever knew his name. Gimme some time."

I went into my office and thought and thought and finally wrote out a report. I still couldn't remember that name.

BY THE TIME of the Maple Valley meeting Bobbie De-Groot's romance with Tim Ogle had collapsed under the weight of George's refusal to stay away from Villa 156. She tried to convince herself that she didn't care, but it was a hard sell.

With Tim gone, the "undercover agent" was a bigger hit than ever around the condo. Suzy Jetley, the lapsing Mormon, still kept her distance, but Sara Amundson and Jenny Graves waited on the star boarder, made him treats, entertained him with skits. George would laugh and applaud with his fingertips as they opened with a few lines from the movie *Dirty Dancing*:

"Hey, Mickey?"

"Yes, Romeo. . . ."

In the mornings, when he came home from his police work and retired to the empty loft, the two eighteen-year-olds would climb halfway up the ladder and serenade him with The Spinners' bouncy hit from *American Graffiti*:

Good night, sweetheart. Well, it's time to go. . . .

Under the circumstances Bobbie wondered why she should even argue about whether he stayed or left. She would always love Tim, but since he'd chosen to end their romance, she allowed George a little hugging and kissing. She also tried going out with other men, but found them boring after Tim and George.

Before leaving the apartment with a nice guy named Brian, she confided that she wasn't comfortable being alone with another man while a killer was loose: "How do I know it's not him?"

George told her she had nothing to worry about. Too many people knew Brian's name and identity. "The killer's a lot smarter than that, hon."

He seemed so sure.

George informed his roommates that he had a date with Dacia Jubinville and left the condo wearing Damien Middleton's dark trench coat. Reconstructing the evening's events later, Dacia reported that they went dancing at Charlie's and she returned George to Villa 156 at a respectable hour. She said he hugged her and kissed her on the cheek like the gentleman he was.

An hour or so later Tamara Francis, the flashy blonde with the slantnose Porsche, was awakened in her apartment. She lived just down the hill from the murdered Randi Levine and had been suffering the same midnight terrors as her neighbors.

Someone was standing alongside her bed. She held her breath and heard shallow breathing. After a while the sound moved away.

She dialed 911 and stayed on the phone for thirty minutes till the emergency operator convinced her to turn on the lights and look around.

She found no signs of entry. Later she told friends that she was sure she'd had a visit from George Russell and that he'd prowled her place before. She didn't know what he was after; "I hardly know the guy." She'd seen him about ten times at Papagayo's, and he'd once invited her to join him in the parking lot for a drink of Rumple Minze, an invitation she'd laughed off. Her lover, an Asian businessman, provided her with four thousand dollars a month in spending money. She didn't need George Russell in her life, day *or* night.

THE NEXT EVENING Tami Grace was at work as a nanny when her roommate Nicole called and said excitedly, "Do you realize there's a serial killer loose and he killed those three women?"

Tami blurted, *"Huh?"*

"He's been targeting women in Eastside bars. I just heard it on TV."

Tami called the Bellevue police and asked for the officers who were handling the murders. A female voice said the detective division was closed for the weekend and took her name and phone number.

"Please," Tami begged. "Listen to me. I'm a regular at a Bellevue bar. Somebody tried to break into my house the other night. I live in the Crossroads area. I'm *scared.*"

The operator sounded calm; Tami got the impression she'd been hearing from many frightened women and had worked out a standard response. "Do *not* go back to that bar," the female voice said firmly. "I'll have the detectives call you."

Tami asked her to make it fast.

AT TWO O'CLOCK the following morning, Sunday, September 9, a sixteen-year-old girl named Nicole DeVita dropped in on friends at the sprawling Landmark Apartments. The complex, less than a mile northeast of Villa 156, had been the scene of a half dozen recent burglaries and the locus of several dozen others, plus so many prowlings that police had lost count. After an hour and a half of Nintendo and conversation, Nicole strolled back to her family's apartment in the same complex—and discovered she was locked out.

It was a quiet night, and she tried to wake up her sleeping brother Tony without disturbing the rest of the family. Her stage whispers only succeeded in annoying a neighbor. She threw pebbles, sticks, then rocks at her brother's open window on the second floor, but he didn't respond.

After nearly an hour she gave up on Tony and walked to the back of the apartment to arouse her parents. A black male emerged from the shadows and said, "Oh? Tony's your brother?" He gave the impression that he was a friend.

When Nicole explained that she was trying to get into her apartment, the man checked the front windows and confirmed that they were locked. She walked around the side and started to climb the privacy fence into the patio. Suddenly she was thrown to the ground. She looked up to see the man lifting a rock. A blow to the head knocked her flat. She yelled, "Stop it! *Stop it!*" He struck her several more times and then dragged her across the lawn, still screaming. Lights blinked on in her apartment. She heard the man grunting as she lost consciousness.

Ten hours later Nicole awoke in a Seattle hospital's intensive care unit with a depressed skull fracture, concussion, and deep scratches on her scalp, neck and hands. She learned that her father and a friend had chased the man off.

As she recovered from her trauma, she was able to provide an impressionistic description of her attacker. "Mixed black, not completely black," a police report quoted her. "Looked like he had a mix of possibly East Indian in him, late 20s in age, about 5-9, scrawny build (not bony, but skinny), had real frizzy approx. 2" long hair (that of a black but somewhat straightened out like an East Indian's and that looked odd), wearing baggy, very loose clothes in dark colors—baggy pants, and a windbreaker-type coat that was somewhat long in length."

A neighbor who'd caught a fleeting glimpse of the intruder described his hairdo as "a short Afro" and his coat as "flapping and heavy by the sound it made." Another had wondered why anyone would wear a trench coat on such a mild night.

It was Dale Foote's wedding anniversary, but he rushed to the scene. Marv Skeen soon joined him, and they set about collecting evidence and arranging still another neighborhood search and canvass. Whether or not Tom Jones had committed the Beethe murder, someone was bludgeoning the young women of the Eastside, leaving no clues, wiping down rooms, disposing of weapons, avoiding obvious mistakes. And he was either losing control or getting bolder—or both.

DETECTIVE RICK BUCKLAND couldn't wait to get back on George Russell's trail early Monday, even though the triple murders were out of the Seattle PD's jurisdiction. He still remembered how hard he'd tried to nail Russell for the concealed weapon and the pistol-whipping. This time there would be no silly legal loopholes. These crimes were aggravated murders, capital offenses, punishable by hanging or lethal injection. Every suspicion Buckland had entertained about the oily young criminal was being verified. But could he make a case?

I phoned a number I got from Mindy Charley. She'd mentioned a friend of George's named Tami Grace, worked up at the Samish Lodge at Snoqualmie.

Tami gave me an earful. She said George hung out at Papagayo's and Denny's Overlake. He was booted out of the Black Angus for calling a waitress a bitch. She thought the name was "Bridgette."

I was taking notes, but she talked so fast I could hardly keep up. She said George always had rings and bracelets and stuff and gave 'em to his friends. Liked to hang with seventeen-year-olds and younger. No permanent address. Carried a scanner, borrowed cars, carried a tote bag with clothes, coke vial, papers, things wrapped in foil. Long fingernails, very strong, kept booze stashed by McDonald's trash compactor, had a good friend named Smitty who hadn't been seen in a while.

The bad news came at the end. She said she'd heard that George was going to California.

I was sure we'd lost him again.

MICHAEL WEISENBURGH, NOW working as a clerk at Payless Drugs, pondered the ethics of the situation. He and Robby Bob Dzurick and Jeff Anderson had begun to suspect that their former squatter George was involved in Randi Levine's killing. The roommates missed their lovely redheaded friend and wanted her murder avenged, but they were reluctant to be tagged as informers.

At 5:30 P.M. on Tuesday, the day after Tami Grace was interviewed by Rick Buckland, "Georgia Mike" finally made his decision:

It was all those weird things about George that got me—the way him and his girlfriend sucked blood when they had sex, sick shit like that. Everything came together: his lifestyle, hanging out at Papagayo's, pushing himself on Randi at her house. I thought, Mo and Robby Bob introduced them, and that son of a bitch went over there without our permission, and then he killed her. I was sure of it, and I was plenty pissed off.

I asked the King County police operator to connect me with whoever was working on the Levine case and she gave me a detective named Wayne Slater. I told him I knew who killed Randi, but I said I couldn't give my name. I didn't have much Georgia accent left and I tried to sound like everybody else on Mercer Island—you know, "I'm just *enor*mously certain. . . ."

He seemed real interested about George. I told him that Randi suspected he stole fifty bucks from her purse not long before she was murdered. He asked me if I knew a guy named Georgia Mike.

I thought, Jeez, these guys did their homework. It made me

feel better about getting involved, and I said, "Yeah, I know him pretty well."

He said, "Do you know how to get ahold of him?"

"I can put you in touch with him real quick."

"How quick?"

"How about right now?"

I ended up telling him everything I knew.

AT ALMOST THE same hour Tami Grace was being interviewed by Detective Dennis Dingfield of the Bellevue PD, who explained that he'd been assigned to find George Russell for questioning.

The night before, Tami had suffered another nightmare about her former lambada partner. She kept asking herself, Why is George around my condo so much if he's not stalking me? The earlier contact with Detective Rick Buckland had only made her more fearful.

All of a sudden I've got cops swarming all over, wanting to know about George. In little ways, they were confirming that he was trying to kill me. Detective Buckland hinted that I was the link between George and some murders, and now Detective Dingfield is telling me that when George looked in that window and saw my blond roommate from the back, he must've thought it was me, and that's why he kept trying to get in the door and windows.

I asked, "Why on earth would George do a stupid thing like that?"

Dingfield said, "From what we know about him, he'd do it for the challenge. If he shows up again, call Nine-one-one."

I said, "That's what I did the last time. He intercepts radio calls on his scanner. You'll never catch him that way."

Detective Dingfield gave me his private phone number and told me to call him direct.

When he finally left, I was so scared I called Mike, and he and Robby Bob rushed over to protect me. They helped calm me down. But not much. . . .

THE NEXT NIGHT, Wednesday, September 12, George Russell and Bobbie DeGroot were back in the sexual trenches. It started in the usual way: too much schnapps, a little hugging and kissing, and a quick retreat by George at the first sign of heat.

"What *is* this?" Bobbie asked as he fled toward the small kitchen in his cool George Russell walk. "Why do you *do* this to me?"

George ignored her and opened the refrigerator. Bobbie walked to the doorway and continued her harangue. Jenny and one of her boyfriends had their ears cocked in the living room, along with young Sheryl Lynn Barthlow, a racetrack habitué who'd been hanging out with George lately. Bobbie was so enraged she didn't care if the whole world listened.

"Look, George," she said, "I want you to tell me what's going on." She knew the Rumple Minze was talking, but she couldn't stop. "Why do you make me feel so frustrated? You're really making me angry!"

He ignored her. She yelled louder, and for the first time in their three-month relationship he returned fire. She backed him into the corner and told him he was *not* leaving the kitchen till he gave her some answers— "because I . . . *deserve* it!"

The rhubarb continued till George lifted his hands in front of his face and shouted, "*No more!*" He turned to Sheryl Barthlow and said, "C'mon, hon, let's take your car and go over to Denny's."

They disappeared out the front door arm in arm.

FOUR DOORS AWAY, in Unit 656, Tami Grace was still trying to calm her nerves.

I'd read an article in the Seattle *Times*, 3 MURDERS WORRY THE EASTSIDE. It advised women to "use common sense in dealing with strangers." Good advice, but what about dealing with a guy that tries to break in your place *and the cops already suspect him of murder?*

Around eleven o'clock I was alone when somebody knocked on my bedroom window. It was insistent—dum da dum dum, dum da dum *dum*. I knew our house noises and this was *not* a cat or a raccoon or a tree branch.

At first I thought, One of my friends forgot something and came back. But then I thought, My friends all know what's going on. They'd *never* scare me like this.

I turned off the light, crawled to the corner and dialed Nine-one-one. The dispatcher kept me on the line till two cops arrived.

First they checked every door and window from the outside. Then the one named Yamamoto came in and said, "Okay, show me where he knocked."

As I started toward my bedroom, he veered off toward the back door. I said, "Where're you going? The knock was on my bedroom window."

The cop said, "Do you realize the screen on your sliding glass door is off its channel?"

I said, "*What?*"

He took me back and showed me. Someone had tried to pry off the screen.

I started to tell him about the first break-in, but just then my roommates came home and Laurie said that George was out front with a girl in a red Volkswagen bug.

I went, "Oh, my God!" I told the cop, "That's the guy who tried to break in!"

Yamamoto ran out the front door. I called after him, "Don't leave me! Call Detective Dingfield. Here's his private number. There's more to this than you realize."

I was convinced George would talk his way out of being arrested and come back and kill me with the same knife he'd used on Mindy's tires.

The officer went out to the parking lot and told George I was accusing him of breaking in. Naturally George had an excuse ready. He said, "I live right here. I have witnesses. We were just going to Denny's for coffee."

He bluffed it out the way he always did, gave 'em the old BS: "I was with my roommates. They'll vouch for me." And one of them did. Jenny Graves told the cops he'd been gone from the condo for "hours." How could he have prowled anybody?

Yamamoto comes back in my place and says, "Mr. Russell didn't even know you lived here, ma'am. And he's been gone most of the evening."

I'm in a panic. I said, "What are you *doing?* If you don't arrest him now, what's to stop him from coming back to hurt me?"

I could've cried. I shut my door and turned off my lights and just sat paralyzed in my room. I asked God to please not let me be killed.

OUT IN THE parking lot, Patrolman Thomas Baker clicked off his radio and informed Patrolman Satoshi Yamamoto that there were outstanding warrants for George Russell's arrest.

Over the objections of roommates Bobbie DeGroot and Jenny Graves, he was handcuffed and placed under arrest on two Seattle warrants dating from his Pike Place Market adventures and two no-bail commitment orders for criminal trespass on Mercer Island. He offered no resistance. He had $132.76 on his person when he was booked into jail just before midnight.

PART THREE

JUSTICE?

I was much too far out all my life
And not waving but drowning.

—STEVIE SMITH,
"NOT WAVING BUT DROWNING," 1957

DALE FOOTE ARRIVED at the station at 3 A.M. and sat
down with George Russell to discuss the Beethe murder.
Early in his career, Foote had developed a reputation as an
overly intense interviewer, but he'd gradually learned to be
supportive, solicitous, catching his flies with honey—
"Yeah? *Yeah?* . . . That's *interesting*. I never *knew* that before. . . . Um-hm, *um-hmmm* . . . Well, I'll be darned. . . . I
really appreciate your help."

The new approach didn't work on George Russell, who
was known for using similar techniques himself. "George
was very collected," Foote recalled. "You could see this
was old stuff to him. He seemed concerned about projecting
the right image—he's cool, you're *un*cool. He was respectful within that need. I was glad that he agreed to talk, but
I didn't get much out of him."

In his faux-friendly way, Russell confirmed that he'd
been kicked out of the Black Angus by a waitress named
G.B. He acknowledged slight acquaintanceships with Randi
Levine and Mary Ann Pohlreich, but claimed that he'd
never met Carol Beethe or visited Cucina! Cucina!, where
she'd served as day bartender.

"When he flat denied knowing Carol, I had nowhere to go," Foote explained. "Marv and Larry Petersen had the other two cases." He arranged to have them notified.

SKEEN'S EXPECTATIONS WEREN'T high when he rendezvoused with Petersen shortly after 6 A.M. He still agreed with Foote, John Hansen and most of the other Bellevue detectives that Tom Jones was the Beethe murderer. On the other two cases, Russell looked to be as good a candidate as any, although cross-racial sex killings were rare and the case against him was completely circumstantial. Sooner or later, Skeen said to himself, we've got to develop something hard, or George is gonna skate.

Larry and I took him into an interview room and I started him out with a list of fourteen standard questions I'd asked every suspect in the Pohlreich case. It's a system developed by the Reid School of Criminology in Chicago.

"We're investigating a homicide," I said.

"I figured that," he said.

"Were you the one who killed her?"

"No, I was not. I did not kill her, any of them."

". . . Do you think she was raped and killed?"

"Who? The paper never said."

"Why do you think someone would kill her?"

"They said she wasn't into drugs, even though I told Detective Barnes different. Someone in the past may not have liked her."

"Did you ever think about killing someone, even though you didn't go through with it?"

"I'm sure everyone has, right? Everyone says at some time, 'I want to kill you,' maybe in a fight or something."

". . . Have you ever been in a situation where you lost control?"

"Angerwise, maybe with my girlfriend. I wrecked a bunch of stuff."

". . . Tell me what you were doing Friday night, June twenty-second."

"Generally, every Friday since Papagayo's opened, I play chess at the Crossroads Mall. There's this big chess set there. I leave home, play chess, arrive early, get a table. I eat first. They bring my drink, a shot of tequila and a Miller Lite, right over...."

He tried to give the impression that he was having an easy time, but his body language told us different. He's sitting in his chair, feet firmly planted, body rigid, face and facial expressions flexible. It's "yeah, yeah, yeah," and "I know this," "I know that," but his body isn't telling the same smooth story. One of the officers who saw him earlier had told us he was handing out a line of jive when he came in—"Gee, guys, I really don't know what you're talking about"; "I'd sure like to help ya"; "If there's ever anything I can do." He didn't try that crap on Larry and me.

After I finished my canned questions, we let him think about it for five or ten minutes and then resumed. He told us quite a lot about Randi Levine, how her truck had broken down and he helped her, how he'd seen her recently at a party at Papagayo's, how he stopped by her house one night and she invited him to go to dinner but he declined. He said he learned about her murder in the paper. He told us about a night she got drunk at Houlihan's and there was a big argument between Robby Bob Dzurick and a guy named Mike Weisenburgh about who would take her home.

It was like he was creating other suspects to divert our attention, an old story with criminals. Most of 'em'll roll over on their mothers. He told us that he knew dozens of police officers; he'd worked at the Mercer Island PD; his mom taught at San Francisco State and his natural father was half British and half black and his stepdad was a dentist. Just a good kid from good stock. It was part of his image, his coolness.

We finally tiptoed back to the murders, and he said he'd met Mary Ann at Papagayo's but she wasn't his type: too tall, too heavy. The night she disappeared, his friend Allen Israel was with him and so was a guy named Smitty. He said they went to Papagayo's in Smitty's truck, and he borrowed the truck just before closing time to go to a 7-Eleven for beer. He visited a female friend but she didn't answer his knock. He was gone about forty-five minutes and missed connections with Smitty when he brought back the truck.

He was still doing a lot of nervous giggling. I remembered what Mike Beckdolt said about Russell borrowing somebody's truck and disappearing with a woman, but Mike still hadn't come up with the owner's name. I'm thinking: if that truck was used in the murder, we might find some hard evidence on it.

I asked, "What's the rest of Smitty's name?"

Russell didn't hesitate. He told me it was Smith McClain and gave his address and phone number on Mercer Island. I thought, This guy's pretty cocky, like he knows we're not gonna get anything off the truck. But we're gonna check it out anyway.

He'd already said he'd be willing to take a polygraph. Now I asked if he'd be willing to give us samples of his blood, saliva and hair.

Bang! His whole attitude changed. He jumped up like he was ejected, crossed his arms over his chest and said, "Shouldn't there be somebody else in this room?"

I said, "You're talking about . . . your attorney?"

He said, "Yeah." He didn't sound friendly anymore.

"You want an attorney?"

"Yeah."

It was eight thirty-seven; we'd talked for over an hour. It took awhile to make the phone connection, and then the lawyer said no more talking and no tests. I got George some breakfast and took him back to the holding cell.

I said to myself, Maybe he killed Carol, maybe he didn't, but he sure looks good for the other two. An innocent man might have hemmed and hawed about the tests, might have said something like, "Do you really need samples?" But George like *levitated* out of that chair. It was like, You *want* war? Okay, man, you *got* war. . . .

Jeff Gomes came in—he'd introduced me to Russell at Papagayo's—and I told him George could be our man. Those big brown eyes almost popped out of his head. He said, "Oh, no! Not skinny George!"

Later we viewed some of the film that Dale Foote had shot from Papagayo's catwalk, and there was George in the middle of the frame. I thought, Yeah, it might be skinny George. But how do we get the evidence?

Aᴛᴇʀ ᴛʜᴇ Rᴜssᴇʟʟ interview, the three lead detectives sat down with Captain Mike Nault of the King County Police and other investigators to discuss commonalities in the three murder cases. The informal task force drew up a list:

All the victims' faces were covered.
All were abused by a foreign object.
All were killed by blunt trauma.
All were nude and posed on their backs.
All had been in a bar not long before death.
All were Crossroads Mall habitués.
All were sexually active Caucasians.
Clothes were completely or partly missing.
Rings had been taken from at least two.

At 10 A.M., when the short session was over, they drove to downtown Bellevue for a conference with Dr. John Liebert, a nationally known expert on sex crimes. The meeting was Nault's idea; Licbert had proved helpful on earlier King County cases and had done some profiling for police. At fifty-four, the forensic psychiatrist was a compact, professorial-looking man, a transplant from Wisconsin, with a flourishing private practice. He'd worked closely with Nault on the baffling Green River case.

Liebert looked at the list of similarities, asked a few questions, pored over color pictures of the dead women. Then he nodded his head firmly and said, "It's one man."

The murderer, he explained, was a so-called lust killer or spree killer, paraphilic, necrophilic and of course sociopathic. Such deviates lacked a conscience and a sense of empathy and sought sexual satisfaction by abusing females, dead or alive. It was apparent that this particular killer hated women, perhaps related to long-standing problems with the dominant females in his life.

In Liebert's opinion, the three victims hadn't been the misogynist's primary anger targets; symbolically, he'd been destroying someone else. Hence the attempts to cover the dead women's heads and eyes. It was an odd impulse, but not uncommon in sex murders.

The psychiatrist was asked how he'd reached his conclusion that one man was responsible. "Several things," he answered after some thought, "but mostly the posing." He emphasized that the phenomenon was rare. The specifics of each posing case were different and constituted a signature unique to the offender.

Nault asked if it wasn't possible that the similarities were just coincidence.

"Maybe in a city as big as L.A.," Liebert responded, "but no—not in Bellevue."

Before returning to their offices, the lawmen discussed whether they should continue withholding details of the posings from the press. Such "holdbacks" might decrease community hysteria and also help to weed out false confessions. Nothing about the fir cone or the gun or the vibrator or *More Joy of Sex* had appeared so far. They decided to risk the wrath of the press.

THE CONDO GIRLS were preparing for work when George called and asked for the phone numbers of his sister Erika in San Francisco and his father's lawyer in Seattle. He said the numbers were in his red gym bag in Jenny's room. He was in jail and he needed them "quick."

Jenny frantically dumped the bag, scattering the contents. She examined dozens of small slips of paper before she found the right numbers. George sounded relieved. He mentioned that he also needed eleven hundred dollars to pay off a fine and gain his release.

After he hung up, Jenny, Bobbie and Sara tried to figure out how to raise the money. Suzy Jetley voted to let him rot in jail.

He called a few minutes later and warned that the cops would soon show up to "toss" the apartment. He asked Jenny to be sure to show them his book *Crime Scene Search and Physical Evidence*. He told her to put his other possessions in a box, seal it with tape and take it to her parents' house for safekeeping. He explained that the local police had a history of seizing his gear and not returning it.

Bobbie DeGroot took the phone from Jenny's outstretched hand, and as soon as she heard his voice she relaxed. He was the same old George—upbeat, contained, *cool*. He chuckled as he told how the cops had stripped him to look for scratches and snapped a full-frontal picture in the buff; he guessed it would wind up in *Playgirl*. He said they'd asked him a bunch of questions from a written list and the first one was, "Why'd you do it?" and he'd snapped back, "Do *what?*"

Bobbie thought, That's George. Always a couple of moves ahead . . .

He sounded patient and reasonable about his old friends the cops. He said they had every reason to be suspicious of him, since he'd known two of the victims personally and was an expert on police procedures and was friendly with many of the people involved. He said the detectives now realized he was innocent and they were just going through the motions of excluding him as a suspect. That was their job. He said he'd be home soon and "not to worry, hon."

Bobbie wasn't worried. If there was anybody on earth who knew how to handle cops, it was George.

SHORTLY AFTER 2 P.M. on that same Wednesday, September 13, Susan Jetley was on duty at M. J. Feet shoe store when three men in business suits arrived.

They introduced themselves as Detectives Foote, Skeen and Petersen and said they wanted to ask some questions. Before they said one word, I knew why they were here: *George killed those women!*

I took my break and we went outside to a bench in the corridor. We talked for a half hour, mostly general stuff—how George came to live with us, how I tried to run him off, stuff about him and Bobbie, a little bit about his background. They asked about the trip to Canada, but I wasn't too helpful 'cause I didn't go. Lately I hadn't been hanging around the condo that much. Summer was almost over and we were all due to move out in a few days. Most nights I was sleeping at my family home at Lake Sammamish. So I was a little bit out of the loop.

The detectives thanked me for my information, and Dale Foote gave me his office and home phone numbers in case I needed to get in touch. They never explained why they were asking so many questions about George. They didn't have to.

While I was on my second job that night at Pietro's Pizza, I kept wanting to help out. I wondered what was happening at the condo. Was any evidence left or had the girls gotten rid of it by now?

I called a friend from my women's support group and asked for her help. We waited till Sara, Jenny and Bobbie wouldn't be home. I knew their patterns, but just to be on the safe side we checked out Denny's window. There they sat, drinking coffee.

We didn't turn on the lights when we entered the condo. Something jumped off the refrigerator and scared us half to death. It was George's cat Sasha.

Nothing looked out of place till we got to Jenny's room. There was stuff all over the floor—papers, cassettes, junk. I wondered why it was so scattered; I didn't know that Jenny had dumped his Olympic Sports gym bag, looking for phone numbers. That bag always gave me the creeps.

We scooped everything up and put it back in the bag, drove to the Bellevue PD and turned it over to a clerk. Then we called Detective Foote at home. He sounded sleepy.

THE LEAD INVESTIGATORS assembled at 6:45 the next morning and agreed that the acquisition of the gym bag was one more proof of a hoary old aphorism: "When I work hard I get lucky." It was only by chance that they'd approached Suzy Jetley instead of Jenny, Bobbie or Sara. The other condo girls, as each admitted later, would never have turned over the gym bag. George was still their friend.

The detectives, parents themselves, avoided passing judgment. The girls were fresh from their senior prom, unschooled in the ways of hustlers like Russell. Almost any teenager would have been taken in, and many others already had. The lawmen figured they were just lucky that Suzy Jetley turned out to be wiser than her age.

"Those girls consider him their protector," Foote commented as he watched Bellevue Detective Dennis Dingfield and King County Detective Wayne Slater inventory the contents of George's gym bag. "He's more like their Svengali."

Lying on the table were music tapes, a copy of a restraining order, a notice to appear for sentencing, several small flashlight batteries, a spoon, and a blizzard of paper slips and cocktail napkins bearing addresses, names and phone numbers, all in George's familiar printing.

Just before 11 A.M. an interdepartmental group consisting of Skeen, Foote, Petersen, Wayne Slater and supersleuth Rick Buckland pulled up at Villa 156 to look for more evidence. They'd hardly entered the apartment before Bobbie DeGroot dutifully handed over the *Crime Scene Search and Physical Evidence Handbook*.

"Here," she said, smiling. "George wanted you to have this."

The Mary Ann Pohlreich poster lay on a shelf in the pantry wall, still blaring HELP in big red letters.

The condo girls proved not only helpful but entertaining. They showed their visitors around, discussed life with George, and pointed out items that belonged to their sha-man, including two paper bags, a watch, some earrings, sample bottles of perfume, photos of women in nightgowns, receipts and a list of phone numbers, some with evaluations like "Judy, Aloof."

Mindful of Tami Grace's prowler of the night before, one of the detectives asked Bobbie if there was any way George could have left the condo long enough to knock on a neighbor's window and return without being seen.

"Two or three ways," she replied. "He could've gone out the back door; all the backyards are connected. He could've gone out the skylight in the loft; he's done it be-fore. Or he could've slipped out the front door when we weren't paying attention. I'd had too much to drink. We'd *all* had too much to drink."

Before the detectives hauled off their bags of evidence, Bobbie, Jenny and Sara insisted on singing a number they'd composed overnight to the tune of Sinéad O'Connor's "Nothing Compares 2 U":

> *. . . It's been several hours and about two years*
> *Since the cops took George away-ay. . . .*
> *Since George has been gone, I can wear*
>   *whatever I want,*
> *I can bring home whoever I choose.*
> *I have to eat my dinner at Pietro's restaurant,*
> *But nothing, nothing can take away these blues,*
> *'Cause nothing compares, nothing compares, to*
>   *George. . . .*

I went to the police and guess what they told
*   me. . . .*
They said, "Keep away from George.
He killed three girls in Bellevue."
Now we don't know what to do-oo.
But they're the fools, 'cause nothing compares
*   to George. . . .*

Back at the station at 1:35 P.M. the detectives agreed that George intended the evidence handbook as a taunt—"in yo' eye."

"He's saying it's a game," Marv Skeen said, "and he'll beat our ass."

They logged and bagged the additional evidence, and Dingfield, the Bellevue PD's computer genius, began punching up a data bank of names, addresses and phone numbers found in the gym bag and the condo.

Skeen shook his head as he contemplated the hours they would have to spend on telephone calls and personal visits to the twenty or thirty people on the lists, not one of whose names rang a bell at the moment. Who the hell was Brian Porter? Deanna Hagerich? Dorothy Bryant, Angela Hans, Korie Gochanour? Betty Westergard? Who were Angela Danielson, David Shea, Michelle Collins? Who was Dacia Jubinville? Who were Kelly West, Fred Bourgette, Jeannie Mizerski, Jeff Saenz, Christie Rider, Terry Miller, Leslie Rosenfeld? Were they George's friends? They couldn't be business acquaintances because George had no business. Were they drinking buddies, classmates, some sort of clients?

More busy seat-work lay ahead.

AT FOUR THAT afternoon Foote and Petersen drove across Lake Washington to the home of Dr. Wonzel Mobley and his wife Kristin. The petite Mrs. Mobley proved gracious beyond their expectations.

After she showed them to comfortable seats, she listened attentively as the detectives explained that they were investigating the Eastside murders and suspected that George might be involved. "We'd appreciate your insights," Petersen said in his mellow voice.

Mrs. Mobley said that she didn't understand George but thought he was "more than one person." He'd been ordered into counseling and went AWOL after a few visits. His IQ was in the range of 180, she said, and he could carry on a conversation "with anybody from a nuclear physicist to a janitor."

The dentist's wife confirmed that George put up a wall when anyone got too close to personal issues, and that he'd always been reticent about discussing his feelings. Foote asked what she knew about his early childhood.

Mrs. Mobley said that he'd been brought up by a grandmother and several aunts after his natural mother decided "she couldn't care for him." She said that little George had felt like a fifth wheel in his grandmother's household. Instead of seeking out playmates, he'd kept to himself. Sometimes family members would find him playing in a ditch a half mile down the road in the ferocious Florida sun.

The helpful Mrs. Mobley said that George believed that his grandmother had taken him in solely because of family obligation, and he "felt deserted, unwanted." As a result, she said, he harbored a lifelong resentment toward his family, his mother, and females in general. To the lawmen it made perfect sense.

WHILE THE DETECTIVES scribbled their notes in the Mobley living room, Bobbie DeGroot was busy wrecking her new Ford Escort a block from the condo. She and her bank had owned the two-door sedan for two days, replacing an ancient Mustang that had become a rolling junkyard. She was hysterical after the accident, and the tow truck driver drove her home. She was still shaking when the phone rang about 5 P.M.

> It was one of the detectives. They wanted me to lead 'em to George's stash in the woods on Mercer Island. I knew I had to get it together somehow, but the timing could've been better.
>
> Jenny and I went in her car and met the cops at a Park 'n' Ride on Mercer. I led 'em toward the place where George found the bag of coins. I showed 'em exactly where to go, but they didn't pay attention. They just started thrashing through the weeds and blackberries, picking up old beer cans and baseball cards and stuff that kids had left from parties.
>
> I told Jenny, "What are those stupid idiots doing in those bushes? Come on." We went straight to the spot.
>
> I yelled, "Look, guys!" It was a dug-out hole in the roots of a tree, hidden by ferns. I said, "This is where the money was." Of course it was empty by now.

TAMI GRACE WAS preparing for bed and trying to shake the memory of the knocks on her window. Two nights had passed since the police handcuffed George and drove him away, and there hadn't been a word about the arrest on TV or in the newspapers. She thought, Maybe they let him out! She felt a spasm of fear till she remembered Detective Dingfield's promise to keep her informed. He'd seemed like a man of his word.

She reached under her bed and pulled out a cardboard box of high school memorabilia. A penciled caricature of a witch stared from the lid: bony figure, sallow cheeks, hollow eyes, full hair, snarly expression. A disembodied hand held a gun to the witch's temple, and a hand-printed caption read, "Are you scared now, bitch?"

She had no trouble recognizing the style.

DETECTIVES RACED THE clock, trying to connect killer and victims. George was safely in custody, but if murder charges weren't brought soon, they would be obliged by law to cut him loose. And formal charges couldn't be brought without tangible evidence, of which there remained little or none.

Mindy Charley was interviewed again, as were other familiar figures from George's recent history: Tami Grace, Georgia Mike Weisenburgh and his roommates Robby Bob Dzurick and Jeff Anderson, the condo girls, Damien Middleton, employees of the Black Angus and Papagayo's, Allen Israel, Tamara Francis, Shay Wilson and the other teenagers who'd accompanied George on the Canada trip, the twin prostitutes he'd picked up in Vancouver, the dancer Lynn Brown, plus others.

A team of detectives checked each name found in the gym bag and the condo. Betty Westergard turned out to be Kristin Mobley's mother in Richland, Washington, and Dorothy Bryant was Dr. Mobley's mother in White Plains, New York. Neither was questioned.

The man named Brian Porter said he'd worked with George at Nintendo and dated his sister Erika.

Deanna Hagerich told police she'd met George at the Mercer Island Denny's and had no idea why he was carrying her phone number.

Neither did Angela Hans, who'd met him on a cruise.

Dacia Jubinville's phone didn't answer.

Patrick Dowling was a casual acquaintance who said that

George told him "the cops are stupid to look for the killer at Papagayo's because he would never return to the scene of the crime."

Cocktailer Dale Kenney recalled that George told her he was tight with the cops and "they'll never mess with me."

David Shea remembered him as someone who drank tequila and tried to deal hot merchandise.

Michelle Collins had dated him and accepted a ring, pin and necklace, but the gifts predated the first known killing.

Kelly West had danced with George at a bar.

Jeff Saenz said he was "surprised and shocked" that George had his unlisted phone number.

Leslie Rosenfeld described herself as "a good friend" and said that George told her he worked for the FBI and that the Green River killer had engaged in postmortem sex.

Nineteen-year-old Korie Gochanour said she'd met George five years earlier at Luther Burbank Park but hadn't dated him; she led the detectives to Laura Green, who described her affair with George and her torturous abortion at fourteen; Laura suggested that the police talk to a couple of her former girlfriends, who in turn recalled Chris Pieretti, who provided the name of Susie Powell, who said she'd once seen George flash a pack of stolen Social Security and ID cards.

The list of names, addresses and phone numbers expanded till Dennis Dingfield's original data bank had doubled in length, then doubled again. Sometimes it seemed that George Russell had rubbed up against every citizen of the Western world, or at least collected everyone's address or phone number. A few of the interviewees recalled being prowled or burglarized, confirming the suspicion that many of the names in George's possession weren't friends or acquaintances at all. They were "marks."

Long-suffering Mercer Island officers briefed the lead detectives on George's various misbehaviors and his love-hate relationship with women and cops, and other Mercer citizens chimed in with so many painful incidents and anecdotes that his dossier began to resemble a modern version of *A Thousand and One Nights*. Police and former room-mates handed over some publications he'd left behind: *Ted Bundy: Conversations with a Kilker*, by Stephen Michaud and Hugh Aynesworth; *Bundy—the Deliberate Stranger*, by Richard Larsen; *Two of a Kind: The Hillside Stranglers*, by Darcy O'Brien; a spy thriller called *The Messenger Must Die*; and Thomas Noguchi's *Coroner*, plus a stack of *Playboys* and *True Detectives* and some pornie videotapes including *Deep Throat* and *Best Chests in the West*. King County Detective Wayne Slater took a little kidding for spending three days screening the pornies for real-life footage that might have been shot by George and spliced into the tape. There proved to be none.

Gradually the detectives began to fill in the brushstrokes of a slow escalation from lonely child to troubled adolescent to antisocial manipulator to sadistic killer. Except for the inside information from Kristin Mobley, they were weak on the details of his first twelve years, but they were now able to enumerate his friends and relatives and describe his activities from his first days on Mercer Island to the fare-well scene with the condo girls on the arrest night They learned his likes and dislikes, his tastes in women, his shoe size and belt size, his preferences in dances, music, books, comic strips, food and drink. They came to know him al-most as they would know a friend, so familiar that they thought of him or spoke of him as ''George,'' despite their revulsion at his crimes.

The dossier lacked one crucial element hard evidence of guilt. The investigators had established a firm connection between George and Randi Levine and a weak connection between him and Mary Ann Pohlreich, but nothing to show that he'd ever crossed paths with Carol Beethe. They had a receipt proving that he'd purchased new pants and shirt at JC Penney the morning of the Pohlreich killing, a titil-lating bit of evidence but purely circumstantial. And they had fat files of biography and gossip, conjecture and coincidences and educated guesses. No prosecutor would dare to bring charges on such a thin gruel. If George was still playing Dungeons & Dragons, as some of the detectives suspected, he was well ahead. Somehow his adversaries had to change the game to The Tortoise and the Hare.

Word came from King County Jail that the prisoner's spirits were high and he was making his usual good adjustment. He'd read his way through Earl Emerson's detective mysteries. He enjoyed discussing crime and especially the triple murders, advancing the theory that a boyfriend had killed Carol Beethe and the cops shouldn't have given up on Damien Middleton and the killer was still loose and why didn't they let him out so he could help catch the guy before he killed again?

The essential problem, he advised admirers, was that the cops were dumb as dirt. He predicted that he would soon be back at his favorite table at Papagayo's, next to the DJ's booth. He admitted that a few of his fellow blacks were giving him heat for being an ''oreo'' and talking like whitey, but he'd served an even two dozen stretches in this institution and when the other prisoners saw that he excelled in chess and other brain games and was an astute jailhouse lawyer to boot, he became everyone's friend, black and white—or so he claimed.

His only regret was that Rumple Minze wasn't available.

ON SEPTEMBER 17, 1990, Marvin Skeen and Dennis Dingfield finally ran down Smith E. ''Smitty'' McClain and his candy-apple red Toyota pickup at an apartment building in Kirkland. It hadn't been easy. As Skeen recalled later, ''When George told us about taking Smitty's truck, he was daring us, living on the edge. Maybe he thought it was safe because Smitty's mom is totally deaf and can't talk on the phone, and that's the number George provided us. Smitty didn't live at home, and George probably figured we'd try a call or two and give up. Or he figured, Smitty's a drunk; what'll he remember? George didn't know that Smitty'd been through alcoholism treatment. He was a new man."

McClain wasn't positive about the exact date of the borrowing incident, but he knew it was the night before his sister Shawn had held the family's annual yard sale, a date that was easily checkable. He remembered his disgust and anger when he looked into his reeking pickup. Smitty wasn't sure how many times the high-riding Toyota had been detailed since the incident, but thought it might be four: he'd taken it to experts twice and cleaned it several times himself with cotton balls and chamois cloths and other agents. This truck, he emphasized as he patted a fender, "is my baby."

Skeen opened the driver's door and peered inside. "Jeez," he called to Dennis Dingfield, "they don't look this sharp in the showroom." They shot a few pictures before leaving for an appointment with Tami Grace. On the way, they agreed that no evidence could possibly be left after so many scrapings and polishings over a four-month period, but they decided to err on the side of thoroughness. Skeen recalled later:

"It took three weeks to finally get that damned Toyota into our garage. We knew it was gonna cost about two thousand dollars to do the job right, and the city was balking at the expense. We knew how close Smitty and George were—good friends for ten or twelve years—and we handled Smitty with kid gloves to keep from pissing him off. He hated to give up his baby, but I told him in a nice way, 'Hey, Smitty, I'm gonna have to take it, but I'll take good care of it. Anything we mess up, we'll replace. Now please, don't clean it again. Don't do *anything* to it. We'll get you a nice rental.'

"He brought it in on October 11, a month after we arrested George. He'd just washed it again! The guy was so truck-proud."

* * *

The red pickup was driven to the Bellevue Municipal Service Center and the interior examined inch by inch by a Bellevue PD scene examiner and mechanic. One pristine item after another was laid on a clean sheet on the floor: armrests, sun visors, seat backs, steering wheel covers, seat belts, transmission and foot pedal covers, the clear plastic from the instrument panel, anything that might have picked up a microscopic droplet of vomit or blood. Fiber samples were snipped from the floor mats.

The marathon examination began to resemble the car-stripping scene in *The French Connection*, where heroin was found in rocker panels after a long search. When the Toyota still retained its secrets after four hours, Skeen and mechanic Kim Svidren peeled apart the layers of upholstery on the immaculate-looking bucket seats.

A faint brownish spot the size of a half dollar came into view on the gauze backing on the driver's side. A matching stain was found on the foam underneath. The stains were fuzzy around the edges, smelled like cleaning fluid, and resembled thinned-down blood.

Skeen marked the items with exhibit numbers and his initials, "MES94" and "MES95," sealed them in plastic pouches, and delivered them to the state crime lab to see if the blood matched Mary Ann Pohlreich's type A. It did, but it also matched 40 percent of the population. Skeen was advised that advanced testing such as DNA genetic blueprinting could take a long time and might not be admitted in court, but he requested the tests anyway. It was the latest act of a desperate sleuth.

MINDY CHARLEY WAS at Bellevue police headquarters when she learned that Smith McClain had just arrived for exclusionary blood tests. A detective said, "He's upstairs, Mindy. Do you mind if he comes down?"

She started to quiver. Smitty was George's good friend,

and he probably considered her a turncoat "Okay," she said. "I'll run into him sooner or later."

When Smitty saw her, he held out his arms. For several minutes they hugged each other and cried. Then they compared stories and cried some more.

"It was obviously just sinking into him that his truck had been used in a murder," Mindy recalled later. "I felt so sorry for him. I thought, Oh, George, you've always hurt your best friends."

As 1990 NEARED an end, tantalizing tidbits dribbled in from the Washington state crime lab and the FBI: the semen found in Mary Ann Pohlreich was also George's blood type, but it could have been contaminated. A hair found on Randi Levine's body proved to be "Negroid," as did hairs found in pubic combings from Mary Ann Pohlreich. And there was a possibility that three hairs found on Carol Beethe's bed had come from an African-American. The detectives regarded the information as exciting but inconclusive: unlike fingerprints, hair wasn't unique. Besides, there was no need to convince Skeen, Foote and Petersen that Russell was guilty. The problem now was to convince the prosecutor, so that George could be formally charged and kept in jail.

The Washington lab made a few more tests and described the Levine finding as a "buckled body hair which exhibits many of the same microscopic characteristics as the control pubic hair samples from George Russell. Mr. Russell cannot be excluded as the source of this hair." There it was, the same old problem: hair evidence couldn't prove guilt; it could only "exclude" or "not exclude."

Carol Beethe's two-ring diamond bridal set was a more promising lead. The jewelry was physical evidence, finite, palpable—and missing. It wouldn't be hard to convince a jury that whoever took the rings might be involved in the murders. But who even knew what they looked like?

After much searching, Carol Beethe's ex-husband Paul produced pictures. The rings had been photographed for an insurance appraisal. The pictures were widely distributed.

The missing Levine ring was a tougher nut. After days of investigating, Detective Larry Petersen located the local jewelry shop where Randi had replaced the original amethyst with a darker one. But there didn't seem to be a single picture of the ring. Friends and relatives described it as gold with a seven-carat dark amethyst in a marquise cut, slightly pointed on both ends, set in the middle of a V. Randi had been proud of the ring and enjoyed flashing it. In fact, she'd shown it off while jokingly giving her friend Kathleen Del Mar "the finger," and Kathleen recalled that another friend had snapped a picture of the occasion. She promised to look for the photo.

Lead investigator Dale Foote still hadn't identified the instrument that caused Carol Beethe's wounds, distinctive Y shapes about two inches long. He showed the gruesome pictures to friends and colleagues, collected a dozen guesses and discarded them all. Dr. Mark Papworth, a retired coroner's assistant from Canada, said he'd handled a case where a broadhead arrow was the weapon, and these wounds were similar.

Foote borrowed three arrows from a sporting goods store and showed them to the King County medical examiner. Dr. Donald Reay said it was an interesting concept, but the Beethe wounds had been made by something heavier.

For the struggling Foote, the biggest problem remained the lack of any connection whatever between Carol Beethe and George Russell. With the finding of the first "Negroid" hairs, he'd finally diverted his attention from her white boyfriend Tom Jones to Russell, but there was still no proof that killer and victim had ever crossed paths.

* * *

Reaching out to everyone involved in Russell's past, Foote called Hawaii and talked to G. B. Coffin. The ex-cocktailer quickly solved his problem.

"George hated me after I had him eighty-sixed," she recalled telling Foote over the phone. "I think he dumped Mary Ann's body behind the Black Angus to get even. And that's why he killed Carol. She was one of my best friends. George saw us together plenty of times. He gave us an ugly look when he saw us talking about him. It was just before he killed Mary Ann. Look, everybody said Carol and I were the same type, same figure, same personality, even looked alike. Don't you think he could've killed Carol in my place?"

Foote agreed it was possible. He couldn't wait to call Skeen and Petersen. Now the three victims were connected by a single thread, however thin. The thread was George Walterfield Russell Jr.

THE CHRISTMAS HOLIDAYS brought a bittersweet surprise for Laura Green. Five years had passed since she'd aborted George Russell's child, and in the interim he'd barely acknowledged her existence. Now she received a long letter from King County Jail, written in his usual pyrotechnics, with extra exclamation points, underlinings, stern advice and biblical references. In a few paragraphs, she was swept back to the languorous summer nights at V——'s house and other trysting spots, talking to the brilliant George Russell about Jesus, Satan and oral sex.

"Guess where I'm at?" he wrote. "And with my family leaving for Hawaii on the 24th too. I'm starting to feel cursed. Hopefully it won't be that much longer."

He warned that "serious conditions" might be coming up and suggested she contact Lynn Brown, his dancer friend—"Lynn knows more." He made several nostalgic references to Mercer Island: the Dairy Queen, 7-Eleven, Pizza Hut, Denny's, Luther Burbank Park.

After some gossipy references to mutual friends, he wrote, "Is Jesus still in your life? How easy it is to let him slip out of our day to day lives . . . he's asked me why he has to keep having me here before I learn that my heart, soul, mind, spirit, and life belong with and to him. He's right of course."

George admitted that God must be "getting pretty tired of my coming to him and leaving him. The message I now get from him is that this is the last time."

Laura couldn't hold back a grin. This was classic George, acting as though God had nothing to do but issue him personal instructions. She wondered how a person became so self-centered.

A few dire predictions followed: "the Middle East crisis definitely looks like the beginning of Armageddon. And all the recent floods, famines, and earthquakes." He suggested that she search her heart, "this could be the start of the end," and closed with, "Love ya much. God bless!!!" A postscript recommended Luke 1:46–55, Acts 3:19, First John 1:9, Isaiah 55:7, and First Peter 1:3–9.

Laura didn't even bother to look up the verses. She was no longer the credulous fourteen-year-old who'd bawled when George talked to another girl. She'd just celebrated her nineteenth birthday; she was studying merchandising at Bellevue Community College—she'd always been good with money—and helping to run a small business on the side.

She reread the letter, trying to fathom his motivation. The phrasing was gushy, cutesy-poo, but that was just his style. She decided that the note was well intended, and she was glad he'd sent it. George was different—everybody knew that—but he wasn't necessarily evil. Hadn't he paid for the abortion?

A few days later she opened the *Journal American* to a story headlined A SUSPECT IN EASTSIDE MURDERS. She read a few lines and said to herself, So *that's* why he's in jail.

The article noted that the authorities were taking hair, blood and saliva samples.

Now she saw the Christmas letter more clearly. "George knows the police'll ask me about him," she explained to a friend. "He's trying to revive my feelings so I'll stick up for him and hold some stuff back, like how he seduces kids. He probably thinks I'll tell them what a gentle soul he is— wouldn't hurt a fly. That's why he put in the stuff about God."

Laura added the cynical note to her thick collection of correspondence from George and bundled it up. The police would be interested.

THE HOLIDAY SEASON was bumming out Bobbie DeGroot. She'd just begun to comprehend that in George Russell's touchy-feely sessions, she'd been nothing but a toy, a gew-gaw, the latest in the woman-hater's list of collectibles and discardables. In some ways she was still a child, with a teenager's tendency toward hurt feelings, and as time went by she saw the full extent to which she'd been manipulated and abused. Worse, she was also forced to endure the mood alterations of pregnancy.

By Christmastime, 1990, she'd stopped singing merry songs about George Russell. She was too busy warding off a breakdown.

> I'd gotten pregnant in October; it was Tim, beyond any doubt. George had been arrested five or six weeks before I conceived, and anyway, George and I had never had inter-course—at least I hoped not.
>
> By the time I found out, we'd all left the condo for good, but we were still tight, and little by little it got back to me that the other three girls were wondering about the color of my baby. I said, "Hey, wait a minute! Something has to happen to have a baby, and that didn't happen between me and George, ya know?"
>
> I began to have nightmares about having a black baby and

not being able to figure out how it happened. Lots of nights George and I had been drinking, and lots of nights we'd slept in the same bed. How could anyone be sure? I also had nightmares that my child would be born psychotic, *Rosemary's Baby*.

I started getting these nasty phone calls from someone close to Jenny; I don't want to give his name. Jenny and Sara still believed that George was innocent, but this guy wasn't *that* naïve. His position was that George was guilty, but Jenny and Sara and Suzy and I shouldn't get involved. Some public-spirited citizen!

He was furious that I was cooperating with the police and prosecutors. He would swear at me on the phone, scream, yell. He'd say, "Kid, you're so stupid you're dangerous. They're gonna get you up on that witness stand and rip you apart. They're gonna convince you that's George's baby."

I got hysterical. I called my mother and told her what was happening. My dad called the guy at work and ripped him a new asshole: "Don't you ever speak to my daughter again!"

The guy tried to apologize, but my dad said, "No! *Never* call her phone number again."

So I had all these problems to handle, and I was dealing with detectives and lawyers, and I was losing it. One night a terrible fear came over me, and even though I was with Tim, I felt very anxious and alone. I was afraid I was gonna be killed; at first I thought George would do it, then Tim. I skittered away from him on the bed.

It made no sense. It was the worst time of my life.

DNA testing is a highly effective investigative tool, but it's only one tool. It is highly persuasive evidence, but it's only one piece of evidence. It's not what everyone seems to want . . . the scientific one-size-fits-all substitute for sex-crimes investigation or juries having to make hard decisions.

—ALICE VACHSS,
SEX CRIMES

Marv Skeen finally began receiving some encouraging serological results. A private lab ran DNA tests and concluded that the thin wash of blood on Smitty's bucket seat was a DQ alpha subtype found in only 6 percent of the white population, including Mary Ann Pohlreich. The sperm on the Pohlreich vaginal smear was of a type found in 8 percent of the black population, including George Russell. The numbers looked convincing, if not overpowering.

On the fourth day of the new year Skeen presented the findings, along with his theory of the crimes, to the King County prosecuting attorney's office. As he and Foote and the other investigators saw it, the Pohlreich killing had been impromptu and the others premeditated. He explained:

George convinces Mary Ann to join him in Smitty's truck for a drink of Rumple Minze. He wants sex, and we know from her personality she would resist. He loses his temper and kills her. Now he has a big problem: a dead body in the truck. George is a thinker, and he still remembers being eighty-sixed by G. B. Coffin, so he offloads the body behind the Black Angus and makes sure it gets maximum media attention by posing her as though she's in her coffin. *Coffin*; get it? That's the way his brain works. Stupid clues for stupid cops . . .

The whole Eastside starts buzzing about this killing, just the kind of attention George wanted. He's always talked and read about the Hillside Stranglers and John Wayne Gacy and Bundy and the lack of black serial murderers. But before he can get to his real target, which is G.B., she skips. He starts thinking, Well, what about a substitute? What about a friend?

That's when he murders Carol Beethe in her sleep. He'd already been burglarizing her place at night. Then he sets up an alibi with five or six kids in his motel room and sneaks out and blitzes Randi Levine the same way, asleep and helpless. She'd rebuffed him twice, and he had some kind of goofy idea that she was cheating on one of his friends. That was more than enough to set him off. For several weeks somebody'd been prowling Randi's apartment at night. It was George. Who else?

The prosecuting attorney agreed that the scenario made sense and brought first-degree murder charges in the Pohlreich case on January 10, the day before Russell would have been released from King County Jail. The next day, Mary Ann Pohlreich's brother Ed and mother Nancy watched as the killer did his cool walk into court to plead innocent.

"I wanted to see what the guy looks like," Ed Pohlreich told a reporter. "Nothing's going to bring my sister back. I still can't comprehend it. She wasn't just a sister, she was a friend." He held up his infant son. "Here is our beautiful little baby she never got to see. She loved kids."

The Pohlreichs promised that the family would attend every court hearing. "I want him to see how much we hurt," the brother said.

The formal charge of murder gave police more time to investigate, but the prosecutor warned that the forensic findings in the Pohlreich case still fell short of proving guilt beyond a reasonable doubt, and if nothing else surfaced, Russell would probably walk. As for the Levine and Beethe killings, there were interesting coincidences and plausible theories, but still not enough evidence to justify charges.

The cases were assigned to Chief Deputy Prosecuting Attorney Rebecca Roe, lauded on the cover of *Parade* magazine as one of America's toughest prosecutors, and there was every expectation that the killer would be defended in court by a similarly high-powered lawyer. There didn't appear to be a shortage of assets in the family. The stepfather, Wonzel Mobley, owned a half-million-dollar home on Mercer Island, a blue Lamborghini Islero and a silver Ferrari 275 GTS, and George's mother was the wife of a university president and herself a highly salaried educator. The accused man had already been counseled by J. Richard Quirk, attorney of record in several cases involving Dr. Mobley. The dentist himself showed his allegiance to his stepson by snubbing Marv Skeen and Dale Foote, explaining after he failed to show up for a scheduled meeting that he had more important things to do.

THE LEAD INVESTIGATORS and their colleagues had no choice but to resume the scut work known as working the list, while frantically juggling their new assignments. With Tom Jones eliminated as a suspect in the Carol Beethe killing, Dale Foote dialed number after number, asking the same questions: Do you know George Russell? Why would he be carrying around your name and address? . . .

Many of the numbers in Dennis Dingfield's data bank had been tried repeatedly without result. Foote had failed on his first five attempts to reach Dacia Jubinville. Then, to his surprise, she called him back.

He cradled the phone on his shoulder and made the usual notes as he listened to the single mother's story: she'd met George at the Black Angus in 1989; he carried a scanner and worked undercover; he was unbeatable at chess and backgammon; he flashed a big roll; he gave her a ladies' ring—

"He *what*?" Foote interrupted.

"Gave me a ring," the young woman said. "He stood me up on a date, so he gave me a ring to apologize."

Foote asked what kind of ring.

Dacia said it was gold with a purple stone. Foote remembered that one of Randi Levine's missing rings had been an amethyst. He asked, "Where is it now?"

"I gave it away," the woman said.

The detective asked her address and learned that she lived in the Cascade foothills but had been staying with her parents down the street from his own home in Bellevue. He snapped his notebook shut and said, "Please, miss, wait right there."

He found her to be different from most of the exuberant teenagers and fast-talking barflies who'd occupied so much of Russell's time and attention.

"I couldn't figure her out," he said later. "She seemed almost nonresponsive. She showed very little concern or emotion about George or the dead women. It struck me as strange, but she gave me what I needed. She said she'd been afraid to get involved after George was arrested, so she gave the ring to a friend named David Vice. She thought he'd left town.''

Foote called Vice's phone number and learned from his mother that the young man was on a hitchhiking vacation with a girlfriend. At the moment, there was no way he could be reached. Foote dialed King County police headquarters in Seattle and was told that Detective Larry Petersen had the day off. The shy Foote was reluctant to bother such an imposing veteran at home. Senior cops were protective of their perks and free time, especially after working long hours on an unbreakable case.

Foote took a deep breath and dialed. ''Larry,'' he said, ''I hope you don't mind me calling you at home, but I got this gal who had an amethyst ring and I'm pretty sure it's Randi's.''

When he finished reciting the details, Petersen chimed in, ''Whattaya mean you hope I don't mind?'' His mellifluous voice turned gruff. ''Listen, Dale,'' he went on, ''you call me at home anytime you get something this good!''

Petersen drove straight to headquarters. Lately there hadn't been much action in the Levine case. His partner Wayne Slater had found a bloodied crescent wrench in the underbrush near her apartment, but the lab tests were inconclusive. Randi Levine's best friend Kathleen Del Mar had promised to look for the photo of Randi holding up her ring finger, but she hadn't produced.

> I called Kathleen and she said, ''Larry, I finally found it.'' I had the picture blown up and you could see a dark stone set in a gold band—not the best ID in the world, but at least you could tell it was a marquise cut and could've been an amethyst.
>
> I called David Vice's mother and said, ''If your son has the ring we're looking for, Mrs. Vice, it can be critically important.''

She said, "Well, David's belongings are right here in the house."

I said, "From what I'm told it's a woman's ring. Maybe he didn't take it with him."

She promised to look. She called back and said, "I've been through all his stuff. I can't find any rings. Maybe he gave it back to Dacia."

I said, "Mrs. Vice, I need your son, and I need him *now.*"

She said David and his girlfriend were riding their thumbs toward the "dolphin institute" in the Florida Keys. David wanted to swim with the dolphins.

I said, "Swim? With the dolphins?"

She explained that there's a place where visitors volunteer their work and time, and in return they're allowed in the tank. She said David and his girlfriend should be arriving any day at the Dolphin Research Institute in Marathon Shores.

I called, but the dolphins were taking the day off. At seven o'clock the next morning somebody answered the phone, and I told 'em it was very important that I get in touch with David Vice. The individual asked, "Who's David Vice?"

It took two days and three more calls before somebody said, "Yes, we have a David Vice here. He's a volunteer." I left my number.

At 12:12 P.M. on Thursday, February 21, our switchboard operator said I had a collect call from a "Kelly David Vice" at Grassy Keys, Florida. The first thing David said was that he wouldn't be home for two months. He sounded like a typical twenty-two-year-old kid with the wanderlust, full of pizzazz, but believable and straightforward. I asked him if he knew a girl named Dacia and he laid out his story.

He said he used to hang out at Denny's Overlake, and about two years ago his friend Dacia Jubinville introduced him to George Russell. After that he ran into George once in a while, but they never became real friendly.

He confirmed that Dacia had given him a ring with a purple stone a few months ago. They'd been sitting at their favorite table in Denny's and she mentioned that she felt uncomfortable keeping George's ring now that he was implicated in the murders. He told her he'd be glad to hold on to it and dropped it into his pocket without even taking a look. A month or six weeks later he felt the ring in the pocket of the same pants and couldn't remember where it came from.

I said, "Where is it now?"

He said that when he and his girlfriend finally reached Florida, they were out of money and he sold his twelve-string guitar and Dacia's ring in Key West. The pawnshop was called Uncle Sam's, and it was in a one-story building on Duval Street decorated by three balls and a couple of tropical trees. He said the clerk gave 'em sixty-five bucks for the guitar and five for the ring. I asked what the ring looked like and he said it was nothing fancy—a gold band with a simple amethyst on top, a pretty dark purple color. That sounded right.

I asked for his number and told him, "Stay near that phone till I call you back. Don't go *anyplace!*"

For the next hour I was on the line to Florida. Lieutenant Frank Sowers of the Key West PD assured me that "Uncle Sam" was a guy named Robert Budakian, and that he was honest and cooperative. Not every pawnshop owner could make that statement. There are places where one inquiring phone call about a piece of jewelry can make it disappear as fast as they can light the torch. I wanted to find the ring fast, but I didn't want it melted down.

I called Mr. Budakian and described the ring. He asked me to hold the line. I'm sitting there drumming my fingers on my desk and thinking, If he finds it, we've got a shot at Russell, and if he doesn't, we're still in the shit.

He came back on the phone and told me he'd found the ring *and* the transaction slip. He said the mounting wasn't worth much, so he'd thrown it into a tray to be recycled. He remembered that he'd had to use a ring cutter to take it off the kid's finger.

I asked him to mark it and keep it in a secure place—"I'll send someone to pick it up." There were still a lot of loose ends and uncertainties, including whether Mr. Budakian picked up the right ring in his discard tray, and if he did, was this the ring George Russell gave Dacia in the first place? I had to move slowly, methodically. We'd been busting our tails too long to screw up now.

I called David Vice and asked, "Do you remember anything else about that deal in the hockshop? Were there any . . . problems?"

He thought for a while and said, "Yeah. My finger swelled up 'cause I'd been playing guitar in the heat. They had to cut the ring off."

I called Lieutenant Sowers back and he sent an officer to pick up the amethyst and secure it in their property safe.

Things were looking better, but I still couldn't prove that this was the ring from Randi Levine's finger. There's something called the chain of evidence, and it has to be followed meticulously or the evidence won't be admitted in court.

I made a few more calls and reached Randi's sister-in-law, Rhonda Renee Levine, in Orlando. She said she'd given Randi an amethyst ring three years ago when they were roommates. Originally it belonged to Rhonda's mother, and Rhonda had worn it for eight years before Randi took a liking to it. She described the ring in detail.

I contacted Les Levine, Randi's father, in Merritt Island, near Orlando. He was like an extra hand on the case, ready to go anywhere, do anything. I said, "I think we found Randi's ring. It's in Key West. How far is that from you?"

He said, "Three hundred miles." Before I could ask, he said, "I'll leave right away."

I suggested that he take Rhonda along. We needed an absolutely positive ID. Who could be more positive than someone who'd owned the ring herself?

At four-thirty the next afternoon my phone rang and it was Les. He was in Key West with his wife and Rhonda and Rhonda's baby. He said everybody was all upset, crying. The ring was Randi's.

DESPITE THE COUP by Petersen and Foote, the individual cases against Russell still looked weak to Rebecca Roe and her cocounsel, Senior Deputy Prosecutor Jeffrey Baird. How could the state prove that Russell had taken the ring in connection with a murder? It was a logical assumption, an interesting *circumstance*, but it wasn't positive proof. Russell could claim that Randi had given him the ring. He could say that he'd found it or bought it on the street, a gambit he'd used to finesse the problem of the stolen gun in the Pike Market incident. Imaginative criminals spewed fountains of exculpatory misinformation, but prosecutors could only counter with facts.

At trial the defense was sure to point out that technicians hadn't raised a single Russell fingerprint from three different murder scenes or found a trace of a weapon. And no certainties, only a string of probabilities, had arisen from the DNA evidence.

Roe and Baird decided to bundle the three cases together and attempt to weave a tight web of circumstantial evidence, the prosecutorial version of the death of a thousand cuts. As a confidential report noted, "The cases had to be tried together because they could not stand alone."

Then the Beethe case firmed up a little. Susan Jetley and a young woman named Shay Wilson told police interviewers that Russell had admitted encountering Carol Beethe at Cucina! Cucina!, refuting his earlier claims and confirming G. B. Coffin's statements that he was well aware of the murdered bartender. Technicians confirmed that complete hairs and hair fragments found in her bed were indeed Negroid in origin, as suspected earlier. The prospects were still unfavorable, but they were improving.

AMONG OTHER AVENUES of investigation, the detectives were still trying to catch up with young Steve Crandall for a routine interview. The search for the beer-drinking comic had been low-priority, but Dale Foote picked up some information that made it urgent.

> I'd been talking to Nicole DeVita. She was recovering, but she had big memory lapses from the skull fracture. Her apartment was only a half mile from Carol Beethe's, and there were other similarities between the attacks—the way the guy "blitzed" Nicole, for instance, using a weapon of opportunity that he could dump.

Nicole mentioned that Steve Crandall was a friend of hers and knew George Russell. I wondered what else Crandall might know about our suspect.

Nicole told me I could find him at McDonald's, but he never seemed to be on duty when I checked. I missed catching him at home because he moved around a lot. I had a description: big, heavyset, long hair cut short on top, a hippie type, twenty-one years old, always wore sweats and tennis shoes.

I made a visit to his latest address and nobody was home, as usual. I was walking back to my car when I saw this big guy shuffling through the Safeway parking lot. On a hunch I ran him down and said, "Hey, Steve! You're Steve Crandall, aren't you?"

He says, "Yeah. Whattaya want?" Real surly.

I could see he'd been drinking. "Steve," I said, "I'm investigating a homicide. Do you know a guy named George Russell?"

He gave a long pause. He didn't look friendly, and yet he didn't shut me out. He says, "Isn't he the guy that was in the paper?"

"Yeah. Let's talk."

I walked him a half block to the Yankee Diner. He was a little wobbly and started acting mysterious. Then he turned challenging. I didn't know what to think.

S TEVE CRANDALL HAD had a few minor problems with the law, but he'd also had problems with George Russell. His emotions were mixed as he confronted the plainclothesman.

I generally distrust cops, period. America is a police state: criminals have rights; victims don't. So I didn't exactly do cartwheels when this detective chases me down in a parking lot. It was scary, and I'm thinking, Why is this guy cornering me?

Right away I knew he was the heat. They all learn the same fuckin' shit at the same fuckin' school. They're about as subtle as a rooster in a henhouse with a minute to live—always running, aggressive, take control . . .

I was wondering what the hell I did wrong. I was *not* the happy face. The smart thing to do when a cop approaches you is shut up. That's what God put lawyers on this planet for. Lawyers are slime, but without 'em you can hang yourself.

He starts asking questions, but I don't rat on people. That's one thing I do . . . not . . . do. But I had to draw a line with myself. Number one, we're talking murder here. That's a fuckin' different story. I figure rape and murder and beating your kids, you got a fuckin' problem. Otherwise it's your own fuckin' business, more power to ya, do your thing and try not to get caught, and I will never *ever* rat you out.

Reason number two was there was a rumor that Russell was suspected in assaulting one of my very dear friends, Nicole DeVita.

I figured, For him I'll make an exception.

FOOTE TRIED NOT to show his fascination with Crandall's information. He didn't want this tipsy young man to realize that he might hold the key to whether George Russell went free or took a lethal injection in his arm.

I asked Crandall the same question I'd been asking everybody: have you ever seen George with any jewelry?

"Oh, yeah," he says. "He tried to sell me some."

I couldn't've been more surprised. Just the day before, we'd given the Bellevue *Journal American* the details on Carol's missing rings, including the insurance photographs her ex-husband had turned up. A reporter named Chris Jarvis was preparing a story. We would've preferred to hold back the ring descriptions, but we needed the public's help.

Crandall told me about running into George in front of Blockbuster Video and being offered a ring for thirty bucks. I said, "Do you remember what it looked like?"

He started drawing a picture. I knew immediately it was one of Carol's rings, the one with the diamond on the band and the little stones off center. He *nailed* the description. It wasn't like he didn't remember certain points; he remembered every detail.

I'd given my only pictures of the rings to Jarvis to go with his story. I called him right away and he was just leaving his office. Crandall and I made the five-minute drive over there and waited in the conference room for the photo lab guy to bring in the pictures. They were already laid out for the next day's editions.

I asked Jarvis to step outside, and I put the pictures on the table. Crandall looked at the first one. No reaction.

Then he looked at the one with the off-center stones. *Bam!* He started pounding on the desk, almost jumping up and down. "That's it! That's the ring!"

I thought, This is the big break. This is *it!*

I said, "Where's the ring now, Steve? Did you buy it?"

He said, "No."

"Do you know where it is now?"

"Don't have a clue."

I guess that would've been a little too much to expect.

W**ITH THE WEB** of evidence tightening, prosecutors Roe and Baird formally added the Beethe and Levine murders to the charges against George Russell. They announced that they would seek life imprisonment; to try for the death penalty would mean a severing of the three cases, upsetting their strategy.

The defendant, still held on $500,000 bail, pleaded innocent. In court, he was represented by the public defender's office. Some wondered what had happened to the expensive lawyers they'd expected his family to retain. Apparently the killer was on his own.

W**ITH RUSSELL AWAITING** trial, investigative reporters took their first long look, at his background. African-American criminals seldom drew analytical attention from the media, but Russell was the only serial killer ever charged in Washington State, boyhood home of Ted Bundy, adopted home of "Hillside Strangler" Kenneth Bianchi, and scene of dozens of unsolved rapes and murders. Northwesterners were as sensitized to serial crime as Oklahomans to tornadoes or Floridians to hurricanes.

The Bellevue *Journal American* quoted Mercer Island Police Chief Jan Deveny as saying, "I guess we had the impression that he was a thief. We didn't see anything that would give us a clue that he would get involved in that type of behavior. He was a charming rascal."

A local publication called *Eastsideweek* scored the first interview with the charming rascal, and reporter Julie Garner tried to pry out some of the childhood information that he'd zealously withheld for years. Garner wrote, "He said he spent his early childhood living with his grandmother, a teacher, and four aunts in West Palm Beach, Florida. He eventually moved to Washington, D.C., while his stepfather, now a prominent Mercer Island dentist, attended dental school. He said that he lived there for about two years, and after the sixth grade, the family moved to Mercer Island. . . ."

Eastsideweek's article offered snippets of information about the years before Russell materialized on Mercer Island walking a St. Bernard, but shed little light on what might have turned him into a serial killer. It also gave Russell a chance to make several self-serving statements, including a claim that he'd been an agent of the Eastside Narcotics Task Force, and that he owned a scanner only because "it's a great way to get invited to parties." He also detailed his itinerary on the night of the Pohlreich killing, omitting anything that made him look guilty.

The most expansive article on the killer's origins turned up on page one of the March 5 edition of the Seattle *Post-Intelligencer* under the by-lines of Gordy Holt and Michael

A. Barber. Veteran reporter Holt, a resident of Mercer Island, had scored exclusive interviews with family members who'd never spoken publicly.

Holt and Barber wrote, "Russell's family yesterday painted a picture of a dysfunctional family upbringing, saying that he was troubled by the absence of his mother, a college humanities professor, who wasn't around much when he was younger."

The killer was quoted as denying that he was a drifter or a fan of Ted Bundy: "I have no aspirations to be like him at all." Nor, George said, did he feel any resentment toward his mother, who was "supportive."

The article continued:

> But some who know Russell best yesterday said he had childhood problems.
>
> Family members said his mother wasn't around. She left 16 years ago while married to Dr. Wonzel Mobley of Mercer Island, a Seattle dentist. And 16 years before that, she had left Russell and his father, George Walterfield Russell Sr., a funeral-home employee in West Palm Beach.
>
> "One day she just left," the senior Russell said yesterday in a telephone interview.
>
> "If I'd known she had left him again, I would have insisted that she send him on down here to me."
>
> Russell [Sr.] said he met Russell's mother, Joyce, one summer.
>
> "We had an affair, she went back to school and then she wrote saying she was pregnant. I told her to stay there as long as she could and then I'd send for her. That's what happened. We were married and she had the baby.
>
> "Then one day I came home and she was gone, gone back to school. She'd left the kid with her mother. He was maybe 6 months old then, and I haven't seen either one of them since."
>
> Mobley said George Jr. was still in high school when his mother last left.
>
> "She just picked up and left us," Mobley said. "George didn't want to be disrupted from school, so she said, OK, I'm leaving anyway, and did. She took Erika, our daughter, who

then was 6, and just left, never choosing to come back and pick George up.''

Russell's mother is now married to Dr. Robert Corrigan, former chancellor of the University of Massachusetts in Boston, who in 1988 became president of San Francisco State University.

Corrigan yesterday expressed shock at hearing the news of the latest charges.

Joyce Corrigan could not be reached for comment.

Soon after his mother left, Russell left Mercer Island High School and would disappear for weeks on end, his stepfather said.

''It was all just suddenly pushed off on me,'' Mobley said yesterday.

''We often asked him why the trouble, what was bothering him? Was he angry at his mother for leaving, for never remembering even his birthdays?

''He always said 'no,' that he loved her, that she was everything to him.

''Now I'm no psychiatrist, but I can read between the lines. Obviously, something has been missing here. We've known it all along, but what could we do?''

After the *P-I* article appeared, George Russell was asked how his mother had reacted. ''She was pissed,'' he said, and quickly added, ''It's not true that my mom didn't remember my birthdays. Maybe Wonzel didn't know, 'cause when my mom phoned I didn't always tell him. She *always* remembered my birthdays. She kept in touch. She's *always* been my mom.''

None of the relatives ever made another public comment about George or his predicament. Joyce Corrigan and Wonzel Mobley ignored requests for information. When George Walterfield Russell Sr. was asked in Florida why there appeared to be no public records of a marriage or divorce between him and George's mother, the funeral home attendant said, ''I'm not angry with you, but I'm just not cooperating. Y'all find out what you want on your own.'' It appeared that he spoke for the extended family.

OLD COURT RECORDS suggested that life inside the Mobley home on Mercer Island might not have been as serene as it appeared to neighbors before "she just picked up and left us," as Dr. Mobley had put it. Apparently a tangle of legal problems had threatened the family's stability as George was growing up. Years after his mother had left for good, she was still squabbling with the dentist about property rights in the Mercer Island home. On January 20, 1981, when she was living in the seacoast town of Hingham, Massachusetts, the English and humanities professor had lobbed a mortar shell of epistolary shrapnel at Dr. Mobley's lawyer, J. Richard Quirk, in response to a property settlement offer:

> My initial impulse, after reading your insulting "proposal," was to either ignore the letter or to advise you and your "client" in graphic terms what you could do with it. Since I am much too busy to engage in petty and blatantly stupid situations such as the one in which you are trying to involve me, I will assume your letter was merely a failed attempt to be humorous.
>
> "Your client" and I have already discussed this settlement, and I will repeat to you, as I have said to him, that my terms are final—$10,000; any negotiations will be higher not lower. He, and you, can take that figure or leave it. I should add that I am totally uninterested in how you arrived at such an outrageous figure. Moreover, since you are apparently handling (euphemistically speaking) *Dr.* Mobley's affairs, I hope he also told you that any agreement I make with him must also specify the payments I will receive for Erika's support—twelve months a year, on time, until she is eighteen—of the incredibly low sum of $230 a month. I am well aware of his record of nonsupport for his two children in Florida. He obviously has no appreciation of my unselfishness in allowing Erika to spend *all* of her vacations for the past six years with him, but if he is unwilling to make the agreement I have outlined, Massa-

chusetts offers many vacation activities for children. I hope the message is clear.

Because your letter raises questions about the intelligence of the people with whom I am dealing, let me be as precise as I can: I do not need a settlement. I do not need an attorney. And, most of all, I do not need the hassle. My daughter and I are presently living a very good life. Since I do not enjoy having it disrupted, Mr. Quirk, I request that you refrain from writing me any more assinine [*sic*] letters. Contact me when the two of you have something rational to say.

The court records indicated that the friction between the Mobleys might have dated to the difficult conditions of their ten-year relationship. The dentist had never married the English teacher, instead remaining the lawful wedded husband of a woman listed as "Quentlyn M. Mobley," mother of his three children in Florida. In court filings, Wonzel and Joyce were pointedly described as "tenants-in-common" of the Mercer Island home rather than husband and wife.

In 1979, with Mobley a year behind in support payments to his wife in Florida, he'd explained to a King County court that his dentistry license had been suspended by the state licensing board on a charge of Medicare fraud. After a similar problem in 1982, Mobley agreed to surrender his license voluntarily for three years.

It was during these stressful times that George Russell had taken to the streets.

The age of the infant when the bonding cycle is broken is critical. The younger the infant the more disastrous the break will be. The first months of an infant's life are the most important for the attachment process. . . .

—DR. KEN MAGID,
HIGH RISK: CHILDREN WITHOUT A CONSEQUENCE

In psychopaths the incidence of illegitimacy and the shunting of the child from one "home" to another is high.

—JOHN BOWLBY,
THE MAKING AND BREAKING OF AFFECTIONAL BONDS

Even after months of investigation the details of the killer's earliest years remained muddled, and his relatives steadfastly refused to unmuddle them. His own romanticized version sounded like a remake of *Cabin in the Sky*, offering no clues to those who believed in such behavioral precepts as "the boy is father to the man" and "abusers were themselves abused." George Russell painted his self-portrait in warm shades of rose, and he gestured and giggled and sometimes guffawed as he denied his misogyny and recounted the pleasant memories.

We're all from Florida, even Wonzel. My mother was born Joyce Dolores Boone, the oldest of five girls. I never knew my real father; he drove a hearse in West Palm Beach when I was born. I'm told he was half or one-fourth British, a Caribbean type. My mother was eighteen. They got married after my mom got pregnant. It says right on my birth certificate that I was born in West Palm Beach to Mr. and Mrs. George Walterfield Russell. That certainly proves I'm legitimate, doesn't it?

When I was a few months old, my mother had an opportunity to go away to Florida A and M, and she took it—and thank God she did! A woman does that today and it's looked at as, Ooh, that's her right as a women, that's her career move, and it's fine. But back then people thought it was strange for a mother to leave her baby to go to college. Well, she *didn't* leave me alone; she left me with family. She said, Hey, I want to go out and make something of myself, make a better life for us.

I lived with my grandmother Ernestine Boone and her daughters, Linda, Pat, Jackie, and Susan. There was a brother, too, my uncle Carl, but he wasn't around. My grandmother was a poet, a writer, an English teacher, an *everything*. We had a genius cousin and other high IQs on my maternal side.

My grandmother had stacks of stuff squirreled away in the attic that she'd written through the ages. My oldest aunt was in high school and the other three were in junior high. My grandfather lived up the road. Except for him there were hardly any men around.

I went to first grade in the integrated school where my grandmother taught the sixth, and she helped improve my reading. It wasn't long before I was reading just about everything.

We moved two or three times during my first six years. For a while we lived in Fernandina Beach, up the coast near the Georgia border. I was a rather rambunctious child. There were big fields separating the houses, and I'd go out in the woods or walk the pipeline and play army or fort. We had to be careful about snakes and spiders.

My mother wrote often, When I had chicken pox, she called long-distance. My aunts took turns tanning me. Believe me, I was *never* abused, never deprived.

We went to church on Sundays and then back home for chicken dinner. I had a bike. On my fifth birthday my mother sent me a record player with slides, like a little TV monitor. It told stories about raccoons and dolphins and other animals. I took it to show-'n'-tell. The teacher told me to bring it back every week 'cause it made the other kids so attentive.

I have close relationships with women nowadays because of my four aunts. They taught me to like women and respect 'em. I was raised totally by females from birth to six years old. We had a relationship where we could sit and play games—no spanking, no abuse. One aunt tried to trick me one day for a candy bar, but that's about the heaviest thing that happened. They were supportive. If one aunt got on my case the others backed me up.

Everybody got along. My youngest aunt, Susan, was seven years older than me. There was no "Oh, get away from us, you little brat. . . ." When adults came to visit I wasn't kicked out of the room. Everything was very open. I have *no* bad memories.

I've always looked for women who were like my aunts and my grandmother, women you could care about. So I would get really ticked off at guys who acted snide with women. I didn't care how big they were; you *don't* mistreat a lady in front of me.

It amazes me how anybody could make comments about how unhappy I was when I was a kid. It has to be their perception, 'cause I never even spoke about Florida to Kris or Dad or complained about my mother leaving. Florida was a Huck Finn–type existence. I look back on it as exciting, great—lots of sunshine, adventures, all my aunts there. If I was mistreated when I was little, would I be smiling and laughing all the time . . . ?

I was six when my mom married Wonzel. I think she'd just taken her master's at UCLA. They arrived in Florida with a U-Haul, picked me up and headed back west for Dad to finish his obligation to the Army at Fort Lewis, near Tacoma. He was a range officer, lost some of his hearing from the gunfire. As a kid he'd been bedridden for a year, picked fruit, toughed it out like other southern black kids.

I saw my first snow in a Cascades mountain pass, felt it, touched it. I asked a million questions: Where's it come from? How come it stays cold? How come the sun doesn't melt it? I'm sure they got bored with my questions.

My mom got a job teaching at Olympic College in Bremerton, took the ferry every day across Puget Sound. I was proud. *My mom's teaching college!* And Dad finished his Army tour and took a temp job as a biologist, helping to clean up Lake Washington and saving money for dental school. Every night he worked on intricate car models; the doors even opened. He said it was good for his finger dexterity.

We lived in an apartment in Seattle. Three houses away there were two sisters, Mary Jo and Sarah, and I was good friends with them. I've always been good friends with women. Here I was in a strange new place, and my first friends were girls.

Then my dad got accepted in Howard University dental school and we drove cross-country to Washington, D.C. He's a man of great discipline. He'd go to school all day, study a few hours, then work all night at the post office. In his spare time he crashed on the couch.

I was already an underachiever in grammar school. They tested me in D.C. and found I had a high IQ, but a lot of school stuff seemed dry and boring. I didn't do well in math.

Grammar was a bore. I liked reading. My mom influenced me to read from six on. She'd say, "I'm going to the library," and I'd say, "Can I go?" It was exciting to walk around and see the books and the people and the pictures.

In the third and fourth grades we lived in an apartment near the zoo. Nice neighborhood. The Washington riots came when I was ten. In the early afternoon the teacher said, "Everybody's gonna be dismissed. Go home on your normal bus."

When our bus pulled out of the parking lot, there were National Guard trucks. As we were driving toward the Capitol, I saw all these ants scurrying around up ahead. It was the rioters. We went a block or two more and the driver said, "Okay, kids, this is as far as we can go. Get off the bus."

Some national guardsmen were gonna walk us through the rioters with their rifles. But within two blocks of the crowds a cloud of tear gas came down, and we couldn't get through. So a sergeant basically said, "You kids are on your own. Please turn around and go back the other way." Most of us were black, but there were a few whites.

I walked to a buddy's house about twenty-five blocks away and called my dad. He had a little Austin Healey then. He put the top down so the rioters could see his color, and he drove through the riots and rescued me. The crowd basically said, "This one's black, let him pass. This one's white, *let's get him!*" And they did! Violent, man, violent!

After the riots, we moved to Silver Spring, Maryland, way up Georgia Avenue. My sister Erika was due to be born, and my parents wanted a safer environment. When Dad graduated from dental school, we went back West and bought our house on Mercer Island. Dad got in on some state-sponsored deal to bring black dentists to Washington. He became friends with Bill Russell, the basketball star. They played golf and raced their sports cars around the island. My parents threw parties, and all the star black athletes would show up: Bill Russell, J. J. Johnson, Downtown Freddie Brown. Heady stuff for a little kid.

We got along fine with our neighbors and friends, but not every black family did. Prejudice was in the air. I remember only six or eight black families on Mercer Island, maybe ten black kids in school. There was a black caucus group and they tried to get my family to join, but my dad was always too busy with YMCA and Big Brothers and other charities, and my mom was too busy teaching at the University of Washington and helping run Black Arts West. So we got nasty phone calls from militant black families.

A few of my white teachers seemed a little prejudiced. One teacher grabbed my by the pants, snatched me out of the lunch line, and threw me through the door. I'm like, What's going on?

He said, "You were supposed to clean out your basket, and you left some paper." And of course we checked and there wasn't a scrap. I thought to myself, Wait a minute. There's people that skip class, that smoke pot and do all kinds of things, but this guy grabs *me*. He called my dad, my mom, trying to get me into trouble. Why? Because I'm black.

After that I did the minimum in school. Then one day my mom goes, "Erika and I are moving back to Maryland. Do you want to come?"

It was a tough decision, 'cause I had friends in Maryland from my D.C. days. It was a toss-up. I was going into my senior year, and I was in with the elite clique on Mercer Island, people like Alice Levy, Mary Strome, Wendy Calvert, Linda Campbell. Those girls ran the high school even when they were juniors.

I said to myself, Are things gonna be the same in Maryland as they were before? You know, you can't go home again. Sure, it might be fun for a while, but it's been six years since you've been around those people.

So I stayed on Mercer with my friends. My sister Erika went with my mom 'cause she was only eight. My mom said she could get me into the University of Maryland tuition-free. When she transferred to Tufts and then San Francisco State, she made the same offer, it's always been open to me. But by then I was busy with other things.

I decided to take my senior year at Inglemoor High School and live with Mike Washington. What a guy! Loved hunting and fishing, and he always took me along. I enjoyed Mike, and I enjoyed Inglemoor—challenging, exciting, good teachers, very different from Mercer Island. Mostly I took drama.

Then just when I was thinking about going to college, an opportunity came up at the disco Tonite's the Nite. I wasn't interested in a big salary that much, but my brother Diron was just born, my stepmom Kris had a job, and this was a way for me to work at night and take care of the baby during the day. Help out my family a little bit.

Kris and my dad would leave the house at seven A.M., and I'd babysit Diron till they got home at four or five. At night I'd manage the disco.

But then Sergeant Booth and Officer Kettells got on my case—you tell *me* why, 'cause I still don't know. Every time a black guy did something wrong on Mercer Island, they hassled me. A bunch of us would be hanging out at somebody's boathouse, and the cops would arrest *me*.

I didn't have a key for Wonzel's house, but he always told me, "Hey, I'd rather have you come home and wake me up and stay here rather than get in trouble."

But I wasn't causing trouble! That was the cops' tunnel vision. Yeah, I raised a little marijuana and did some partying. Who didn't?

One day Sergeant Booth said, "I want you to level with me before I take you to the station."

"What about?"

He said a lady at the Safeway had found her dog missing from her car and a note, "If you ever want to see your dog again, you owe me one fuck."

I'd shopped in the Safeway earlier, so naturally I had to be the guilty one, right?

Later the lady gets home and finds out her husband left the note as a prank. But I took the heat. That's how it went till I finally left Mercer Island for Bellevue. The cops were just as bad over there. Everybody knows the rest.

PRETRIAL HEARINGS OPENED on August 2, 1991, in the rococo bird-stained King County Courthouse, a few blocks from Puget Sound in the oldest part of Seattle. Reporters crowded into the muggy courtroom to cover the first serial murder case ever tried in the state.

At issue was the admissibility of a new type of DNA evidence. For three weeks expert witnesses filled the courtroom with soporific phrases like "polymerase chain reaction," "gel electrophoresis," "Chelex extraction protocol," "major histocompatibility complex," "allelic dropout," "enzymatic amplification" and "HLA genetic structures." In fine courtroom tradition, the state's experts declared the new techniques a great leap forward in forensic science, while the killer's experts derided them as "snake oil." Superior Court Judge Patricia Aitken, one of the few local judges capable of understanding such complex testimony, finally ruled that the DNA procedures used in the case were "generally accepted in the scientific community" and that a jury could hear the evidence.

The issue of whether the three counts would be tried simultaneously was equally important to both sides; many observers believed that the outcome of the case would hinge on these two pretrial issues.

Russell's energetic public defenders, Miriam Schwartz and Brad Hampton, who'd been court-appointed after he was unable to raise a $30,000 retainer for private counsel, argued that the Pohlreich killing was clearly demarcated from the bedroom murders and should be tried separately. For the state, Rebecca Roe and Jeffrey Baird insisted that the murders and posings bore the signature of a single killer. Privately they were afraid that the splitting of the trials could result in still another Pacific Northwest failure to put away a serial killer. It was becoming a stigma.

Both sides wheeled up their big guns.

Normally, Crawford looked like a fit, middle-aged engineer who might have paid his way through college playing baseball—a crafty catcher, tough when he blocked the plate. Now he was thin, his shirt collar was too big, and he had dark puffs under his reddened eyes.

—THOMAS HARRIS,
THE SILENCE OF THE LAMBS

After waffling for months, FBI headquarters endorsed the single-killer theory and agreed to send John Douglas, the high-profile chief of the bureau's National Center for the Analysis of Violent Crime and model for the avuncular Jack Crawford of fictional fame. Douglas, coauthor of a definitive text, *Sexual Homicide: Patterns and Motives*, enjoyed an international reputation as an expert on criminal behavior and profiling. He was a faculty member of the University of Virginia, a senior research fellow at the University of Pennsylvania, and a frequent prosecution witness.

Countering the FBI's best-known behaviorist would be his old mentor and *Sexual Homicide* coauthor, Robert K. Ressler, retired from the bureau after a long career in the Behavioral Science Unit, and creator of the agency's Criminal Personality Research Project. Though once friends and colleagues, the two experts were now at odds. Ressler conspicuously omitted his protégé from the acknowledgment section of his own book *Whoever Fights Monsters*, and dismissed him in the text as "flamboyant," a harsh epithet in the FBI lexicon. It was said that Douglas was reported to be both baffled and annoyed that the likes of Bob Ressler would agree to testify on behalf of the likes of George Russell, especially after word got out that Ressler intended to shoot down the one-killer theory.

Detective Marvin Skeen, ever the bare-bones realist, predicted "the battle of the big egos."

Testifying against the motion to sever the three counts, the well-spoken Douglas explained the difference between "staging" and "posing." Staging, he informed the judge, appears in crimes "where the offender is attempting to throw off the investigation," as in cases where a husband kills his wife and tries to make it look like a bungled burglary. But posing, Douglas testified, "is an extremely unique characteristic. . . . Posing is where a subject is treating the victim like a prop and is manipulating the body after death for a specific message. . . . It is a position where the subject wanted the victim to be found."

The behavioral expert described the typical poser's motivation as "degradation and manipulation of the victim, and showing a heck of a lot of control. . . ." He added, "It is the thrill of the hunt, it is the thrill of the kill, and it is the thrill afterwards of how that subject leaves that victim and how he's basically beating the system." The murderer's message in the Pohlreich posing, he said, was that women "were like trash, like garbage."

As Douglas spoke of Mary Ann's savage treatment, the victim's mother Nancy squeezed back tears and repeated to herself, "The battle belongs to the Lord," a reminder that there was a higher court. She listened attentively as Douglas said he found a commonality in the way that the victims were "penetrated vaginally, anally or orally with some type of device, foreign object."

The state's star witness was asked if this sort of sexual abuse was unusual.

"It is *very* unusual," Douglas replied. "You don't see that. I can't tell you the numbers, but it is very, very rare. . . ."

He pointed out that the time frame of the murders also suggested a single perpetrator—"Between the first and the last case of homicide here we have just over sixty days"— as did the fact that the killings were committed in a concentrated area and involved similar victims.

The Douglas pretrial testimony was concise and professional, and the general feeling in the courtroom was that only a bravura performance by his ex-colleague Robert Ressler could save the defense's motion for severance. But Ressler surprisingly pleaded other commitments and dispatched a handpicked replacement, Russell Vorpagel, a California private investigator, alumnus of the Behavioral Science Unit and holder of degrees in psychology and law.

Vorpagel was a big man, six-four, 260 pounds, a former Milwaukee detective and twenty-two-year veteran of the FBI. He was described by Ressler himself as "a legend in the Bureau." On a week's notice, Vorpagel managed to confer with Ressler by telephone for an hour and fifteen minutes, digest the voluminous paperwork, and develop several alternative theories about the murders, each tending to exonerate George Russell.

The expert witness's courtroom dignity was threatened when his pants split, necessitating a hasty cover-up. He testified that Mary Ann Pohlreich had not been "positioned to degrade. Her legs are not spread. Her private parts are not there to shock and dismay people that find the body. She is placed in what we would call a relatively pleasant position, a comfortable position. She hasn't been thrown down, twisted." He had to admit, however, that the fir cone in the victim's hand was "somewhat unusual."

Carol Marie Beethe was definitely not killed by the same person, the criminologist continued. He cited the many differences between the crimes, including the fact that "Ms. Beethe has been killed in her own home. She has received massive beatings about the head. She has not been sexually assaulted. She has been infarced—by that particular term we mean something has been stuffed into body cavities. . . . She has definitely been positioned to degrade. . . . I do see one bizarre thing in that particular case, that was the red shoes that she was wearing. I felt that was a little unique." The insertion of the gun barrel, he said, suggested that the murderer was an ex-husband or boyfriend.

As for the Levine killing, he couldn't be sure if it was connected to the Beethe case, but there was certainly no connection to Pohlreich. A main difference was the series of stab wounds, described by Vorpagel as "a sexual experience called piquerism" and "little cuts that are fun to make, to the perpetrator." He reminded the judge that there'd been no such injuries on the other two bodies.

The killer's star witness sent a stir through the courtroom by adding, "I also felt there was a possibility that Levine had been killed by a female instead of a male" because of "the type of markings, the scratches, the cuttings, no sexual assault, no vaginal assault, and the fact that something has been placed in her mouth. She does use a dildo.''

He continued, ''I found from one of the reports that there had been prowlers reported outside of her window. That tells me that quite possibly she may have been assaulted by a voyeur who was a piquer. He could have come there, watched, masturbated, or saw her masturbating, was incensed, went in and stuck this dildo in her mouth.''

He disagreed with John Douglas that posing was a common denominator in the killings, or that posing and positioning of bodies was rare: ''I would say that approximately twenty-five or thirty per cent of the cases I've worked on in the last fifteen years have involved some sort of positioning . . . [in which] the body has been exhibited in some particular way that doesn't even involve the killing of the victim. They've been placed in a particular manner to challenge or to degrade.''

On cross-examination, coprosecutor Rebecca Roe, an attractive feminist who played down her trim jogger's figure with schoolmarmish dresses, delivered an interrogatory attack on Vorpagel's credentials as an expert, then zeroed in on his statement that Mary Ann Pohlreich's body had not been in a position to degrade. ''We have a woman here who has been strangled, beaten about the head, raped, dragged,'' she told the witness in her sharp voice, ''and yet is lying in essentially a peaceful kind of pose. Does that not smack of mocking or degradation to you?''

Vorpagel replied, ''That does not fit the criteria that we have established for degradation.''

Roe inquired, ''What is the criteria for degradation?''

''The criteria for degradation is deliberately exposing the genitalia of a victim for degradation of the victim. By lying somebody down, by dumping them from the car, by dropping them, we don't consider that.''

''What definition is that and where is it contained?''

"It is an arbitrary definition that those of us who work in the field use."

The former FBI agent suggested that the killer might have inadvertently crossed the victim's hands or legs as he dragged the body—"if he's dragging this body face down or abdomen down, then he turns the body over to drop it or get rid of it, maybe because he suddenly sees headlights coming into the parking lot late at night or early in the morning. If you are dragging somebody, turn them over and drop them, the legs will frequently cross. I don't see this posing as degradation."

He agreed that there was a strong likelihood that the fir cone was deliberately placed in the victim's crossed hands by the killer, but "I do not see it as the same type of posing or degradation that we see in the other [Beethe and Levine] pictures."

Roe asked what he made of the plastic lid that had covered one of Mary Ann Pohlreich's eyes. Vorpagel answered, "I thought that was just one of these unusual situations that happens at crime scenes that is unexplainable all the time. This is a trash area. There is a Dumpster there. There is other residue of trash lying there. She has some caked blood on her body. My feeling was that probably it blew there and stuck on the side of her face."

And the plastic wrapping around Carol Beethe's head?

Vorpagel said it could have been an act of "psychic erasure." He explained, "Quite frequently we have individuals who act—we'll call them an obsessive, compulsive, violent personality, and they will act in haste and shortly thereafter regret it. Therefore, they sometimes will subconsciously perform some act at that scene that hides or covers what had taken place."

"Is it your opinion that the pillow placed over her head may have been this expression of remorse?"

"It could have been that expression."

In Becky Roe's everyday job, she headed a unit that specialized in prosecuting crimes against women, and some of her well-known animus toward sex criminals seemed to creep into her voice as she asked George Russell's witness, "Could it have been the same expression of remorse that had led him to insert a shotgun and cock it in the vagina?"

Vorpagel hesitated, then said, "I don't see remorse at that moment. What I see is the individual has anger, has hatred, wants to injure, wants to revile. He does this and then for a brief moment regrets what he has done, maybe wants to cover it up. This is similar to what we see in many of our rape cases, where a man rapes a woman, then sends her a letter of apology."

Roe asked for his personal interpretation of the placing of the gun barrel. "There are many ways of placing things into body orifices," Vorpagel began. "Many of them show extreme anger, where the item is jammed in several times to hurt and harm, many times in a victim who is still alive. There are other times that a weapon is placed in the vagina, along with other acts on the body, that will defeminize the female. However, in this case a long shotgun wouldn't do that. But there are many different reasons, ways and types of inserting items in the vaginal canal or vault. We find one is done out of curiosity. We will see certain young Pennsylvania men who are psychotic who—"

Roe interrupted. "Could we stick to the facts of this case? We don't see evidence of curiosity, do we?"

"You asked why this is significant to me, Counsel. If I am not allowed to explain why it is significant to me, the question is useless. May I continue explaining?"

"If you could give us a direct response."

"I'm trying to give you a direct response. . . . I'm showing you there are many different types of persons that place things in the vagina. One is the type of person that does it out of the curiosity, to see its depth. Another is a type of person suffering from a major mental disorder wherein he is defeminizing, where he will remove both breasts and place something in the vagina. In his sick fantasized mind this is no longer a female, it is a male, therefore no longer a threat to him. In the antisocial or psychopath or sadistic person, these things are jammed in with violence, eight, nine times, sometimes with such violence that a rifle might come out the shoulder. In this particular case, we see it placed there not for any of those reasons. None of that is done. None of that shows up.''

He paused, then attempted to shift suspicion toward Carol Beethe's ex-husband: "Therefore there is some other special significance of this particular act. He's placing it in there because it either means something—I don't know if they ever used it, ever went hunting, he asked her for it when they got divorced—I don't know if they are divorced or just separated. But we don't see the usual reason for jamming that.''

As for Mary Ann Pohlreich's anal tear, Vorpagel noted that there'd been a beer bottle at the scene, but it hadn't been collected by detectives.

"We have a tear," Roe said, "so it is pretty clear *something* was there. Correct?''

The witness said it depended on where the sexual act took place. "I have seen cases where people have been in automobile accidents, wherein they have fallen or been thrown on the stick shift and we have tears in the anal canal. . . . It could be possible that the victim inadvertently was sat down on a stick shift in a car.''

After an edgy colloquy about the definitions of piquerism and mutilation, the prosecutor returned to Vorpagel's suggestion that Andrea Levine might have been murdered by a female. She asked, "Why is the lesbian aspect of it, which I believe you referred to on the phone yesterday as dykes— why is that important?''

Judge Aitken ordered the question stricken, and Roe rephrased her question to ask why Vorpagel had raised the issue at all.

"The lesbian issue was what I mentioned to you on the phone,'' the private detective answered. "If I knew more about this particular victim, I would say that there was a possibility that there was a lesbian relationship because of the type of wounds, the lack of attack in the vaginal area,

the slashing and cutting, not a great deal of violent stabbing, and the placement of the dildo and the book, *More
Joy of Sex.* I don't know what that book is. I said I would
like to know more about his victim's background. I would
like to know more about what type of literature she was
involved in, what type of relationship she had with other
people. I posed it only as a possibility, that this could have
also been a lesbian relationship, especially when we think
about the dildo vibrator that has been used.''

Just before the close of cross-examination, the expert
witness introduced a final hypothesis: a ''copycat killer''
might have committed some of the crimes.

In the hallway after the testimony, Marvin Skeen was
seen to confront Vorpagel, and the two investigators exchanged sharp words.

Judge Aitken denied the defense motion for severance
and instructed the lawyers to prepare for trial.

MINDY CHARLEY WAS pleased that she wouldn't have to
testify. In legal terms, anything she might have said was
largely irrelevant, since it didn't bear on the murders themselves.

She wondered if the Mobleys would be dragged into the
courtroom spectacle and how they would take it. She wrote
a letter (and later reconstructed it from memory):

> Dear Kris, I'm really not trying to intrude or any-
> thing. I just want to say thank you for helping me
> start my life over by getting out of a bad relationship
> and I just hope you all are doing well. I hope that all
> the publicity hasn't caused problems for the family,
> and I wish all of you all the best.
>
>   Love,
>   Mindy

There was no reply.

TRIAL ON THE merits started on Friday, September 13, 1991, and lasted five weeks. The testimony proved bizarre, repugnant, sickening, but mainly anticlimactic. Court reporter William Kramer called it "the most gruesome trial I've seen in twenty-one years."

With the three cases joined and the DNA evidence admitted into evidence, the state's prospects seemed improved. Public defenders Brad Hampton and Miriam Schwartz could hardly be expected to match the skills of the two heavy hitters from the King County prosecutor's office. But Russell's attorneys put on a dogged display, attacking police procedures and impugning the credibility of key prosecution witnesses like the condo girls, the waitress G. B. Coffin and Steven Douglas Crandall. After the loquacious young comic testified about identifying a photograph of Carol Beethe's stolen ring, Hampton asked him point-blank, "The reason you're here today is because you want to see Mr. Russell convicted. Is that fair enough?"

"No," Crandall said softly. "It's not fair enough."

"You do want to see him convicted, don't you?"

"No, I want—he's entitled to a trial. . . . I'm here to testify that he tried to sell me a ring—beginning and end."

When the defense lawyer asked why there were contradictions in his statements to police, Crandall replied that a lot of things had been "tooken out of context." By skillful phrasing of his questions, Hampton created the impression that the witness held a long-standing grudge against Russell and was lying out of spite. The clear implication was that Crandall had made a phantom identification of the Beethe ring.

On redirect examination, Jeff Baird attempted to rehabilitate the state's mercurial witness by reminding jurors that Crandall had accurately described the ring *before* seeing its picture.

Q: Mr. Crandall, I've got a ring in my pocket right now.

A: You're a lucky man.

Q: Can you describe it to me?

A: Are you sure it is your ring? No, I can't, because I haven't seen it.

Q: Do you know whether it has a gold band or a silver band?

A: No. I don't know what it looks like at all.

Q: Do you know how many stones it has? . . . You can't describe it because you haven't seen it?

A: Exactly.

Q: If I bought you twenty bucks worth of beer . . .

A: For twenty bucks of beer I would describe half the things in America.

Q: Would you be able to accurately describe something you haven't seen?

A: No . . .

Q: If I threatened you, would you be able to?

A: No, I still couldn't describe it. I would be in jail and be unhappy.

Q: If I promised you anything you wanted, would you describe a ring. . . .

A: Anything I wanted?

Q: Yeah.

A: Oh, yeah!

Q: You would not accurately be able to describe something you had not seen under any circumstances?

A: No.

Q: Why would you accurately describe the ring in this case?

A: Because I had seen it.

Defense counsel Hampton took several more runs at the state witness, but was unable to shake his story.

As the trial went on, it became clear that Russell's lawyers were placing heavy reliance on the "wrong man" argument, attempting to focus the jury's attention on cat's-paws like Tom Jones and Paul Beethe. The strategy was seriously weakened when John Douglas returned to the stand and threw the prestige of the FBI behind the single-killer proposition, strongly implying, of course, that the single killer was the relaxed young man at the defense table.

Miriam Schwartz, a tough lawyer with a voice so incongruously soft that spectators had to lean forward to hear her questions, seemed unimpressed by the distinguished witness from the FBI's shrine of crime psychology at Quantico, Virginia. Her attack started obliquely:

Q: Did you get involved in the Green River murder investigation back in 1983?

A: Yes, for a couple of years. I was involved off and on.

Q: You made a trip out here?

A: Several trips.

Q: When was your first trip?

A: I think 1981 was my first trip, '81 or '82. I'm not really sure.

Q: That was to assist law enforcement authorities here in their investigation of that Green River series?

A: Yes, it was. The first trip was when we had seven or eight victims in the Green River, actually found in the Green River. That's when I came out.

Q: Before you came out here you had a premonition about what was going to happen when you came out here?

A: Premonition?

Q: Didn't you say you had a premonition you were going to become ill and you bought life insurance policies?

A: If you don't want to tell the whole story, I would like to. That was not the time. . . .

Q: You did have a premonition, is that right?

A: I had a very good premonition. I was speaking before three hundred police officers in New York City, and the amount of cases—I was primarily the person who was doing this work for the FBI and basically was getting burned out from working several hundred cases a year. As I was speaking before the New York city police, I felt—basically I had an anxiety attack. I came back and told my wife and children I took out this extra life insurance, because I felt something was going to happen to me. Sure enough, I went before the [Green River] Task Force and ended up in a coma after collapsing in the Hilton. I was in a coma for a week and hospitalized at Swedish Hospital [in Seattle] for a month, out of work for five months.

Q: Was that sort of going back to before you came out here, this was sort of almost a psychic feeling?

A: No. It was not a psychic feeling at all.

Judge Aitken sustained Rebecca Roe's objection to the ad hominem questioning, and Schwartz asked whether political pressure had been brought to bear in the Green River murders. Douglas quickly foreclosed another prolonged discussion by stating emphatically, "There is *always* tremendous pressure to solve cases."

Courtroom scorekeepers voted the shoot-out a draw. It was true that the FBI demigod had been exposed as a frangible human being, subject to the same frailties as other stressed-out lawmen, but he'd also come across as a dedicated cop who worked himself into the hospital.

* * *

Throughout the proceedings, George Russell's demeanor seemed to vary between detachment and bemusement. He slumped slightly backward in his chair, the index finger of his left hand tickling his cheek, his thumb cradling his chin. He frequently referred to his trusty literary companion, *Crime Scene Search and Physical Evidence Handbook*, took notes, and smiled pleasantly at witnesses. Sometimes he seemed involved in another proceeding, one going on in his head—"imperturbable, as though he's deaf or doing homework," as his former classmate Michael O'Hara noticed one day.

To O'Hara, the defendant was "the best-dressed person in the courtroom. On the opening day of trial, he looked great in a navy-blue sports jacket, gray slacks, white shirt, and tie. Altogether, he wore about five different suits. Sometimes he looked like a page out of *Esquire* in his polished brown shoes, dark brown checkerboard jacket and dark brown pants. Understated, fashionable, *cool*. I never looked at him without thinking of what he could've been."

Now and then Russell even appeared to nod off.

Glendon Booth was one of only a few prosecution witnesses who seemed to irritate the defendant. The Mercer Island sergeant went home from the trial and told his wife, "Georgie got shook when I testified that he used to wipe blackboards for us cops. He acted like I was insulting him. He stared hard at me, and the minute I began describing him as a little bitty kid, his feet hit the floor and he sat right up. He grabbed his pad and wrote a dissertation and shoved it in front of his lawyer."

Mercer Island Patrolman Tom Kettells took a seat directly behind the defense table and stage-whispered, "Hi, George. How ya doin'?"

Russell saw his nemesis and quickly turned away. But he acted friendly toward his former roommate and fellow barhopper Michael Weisenburgh. When he was led past

Georgia Mike in the corridor, George called out, "Hey, how's it going?"

The irritated Weisenburgh told a friend later, "I just stiffened. I almost started to lunge, didn't know I was doing it. Ended up I didn't say nothin'. He just kept walking. Always cool."

Sometimes Russell could be seen bantering with the bailiffs as he entered the courtroom in handcuffs. He'd always had a rapport with men in uniform.

One day a handsome pair of African-American women took seats and watched the proceedings attentively, then quietly disengaged. Reporters learned that they'd been in the presence of Professor Joyce Corrigan of San Francisco State University and her sister Patricia, who resided in Spanaway, Washington, about thirty miles from the courthouse. If Dr. Wonzel Mobley, his wife Kristin or his daughter Erika made an appearance, it went unrecorded.

G. B. Coffin flew back from Hawaii under the impression that she would be asked to tell everything she knew, especially since her information shed light on the motivation for the murderous binge. But she was quickly shot down by the justice system's built-in solicitude for defendants. In the end she wished she'd stayed home.

> I spent my first morning in the prosecutor's office being told what I couldn't say in court. They said, "We're seven weeks into the trial, and we *don't* want a mistrial. Do *not* talk about these things; the judge says it wouldn't be fair to George." I thought, *Fair to . . . George?*
>
> They had a blackboard listing the things I couldn't say. I couldn't mention that George threatened to kill me. I couldn't even hint that he claimed to be a police informant. I couldn't give the reasons he was kicked out of the Black Angus or why the murders ruined our business. I was pretty much restricted to saying that he was eighty-sixed, that's all.
>
> I sat in the hall for five days before I was called to testify.

One day I was talking to my mom on the pay phone and I turned around and the elevator opened and it was George and the bailiffs. I jerked away so I wouldn't have to look at him. I wanted to throw up. Here's this guy that always had scruffy hair and long fingernails and high-topped sneakers, and now he's in a suit, all cleaned up.

That night I went over to visit Carol Beethe's daughters, Kelly and Jamie. They were living with their dad, Paul, and he went out for a while and left us alone. It was the saddest experience; it ripped me apart. The girls kept every light on, the TV, the radio. I thought, My God, these poor children are still scared. Two years later!

Kelly was thirteen and very withdrawn. She still didn't want to believe that it happened. I don't think she ever will.

Jamie—she was the nine-year-old—kept wanting to know what I remembered about her mom. She showed me Carol's favorite clothes that they'd saved, pictures of Carol. It was hard.

It got late and I told Jamie she should go to bed. She went in and laid down, and I heard this sound. It was a sleep tape she had to listen to, counting, a soothing noise that her therapist had given her. I went in to tuck her in and every light was on.

When I walked to the witness stand the next day, George looked like he was gonna spring right out of his seat. It was almost like he was trying to intimidate me.

My testimony was so weak. Afterward I cried and cried about it. I told my mom I wanted to do something for those girls, for everybody that George Russell hurt. And I wasn't allowed to.

That's the system, I guess. A killer has all these rights.

THE CONDO GIRLS, with their divided loyalties, were potential booby traps for both sides and had to be handled with care. Jenny Graves, the first to be called for the prosecution, spoke in a small, hurried voice that served to em-

phasize that she was not testifying voluntarily. She'd visited
George twice in jail. Under oath, she characterized the two
of them as "the closest of friends."

She told the jurors about the night they met: "He was
extremely nice. We immediately liked him a lot." She described him as an asset to condo life and a good influence
on four teenage girls: "George usually put a limit, made
sure we didn't drink too much. He didn't like people to get
out of hand. . . . If we all had our limit or too much,
sometimes he would hide it." She was asked if she'd ever
seen him with a scanner and answered, "Not that I remember."

But despite her air of partisanship, Jenny told about
George's switch into dark clothes when he went out at
night, his claims of being an undercover cop, his dabblings
in money, the trip to Canada, the Crown Royal bags that
had probably come from Carol Beethe's dresser, his preoccupation with murder, his odd relationship with Bobbie
DeGroot.

Jenny's testimony about his attitude toward Andrea Levine seemed especially damaging to the defense: "He
didn't talk about her in a good way. He told me how she
was going out with one guy . . . and sleeping with another
guy who was friends with the one guy. How he thought
that was a terrible thing to do, kind of."

Bobbie sat on a wooden bench in the hallway, holding her
infant son Jake, a dead ringer for his father Tim. She was
curious about how George would look after all this time in
jail, but she didn't want to confront him. Lately she'd converted to a total belief in his guilt, and she was suffering
from retroactive terror at how tight she'd been with an un-
speakably evil man.

The heavy courtroom doors opened and out he came,
flanked by two deputies. At first he seemed to be smiling,
but then she realized it was more like a smirk. As he walked
in front of her, he seemed amused.

Bobbie wished she knew what he was thinking. Was her

little family *humorous* to him? Were they a joke to his twisted mind? Or was he smirking because she'd married Tim, as promised? She was confused. He'd always had that effect on her.

When she took the stand against George, it didn't take long for Rebecca Roe to ask about their personal relationship.

"We were friends," Bobbie testified, choosing her words carefully. "Maybe a little bit more. Him staying in my room was completely platonic. As far as I know, he didn't have any romantic feelings for me and never tried to push himself on me or never tried anything with me."

Roe asked, "You had romantic feelings for him, didn't you?"

"Sometimes," she said, then added, "It wasn't all the time."

"Were there occasions when you shared a bed?"

She took a deep breath and said, "Yes."

After the questioning, she couldn't wait to rejoin Tim and Jake and get back home to the Eastside. Compared with her love for them, any feelings she'd ever had for George Russell were inconsequential.

Susan Jetley, the roommate who'd despised George from the beginning, was one of only a few witnesses who could connect him to Carol Boothe, the weakest count in the state's three cases. Prosecutor Jeff Baird asked, "Do you remember anything that Mr. Russell told you about that killing or about the victim?"

"She was an acquaintance. She was at the same social spots he was."

Suzy also linked Russell to the final victim: "Andrea Levine had dated a friend of his. . . . He had some pretty cruel things to say about her. . . . [He said] she slept around, she was a whore, she used men." She recalled that "more than once" George had said that the police were stupid and the victims "were all promiscuous, that they were sluts, that they used men."

* * *

Sara Amundson wasn't called by the prosecution; her belief in George Russell's innocence remained firm, and she too had visited him in jail. As a defense witness, she testified about George's negative reaction to her backless dress, thus reinforcing Jenny Graves's courtroom depiction of the killer's high moral standards. Sara's only other apparent purpose as a defense witness was to mar the credibility of a key prosecution witness.

"How long have you known Susan Jetley?" she was asked by Miriam Schwartz.

"Three years."

". . . Do you know other people that know Suzy Jetley?"

"Yes, I do. . . . "

"Does Suzy Jetley have any particular reputation regarding her truthfulness or non-truthfulness?"

Observers anticipated an objection, but Roe and Baird remained silent.

"Yes, she does," Sara went on. "She's regarded as a non-truthful type of person."

On cross-examination, Sara was asked if she liked George Russell.

"I did like George," she replied.

"He was very charming?"

"Yeah."

"He listened to you and your friends and advised you on your personal lives, shared with you?"

"Yeah."

"Is it fair to say that sharing only went one way? It was [you] guys talking about your problems and getting very little information from Mr. Russell about himself?"

"Well," Sara answered, "I don't think we ever really asked him about himself."

The teenager testified that she "didn't really care" that Russell moved in, that she'd never seen him count silver dollars on the condo floor, and that she hadn't heard him talk about the triple murders. Nor did she recall a poster of

Mary Ann Pohlreich that he'd posted on a shelf in the pantry.

She was asked, "Mr. Russell never told you he had this poster because he was trying to help the police find the killer?"

"No," she replied, then added shyly, "I probably wasn't paying attention."

After Sara stepped down, Jenny Graves made her second appearance of the trial, this time as a defense witness. She was asked how long she'd known Suzy Jetley, and she answered, "Years."

"Among your common friends," she was asked, "does Suzy Jetley have any particular reputation regarding truthfulness or untruthfulness?"

"I would say untruthfulness," Jenny responded. "A lot of times, she's very untruthful."

Jeff Baird seemed irritated when he took the witness on cross-examination.

Q: Last summer you lived with George, right?

A: Yes.

Q: You considered him a good friend, didn't you?

A: Yes.

Q: A close friend?

A: Yes.

Q: You talked a lot with him, didn't you?

A: Yes.

Q: He got to know you pretty well?

A: Yeah.

Judge Aitken overruled an objection by Miriam Schwartz, and the questioning hardened.

Q: You didn't get to know him all that well, did you?

A: Apparently not.

Q: You did consider him a protector of you?

A: In a lot of ways, yes.

Q: You considered him somebody who was older and wiser?

A: Yeah.

Q: You let him regulate such things as how much you had to drink?

A: Uh-huh.

Q: In fact, it was comforting, wasn't it, last summer, to have a protector in your house?

A: Yes.

Q: Because it was scary last summer, isn't that right?

A: Yes.

Q: Because somebody was going around killing women last summer, right?

A: Yeah, in the area we lived in. It was scary. . . .

Q: One of the reasons that you considered Mr. Russell good protection was because he told you he was working for the police, didn't he?

A: He did, but I don't think that really made me—had anything to do with how I felt.

Q: You believed him, didn't you?

A: Sometimes I did, but sometimes I had doubts. It didn't matter to me.

Q: . . . It is true you protected George on at least two occasions?

A: What two occasions? I can't remember.

Q: The first occasion was when there was a little bit of disagreement in your house about whether or not George should be there or not?

A: Yeah, yeah. I know what you are talking. I guess I did.

Q: . . . For a while, Mr. Russell left, isn't that right?

A: Yeah.

Q: You invited him back, isn't that correct?

A: Uh-huh.

Q: You knew that Suzy didn't really want him there, didn't you?

A: Uh-huh.

Q: You have to say yes or no.

A: Yes, yes, *yes!*

Q: . . . Now, it's true in fact that when Mr. Russell became a suspect in the three killings, you protected him then, too, didn't you?

A: I don't know how I could have protected him.

Q: Do you remember the first time the police came to your house?

A: Yes. Okay. Yeah.

Q: Do you remember that? Do you remember them saying where is Mr. Russell?

A: Yeah.

Q: Do you remember saying he left hours and hours ago?

A: Yeah.

Q: He hadn't left hours and hours ago?

A: He had just walked out the door, not even minutes.

Q: It is fair to say, isn't it, Ms. Graves, you *lied* to protect Mr. Russell?

A: Yeah. . . . It took me by surprise, having a cop at the door asking me that. I didn't know what to say. I don't know why having said he left two hours ago would have helped him or anything. I just said that he left a long time ago. I guess I got caught off guard, I don't know.

Wɪᴛʜ ᴛʜᴇ ᴘʀᴏᴄᴇᴇᴅɪɴɢꜱ winding down, the Bellevue *Journal American* continued its daily coverage, but the Seattle *Times* and the *Post Intelligencer* seemed to have lost interest. Both newspapers customarily underplayed crimes involving African-American killers or victims. It was standard journalistic practice.

Just before the defense rested, Russell's lawyers announced that their client wouldn't be taking the stand. Judge Aitken asked him directly, "You are electing not to testify in this matter?"

"That is true," the killer said, half rising. He looked like a relaxed, assured young lawyer.

The judge asked if had any questions, and he said, "None at all."

During a recess Miriam Schwartz explained to reporters that the defendant's appearance on the witness stand would have changed the tenor of the trial: "We don't feel the state has a real solid case. . . . We're not saying he isn't credible, but it shifts the entire focus of the trial. We feel there are some problems with the state's case and we want to keep the focus on that."

When reporters asked her what the problems were, she promised to detail them later. Cocounsel Brad Hampton cracked, "Why don't you guys give us some ideas?"

Jeffrey Baird, an energetic thirty-eight-year-old with sharp features and a shock of black hair, brought the last threads of the state's case together in his closing argument, reaching levels of emotion that might have seemed inappropriate except for the gravity of the crimes. The dark suits that hugged his athletic frame seemed to hang a little lately; observers were sure that he'd lost more weight in the course of this trial than he'd ever lost climbing the sheer cliffs of his beloved Cascades. All four lawyers showed the strain of two and a half months of infighting. Only the defendant appeared unchanged.

Baird opened by pointing to pictures of the three women. "Mary Pohlreich, Carol Beethe, Randi Levine," he said as though intoning a roll of saints. "This is the way they looked when they were alive. This is not the way they will be remembered. We will find ourselves for a long, long time to come, at inopportune and unexpected moments, remembering them the way Mr. Russell intended us to remember them. . . . He made caricatures of them; he made cartoons, grotesque, obscene, cruel—and unforgettable. This is the creative work of George Walterfield Russell."

The jurors tilted their heads, frowned, scribbled notes.

"I'm going to talk today about Mr. Russell's work," Baird continued, "about the themes we see in his work, about the materials he used, the terms he used, the tools he employed, the gloves he used, and the paint he had to work with.

"I'm going to talk about the little pieces of himself that Mr. Russell left accidentally in his work. I'm going to talk about the little pieces of each victim, a poster, a couple of rings, that Mr. Russell took with him and passed around like prizes.

"I'm sure Mr. Russell himself is flattered by this analogy to the artist, the personal self-expression that is evident in his work, the fine detail work visible even on the soles of Randi Levine's feet, the broad sweeping strokes that he used on Carol Beethe's head, and the satisfying subtle character sketch of posing Mary Pohlreich, her battered body, in a position of repose.

"In this argument, I'm going to suggest that Mr. Russell's signature, not his name but his signature, is visible in his collected works."

Baird talked for almost two hours, returning most frequently to the posing of the bodies, describing it as "a message that cannot be translated because we have no words for that level of hatred." He noted the variations in the poses. "He didn't use a shotgun on Levine. He didn't use a pine cone with Beethe. He didn't leave a sex manual with Pohlreich. That's right, they are different. He used to write with whatever he found.

". . . Now what he wrote varied, didn't it? From scene to scene? Undeniably, they are all different. But he wrote in each case on the same surface, didn't he? He wrote on the broken bodies of the women he killed. He wrote, I suggest to you, the same thing each time: a message to the victims, a message to the families, a message to the police, and a message to all of us . . . and what he said was 'Fuck you,' and he said it three times."

Baird reminded the jurors of some of Russell's comments to the condo girls. "Mr. Russell said some very curious things about the killer and about the police who tried to catch him. To Bobbie DeGroot he said it was ridiculous that the police couldn't tell the same man killed all three women. . . . He told Suzy the cops were stupid not to make the connection. Indeed, one of the great ironies here is that it did appear to disturb Mr. Russell greatly that the police were never quoted in the paper as talking about these poses. . . .

"As far as Mr. Russell could tell, these police were incredibly stupid. They stumbled into the scene, packaged up the bodies, dragged them away, and they ignored Mr. Russell's handiwork. For all they knew, they were dealing with a run-of-the-mill murderer. They didn't even acknowledge that it was one man, one special man who did these killings. So it's no wonder Mr. Russell was telling everyone who would listen how stupid the police were. He was insulted! He had gone to considerable time and trouble, hadn't he, and risk to him, to pose these women in positions so they would never be forgotten?

"He left his signature at the crime. He signed it anonymously, if you will. He didn't want to be caught, but he wanted to create an effect. He wanted to make the headlines, 'Serial murderer strikes again.' And the headlines never came."

The prosecutor argued that this same sense of frustration

had led to overconfidence and eventually to Russell's downfall. "He tried to sell Crandall the ring. He gave Dacia Jubinville a ring. When he learned that the police were going to search his residence, he called Jenny and said, 'Jenny, I would really appreciate it if you took my stuff to your folks' house. There is nothing there the police will want. You make sure they get that evidence handbook. You make sure they get that, Jenny.'

"Mr. Russell wanted the police to know what he wanted the world to know, and that was they weren't just dealing with anyone. They were dealing with somebody *special*.

"How special Mr. Russell really is, is ultimately your decision. It seems to me you have two decisions: you can agree with the defense and you can look at this case as nothing more than coincidence after coincidence after coincidence, stacked one on top of the other, hundreds deep, all pointing toward Mr. Russell, and all pointing toward Mr. Russell just by chance.

"You can agree with the defense that as a result of this miraculous set of coincidences, George Walterfield Russell is just the hapless, helpless, dumb dupe of faith. . . .

"Or it seems to me you can agree with your common sense, with the prosecution and with Mr. Russell himself. You can find that he really is something special—something specially dangerous. Something specially powerful. Something specially cruel. And guilty as charged.

"Mr. Russell was going to California, San Diego, I think he said. If you have a reasonable doubt that he killed these women, let him go. He'll find new friends. There is no shortage of naive, trusting, foolish young people in the cities of this country. He will settle in. He will begin looking for work. You could say he will be hunting for a job and he will find it. If you have a reasonable doubt that he's the killer, let him go."

He turned again to the pictures of the victims. "Mary Pohlreich, Carol Beethe, and Andrea Levine. Mr. Russell has had his success. You will never be able to hear these names without seeing and feeling images of cruelty, de-

pravity. That's why I'm going to end the way I began, with
the photos of these women in life. It's the least I can do.
Individually, he murdered them. Together they are the collected works of George Walterfield Russell.''

A FTER TWENTY-TWO HOURS of deliberation, the jury returned verdicts of guilty of first-degree murder in the Pohlreich case and aggravated first-degree murder in the cases
of Levine and Beethe. The only African-American juror,
Patricia Montgomery, assured reporters, ''At no point was
race an issue.'' Juror Colleen Felling said there'd been little
disagreement about Russell's guilt; ''we just wanted to talk
about everything.'' One of the talking points was whether
the funereal pose of Mary Ann Pohlreich had been inspired
by G. B. Coffin's name or the occupation of the killer's
natural father in Florida.

George took the decision with his usual aplomb, causing
Mary Ann Pohlreich's mother Nancy to comment, ''I'd like
to have him say he's sorry. But he doesn't think like we
do. He doesn't feel like we do.''

At the formal sentencing hearing, Judge Patricia Aitken
asked if Russell wished to speak in his own behalf. The
court reporter typed, ''Defendant shakes head.'' The judge
imposed the mandatory sentence of life imprisonment without possibility of parole.

Through tears, Nancy Pohlreich said, ''I feel like I could
almost fly.''

The killer quickly leaked word to the media that he'd been
railroaded by police because of his color. Of course he
would appeal, he said. What choice did an innocent man
have?

In one of several interviews later, he suggested to
KOMO-TV's John Sharify that the serial killing of three
Eastside women was no big deal: ''Not to be desensitized

or anything, but this area for years, since Bundy and everything, has had astronomical amounts of bodies being found in the woods or in clumps or whatever. . . . It's something that's in the paper every day. It's almost common."

His hands resting on a Bible, he seemed unperturbed about his conviction. Asked what he thought about the prospect of spending his life behind bars, he gave Sharify a typically judicious answer: "I have to assess my feelings and see where to go from there."

Rebecca Roe, a longtime trench warrior in the fight against sex criminals, weighed in with an incisive public comment of her own: "Since the verdict, Mr. Russell has been giving a lot of interviews that really amount to speeches by him, and I think you can see how articulate, manipulative and perhaps persuasive he is. He chose to remain silent at trial . . . and I think probably his silence at trial is as eloquent as his speeches are now as to what kind of person he is."

AFTER THE CONVICTED man had been driven across the Cascades and the Columbia to "The Walls," the maximum-security prison in the sagebrush-and-onion community of Walla Walla, Mindy Charley was engaged in one of her periodic orgies of housecleaning when she heard a rattling sound inside the arm of her sofa. She'd noticed the noise several times since George had moved out in the spring of 1990, but it just sounded like a loose bit of metal.

She reached under the armrest, felt a slit in the fabric, and drew out a pocket knife. At Bellevue police headquarters, her friend Detective Marvin Skeen, whom she now addressed as "Marvelous Marv," examined the weapon and told her it had been altered so that it could be flipped into a locked position, making it illegal—and lethal.

Mindy was vexed. She thought, They put George away for life and he's *still* intruding on me.

Almost a year earlier she'd come across three pairs of

earrings, hidden in a Christmas tree ball. Then a foil containing marijuana had floated up when she watered a potted plant. She'd begun to have recurrent dreams of running from room to room in her childhood home and confronting George at every door, casual, smiling, saying, "Hey, Min," or, "Hi, hon." She would awaken with a trapped feeling and have trouble getting back to sleep.

A week after finding the knife, Mindy discovered that an ace of spades was missing from her canasta deck. She felt "freaked," as she complained to her husband Mark. "Do you think," she asked, "I'll be finding George's stuff for the rest of my life?"

The situation left her shaky. When Mark went to work, she examined pockets and seams in her clothing, squeezed the mattress, opened toiletries, and poked a flashlight into crawl spaces, cracks and openings, including the ones in her car. As she ripped the gauzy covering off the underside of a sofa, a pair of panties fell to the floor. She reached into the springs and drew out a soft, pliant package. As she removed the toilet paper wrapping, the letters "SPD" came into sight.

She hoped the navy-blue police cap would be the final remembrance of her ordeal, but she wasn't optimistic. Someday, she said to herself, I'll be dusting a closet and I'll come across a bracelet, an earring, a slip of paper with a phone number, a roach, and that'll be it, at last, *finito*, the end of George. It couldn't happen too soon.

EPILOGUE

AFTER EIGHT MONTHS in the penitentiary, George Russell's dark brown complexion had grayed, as though covered with a fine sift of ash. In the large visiting room, everything clanked or scraped. There were some sixty tables. Chairs were welded together to discourage spontaneous sex and the passage of contraband. Vending machines lined a wall: pop, candy, snacks. Visitors—restless children, parents, wives, girlfriends—strolled about as though in a shopping mall. Guards, euphemistically known as correction officers, watched from elevated posts in the corners.

When his guest was escorted into the big room, George was leaning against a wall next to a cigarette machine, face slightly turned in a half-smile, watching at an angle before offering a hard handshake. In the dispiriting environment he seemed as relaxed as ever. He wore tight Lee blue jeans that looked as if they'd just come off a rack at Belsquare, a button-down shirt open at the collar, polished brown shoes. As always, his hair was in a short, neat "natural." His fingers were long and slender, the nails slightly longer than normal.

A guard assigned Table 43, and George started out in the wrong direction, as though unaccustomed to visitors. The guard steered him and said lightly, "You're here, where we can keep an eye on you." It was almost as though they were friends.

With his usual animation, George started right in on the

major themes of his ruined life: I'm fine; I'm cool; it's no big deal. He'd developed a twitch in mid-forehead. As he talked, he frequently looked down, but sometimes his dark eyes rolled back in his head: an unsettling affliction. He crossed and uncrossed his legs, made expansive gestures, giggled and laughed at the slightest provocation, appeared quick of thought, friendly, funny, glib. The word "foxy" also came to mind. He said his sister Erika had made the long journey from Georgetown University Law School in Washington, and his mother and stepfather had also visited. He stressed that money was no problem and his needs were filled at the prison commissary.

"This is like being in a college dorm," he said with his trademark smile. "I just put on my headphones, get a book, and I'm back in school. I play a lot of basketball. I coach our Christian basketball team. It's weird; with my broken femur and snapped tendons and all my injuries, I probably jump only two inches less than I did ten years ago."

He described the prison cuisine as "great, exceptional," but later he grimaced and said, "The diet here is a lot of starches. I eat dinner and then about one A.M. I have a snack: Top Ramen soup with sausages, potato chips, peanut butter, crackers, candy bars, stuff like that. I have breakfast about once every three weeks, but I never eat lunch."

A pattern of minor contradictions continued as he talked about his adjustment to prison life. He said he had good cellmates, listened to music, wrote letters, spent most of his time at chapel reading religious books. But he also spoke knowingly about books on murder, said that he'd just finished *Unanswered Cries* and *Deadly Weapons*, and claimed to know all about "the Red ripper," the Ukrainian serial murderer: "Killed fifty-two women, didn't he?" In between Genesis and Revelation, George was keeping up on his field.

He claimed that he seldom watched television, then launched into a lengthy analysis of a George Carlin appearance on HBO and the plot line of *Beverly Hills 90210.*

He said that one of the stars of the show, Shannen Doherty, resembled Mindy Charley. And as though he'd completely forgotten his earlier words, he abruptly complained that he wasn't getting along with his "cellies" because they were irreligious and lacked a proper understanding of morality. Besides, they watched too much TV. He seemed to be editing his script as he went along.

He said he was pleased that the bureaucrats at King County Victims' Relief hadn't been able to get their hands on the $10,000 insurance settlement he'd won for injuries suffered in one of his accidents. "I hid it good," he said. "They got some, but I moved the rest out of state, and I only keep a minimum." He seemed as proudly crafty as ever.

He expressed emphatic opinions on the state of the world. "Look at crime, look at the guns in schools, look at the low level of morality and religion. The world is dying because the rain forests are being depleted." He said he had fond memories of Mercer Island, "but it's dying, like everyplace else."

He explained that he couldn't discuss his murder convictions because he was working on an appeal in the prison law library. But once the subject was broached, he rambled on for an hour, showing deep self-involvement but no emotion, referring to the victims as "Beethe," "Pohlreich," "Levine"—cold, clinical, legal. It was obvious, he said, that Tom Jones had killed Beethe. But Tom Jones wasn't black, so he got away with murder.

He trotted out his alibis, complained about police behavior ("That Skeen sneered at me during the trial, and I didn't like it one bit"), accused prosecutors and witnesses of planting and suppressing evidence, suborning perjury, and lying about him and the case. "That Crandall's a liar," he said. "Did you know he tried to kill his brother with an ax?"

He insisted that he'd intended to take the stand himself to correct the record, but "that would've just given them an excuse to bring up more lies about me." He described his trial lawyers as "bumblers." Next time around he would represent himself, *pro se*, every narcissistic criminal's fantasy. He pointed to some of the other inmates and spoke of the raw deals inflicted on each, as though he'd reviewed their cases in his role as chief jailhouse lawyer. "That guy over there got twenty-five years for assault," he confided, "and the victim lived. *Twenty-five years!* He's really getting screwed."

After a while it became apparent that cool hand George was still involved in a human chess game, with himself as puissant king and others as lesser pieces. In his long-winded disquisition on his case, he showed no anger about the miscarriage of justice he was describing or the life sentence he claimed he was serving for other men's crimes. Instead he took the sociopath's approach of explaining how he *couldn't* have done the killings; it was illogical; every clue pointed to others; the whole thing was ridiculous. A small speck of honesty or reasonableness (or perhaps a fear of sounding uncool) seemed to keep him from coming right out and declaring, *I'm an innocent man.* . . .

At the end of the three-hour visiting period the correction officers arrayed prisoners on one side and guests on the other for a head count. Inmates and loved ones stared hungrily across fifteen or twenty feet of floor. Children broke ranks for a final hug and guards indulged them. Fathers who would never see their families in another setting leaned a few inches closer. Everyone looked forlorn.

Except George. He was busy kibitzing with another inmate, chuckling, gesturing, eyes cocked toward his departing visitor. As the guest walked through the big metal door, George shot out one of his long delicate fingers, as though to say, *Gotcha!* . . .

His face bore a sharp, tense smile.

THE KILLER'S SURVIVING victims (those who weren't too terrified to discuss him) seemed neither as glib nor as cheerful. Some had been subjected to a kind of emotional death and seemed unlikely to make a complete recovery. Some were scarred but healing. A lucky few seemed to personify the Nietzschean precept that whatever doesn't kill one helps one.

Tami Grace found comfort in her religion, with a helpful assist from Detective Marv Skeen. "I was scared enough when George tried to break in," she recalled, "but when he was convicted of murder, I was shattered. I thought about the sexy dances I did with him, and what he'd done to those poor women. I was convinced he'd come back and get me. I hid out with friends. I told myself, If I die, it's God's will. If God means for me to die, *then I will die*."

She wondered, Why me as a target? Skeen, every victim's best friend, explained that George's animosity wasn't personal; it didn't derive from a bad move or an indiscretion on her part. George simply enjoyed killing females and abusing their dead bodies, as other men enjoyed fly-fishing or poker, and he picked his victims from women he knew. If he didn't have a genuine reason to be angry enough to kill, he invented one. The simple fact that Tami had discussed him behind his back could have set him off, or that she was tight with Mindy and Mike Weisenburgh and some of George's other detractors. "And don't forget," Skeen told her, "you were a handy target, a few doors away."

For almost a year after the murders Tami suffered from anxiety attacks, a Henny Penny fear that the sky was falling. She was afraid to go out, afraid to get in her car; she couldn't shake the idea that George would arise from the floorboards. The only man she trusted was her minister.

Recovery began when her fear turned to anger. She

started asking herself, How dare that man keep intruding on my life! Or *any* man!

She bought a battery-operated stun gun and carried it at night. The high-voltage shock would floor a steer. "After that," she explained, "I began to get better. God provided for me. He always has."

Tami's former boyfriend Mike Weisenburgh advised her not to waste time worrying about George Russell. "Somebody'll kill his ass," Mike declared. "Convicts recognize bullshit quicker'n anybody. It isn't like the outside where people aren't expecting a steady stream of lies. George never gave a straight story in his life."

Georgia Mike was still enraged about the killing of his friend Andrea Levine. After he testified at the trial, the prosecutor's office offered to put him on a victim notification list so that he would be warned if George was released from prison.

Mike declined the offer. "I'm not letting anybody have that much control over my life. If George ever gets out, he's more than welcome to come by. He can walk right in through the front door. But he ain't gonna walk out the same way."

LIKE TAMI GRACE and some of the other victims, Laura Green sought comfort in the Bible, but she'd been more seriously damaged than most and was slower to recover. In high school, two years after aborting the woman-hater's child, she'd been diagnosed with a chronic intestinal disorder. A specialist briefed her on the disease, told her it was manageable, incurable, and at least partially psychosomatic. Now that she was in her second year of college, Laura thought of the problem as "my heritage from George."

I still feel *incredible* confusion about him. He was my first
love. Our baby would be five years old now. If George had a
child of his own, maybe he wouldn't've done what he did. I
think about that a lot.

But the way he treated me, all that talk about my life, religion, Satan, the Holy Ghost—he's made me suspicious of boys.

George always seemed so interested in my girlfriends and
I. Our problems, every detail of our lives. He couldn't have
been faking. Not night after night till five in the morning.
Could he?

I met a real nice boy in college, and as soon as he started
talking religion, I distrusted him. He sounded like George on
V——'s bed, scaring us with his stories, getting me to throw
away my mom's Ouija board.

Sex was something important that George and I had, one of
the things that kept us together. At the time it was great; it
was like there was no age difference. I'd probably do it again
if I was fourteen, even though I regret it now. But that abortion—the pain, the shame! The main thing it taught me was
to use protection. I'm always telling friends, "Condoms, condoms, *condoms!*" I know I've helped some of 'em. I wrote a
report for my English class on AIDS, pregnancy and protection. I got a B.

George hurt my pride, my valuation of myself. Nowadays I
find myself in sexual situations more quickly than I want. Sex
feels a lot more casual. I wish it wasn't that way. I think it's
wonderful to wait till marriage. I didn't have that option. I
wish I hadn't done it with George, 'cause I got used to sex
too early. He made me feel that a man won't like me unless I
give myself physically. I think of myself as stained.

Now that I'm in college, George has become a big deal
between my boyfriends and I. It's hard for them to see how
young I was, takes 'em awhile to comprehend that I had sex
with a murderer and aborted his child. They say, "My God,
are you *serious?*"

I try to describe our secret meetings, going to the beach,
hugging on the bed, his letters from jail—"You are my one
true love, otay!!?" All those exclamation marks and happy-
faces . . .

My boyfriends listen with their mouths open, and when I

tell them George killed three women, they freak.

My parents still know nothing about George and I. After he was convicted, they asked me if I had ever run into him on the island. I said no. They're bright, understanding people, but they'd *never* understand George.

My older sister said that he was just using me. I said, "Yeah, well, I guess you're right."

Then she said, "No, not totally. I think he cared for you a lot."

So I thought about him and realized maybe he really did love me. It bothers me to be loved by somebody like that. It's hard for me to see what he's become. That's not how I knew him.

It hurt me when Mary Ann Pohlreich's mother said it ripped her heart out to see George smile. It's so painful to reread his letters. How can I feel nostalgia for this person who ruined so many lives?

I cried about him for a long time. I don't cry anymore. That's something else I worry about. Maybe he made me hard.

KATHLEEN DEL MAR, the outspoken young secretary who'd noticed that Randi Levine's amethyst was missing, listened to a few theories about the origins of George Russell's behavior and lost her patience.

"Listen," she said, "I don't want to hear a bunch of crap about how he had a rough childhood. Yeah, yeah, I know—some psychologist'll say, 'Well, he's this way because he wasn't treated right as a child.' I don't care; I really don't. Lots of people have bad childhoods. I'm sure I'm dysfunctional, too, but you don't see me slashing people. I don't think that's an excuse."

Kathleen was still upset about her friend's cat Missy. Randi's older pet, Sambo, had found a happy retirement home with her parents in Florida, but Missy had been torn apart by raccoons or coyotes. It seemed like an intolerably cruel end for a pet that had seen its mistress stabbed so many times.

"A<small>M</small> I <small>THE</small> only one who thinks that summer was a horrid mistake?" asked Sara Amundson. Most introspective of the four condo girls, the one who seemed almost detached from events, she seemed as much a Russell victim as any of her former roommates.

It was total chaos, awful. I don't need any more of that kind of life. People ask do I think George is guilty. For a long time I didn't. No way. Now I have no idea. I guess he is. He was convicted, wasn't he?

I think that somewhere along the way, something went wrong in George's life and he tried to relive it. But he got it wrong all over again, and look what happened.

I'm not as upset as I used to be. For a long time after the murders I was scared to be alone. I couldn't take a shower without someone in the house—and I never saw the movie *Psycho*. It went on for a year. I had a strange fear of a black man being burned in a fire and all of his skin came off and he would run to my house. Do you understand why it makes me giggle? Nervous laughter, I guess. This black man, he'd run right by my bathroom.

I took my fears to my job every day. Where I worked at Belsquare, you go down this long hallway to dump the garbage, and I was always scared that this burnt black man was waiting for me.

Then I started dreaming about George's head. I'd be sitting with my parents in the living room and George's severed head would be sitting in the middle of the floor. My people are all Norwegian and they believe that whatever happens is supposed to happen, and someone would say in my dream, "Well, that head's supposed to be on the floor, for goodness' sakes! Look at what he *did!*"

I dreamed I'd lift the toilet seat and George's head would float up in my face. I still dream about men breaking into my house, usually with a weapon. I wake up in the middle of the night and can't get back to sleep. And I still have fears of being raped, and I still hate to be alone. I'm in counseling.

BOBBIE DE**G**ROOT **O**GLE also saw a counselor, for a few months. The therapy didn't seem to help. She was convinced that marrying Tim and giving birth to Jake did more for her mental health than counseling.

We four girls had planned to go on to college, but that summer changed us all. Sara changed her mind three or four times about what she wanted to do. When I first moved into the condo I was gonna go to the Art Institute of Seattle to learn acrylics and watercolors, but after that summer I was so screwed up it wasn't even a consideration anymore. I knew I'd be affected by George for the rest of my life. He made me suspicious of everybody. My attitude toward strangers changed horrendously. I'm always afraid, extremely cautious.

At night I can't be alone outside. It scares me to death. Someone like George could be out there. And you can't tell what a person's really like, can't be sure of anything. Can't relax for a second. I walk past a priest and I think, *Could he be a murderer?*

Our parents never knew George was living with us and can't understand how we didn't spot what kind of person he was. They have no frame of reference. They've never been involved with anyone like him.

Now we just don't talk about him. The subject is *never* discussed, 'cause the few times that we tried, everyone got upset. Somebody told me that psychopaths are famous for doing this to people. They're like a cloud that settles over a family, and nobody's the same again. Every relationship changes.

I had nightmares for a long time.

SUZY **J**ETLEY'S BAD dreams were recurrent and specific. Night after night she dreamed that George would do to her what he'd done to the others. Sometimes she imagined she saw him on the street, even though he was behind bars in the southeast corner of the state, three hundred miles away.

Late one night after the sentencing, a friend and I were driving in downtown Bellevue when we saw a black man who looked like George. He was wearing a cap and carrying a paper bag. We watched him get on a bus that went out toward my parents' neighborhood. We followed all the way to Lake Sammamish, watched him get off. It was two A.M., perfect timing for George, and he headed straight for Jenny's house. The closer he got, the more we were convinced it was George. But of course he wasn't.

I didn't make my daily run for a year; I was so frightened of men and afraid to be outside. Now I carry Mace whenever I'm out, even walking to my car. I tell my friends, If you run into me walking at night, don't try to talk to me; you'll get Maced. And I never respond to questions or comments on the street. I look 'em straight in the eye so they know I could pick 'em out of a lineup, and I walk faster.

When we all split from the condo, I had to get away from Bellevue. It's such a small town. Strangers would stop me on the street and say, "Tell me about that murderer you lived with." I moved to Seattle and got a new job and started college.

Sara and I are still distant friends. I went to Bobbie's wedding, but I don't see her otherwise. Jenny and I talk if we run into each other. Everything's different since George.

I never thought I'd see the day when any of them would admit that he was guilty. Even after he was charged, they were corresponding with him and visiting. What power he had! We were all relieved to see that Bobbie's baby was white.

Some of my friends still waste time playing that old party game: what made George kill? The truth is, we'll never know; he probably doesn't know himself. He's got that huge wall of denial—life's just one big happy experience, no problems— *Hey, dude, look at me. I'm cool. . . .*

Personally, I never bought the mommy theory. There's too much mommy-bashing anyway; it's too simple, too easy. The newspaper pointed to George's mom and suggested if she hadn't abandoned him he wouldn't have killed. What a leap!

I believe there was something neurologically different about

him from the beginning and he would have gone to this lifestyle anyway. But the truth is no one will ever know. It's all
a big guessing game. He's probably guessing himself.

It took almost a year, but Jenny Graves finally came
around to agreeing that George was guilty. "From the beginning we thought it was possible," she admitted, "but
then we thought it was too weird. No, no, *no*, it couldn't
be George. But the evidence was overwhelming."

Jenny was the only condo girl who didn't appear deeply
disturbed by the events of the summer. A friend explained,
"With Jenny the tide goes in and the tide goes out. If you
stand next to her, you can almost hear the beach. Her attitude is, Maybe it'll faze me later, but it doesn't now, and
I don't want it to. It's hard to tell whether it's a blocking
mechanism or just the way she is."

And the detectives?

Larry Petersen earned a slap on the back and a few days
off from his boss, Captain Michael Nault, who was praised
by his own chief for helping to achieve the state's first
serial murder conviction.

Marvin Skeen belatedly became Bellevue's "Officer of
the Year," thus catching up with Rick Buckland and Dale
Foote, who'd previously won similar honors and enjoyed
needling him about it.

Buckland saw to it that Patrol Sergeant Doug Vander-
giessen won a commendation for steering him toward
George Russell in the first place. In turn, Foote, Skeen and
Petersen awarded Buckland a spaghetti dinner, where the
celebrants laughed at a list called "The Serial Killer's Top
Ten Peeves," which included "Hefty bags that leak,"
"They never have Serial Killer Day at the ball park," and
"The movie version of *The Silence of the Lambs* turns out

to be not as funny as the book.'' It was typical police humor, grisly and morbid, but somehow soothing to men involved in violence and death on a daily basis.

The four investigators relaxed over their spaghetti and jokes, then returned to work. There were other killers to catch.

AUTHOR'S NOTE

IN RECENT YEARS, two distinct schools of "true-crime" writing have developed, each as legitimate as the other. In such classics of fictionalization as *In Cold Blood*, by Truman Capote, and *The Onion Field*, by Joseph Wambaugh, the authors employ imagination and creativity to augment the basic story. Members of the other school—journalists, for the most part—try to remain within the facts. *Charmer* is of the second type.

Certain characters in this book are necessarily pseudonymous: Boris Brockett, Tom Haggar, Laura Green, Tom Jones, Lynn Brown, Tami Grace and Susan Jetley. I have altered a few insignificant details to protect the privacy of those who preferred not to be linked to George Russell in a public document.

I gratefully acknowledge the assistance of several fine journalists: Christopher Jarvis of the Bellevue *Journal American*, Gordy Holt of the Seattle *Post-Intelligencer*, and free-lancers Sally Deneen of Fort Lauderdale and Mark McNamara of San Francisco. A special debt is owed to George Russell's friend and classmate Michael A. O'Hara, whose reportorial and mnemonic skills were of incalculable value in my research.

—JACK OLSEN
BAINBRIDGE ISLAND, WASHINGTON

INDEX